Pharaohs on Both Sides
of the Blood-Red Waters

Pharaohs on Both Sides of the Blood-Red Waters

Prophetic Critique of Empire: Resistance, Justice, and the Power of the Hopeful *Sizwe*—a Transatlantic Conversation

Allan Aubrey Boesak

CASCADE *Books* • Eugene, Oregon

PHARAOHS ON BOTH SIDES OF THE BLOOD-RED WATERS
Prophetic Critique of Empire: Resistance, Justice, and the Power of the Hopeful *Sizwe*—a Transatlantic Conversation

Copyright © 2017 Allan Aubrey Boesak. All rights reserved. Except for brief quotations in critical publications or reviews, no part of this book may be reproduced in any manner without prior written permission from the publisher. Write: Permissions, Wipf and Stock Publishers, 199 W. 8th Ave., Suite 3, Eugene, OR 97401.

Cascade Books
An Imprint of Wipf and Stock Publishers
199 W. 8th Ave., Suite 3
Eugene, OR 97401

www.wipfandstock.com

PAPERBACK ISBN: 978-1-4982-9690-8
HARDCOVER ISBN: 978-1-4982-9692-2
EBOOK ISBN: 978-1-4982-9691-5

Cataloguing-in-Publication data:

Names: Boesak, Allan Aubrey, 1946–

Title: Pharaohs on both sides of the blood-red waters : prophetic critique of empire ; resistance, justice, and the power of the hopeful *sizwe*—a transatlantic conversation / Allan Aubrey Boesak.

Description: Eugene, OR : Cascade Books, 2017 | Includes bibliographical references and index.

Identifiers: ISBN 978-1-4982-9690-8 (paperback) | ISBN 978-1-4982-9692-2 (hardcover) | ISBN 978-1-4982-9691-5 (ebook)

Subjects: LCSH: Theology. | Social justice. | Religion. | Human rights.

Classification: BT28 .B6184 2017 (print) | BT28 .B6184 (ebook)

Manufactured in the U.S.A.   07/10/17

To Elna, the one of unbending strength, unfading beauty, and delightful intellect, after twenty-five years—"anniversary" is saying far too little.

I felt like Sojourner Truth was on one side pushing me down, and Harriet Tubman was on the other side pushing me down. I couldn't get up.

—Claudette Colvin, (1955), 2009

Cowardice asks the question—is it safe? Expediency asks the question—is it politic? Vanity asks the question—is it popular? But conscience asks the question—is it right? And there comes a time when one must take a position that is neither safe, nor politic, nor popular; but one must take it because it is right.

—Martin Luther King Jr., 1968

The greatest ally of the oppressor is the mind of the oppressed.

—Steve Biko, 1973

For Mohamed Bouazizi to remain the martyred witness of a revolution that will not replace one dictator with another, one false prophecy of freedom with another, there is only one logical and lasting measure: the people.

—Hamid Dabashi, 2012

Contents

Preface | ix

Acknowledgments | xxvii

Introduction: Seeing Satan Fall Like Lightning from Heaven: The New Militancy and the Hopeful *Sizwe* | 1

1. Pharaohs on Both Sides of the Blood-Red Waters: Why We Cry, How We Cry, and Who Can Cry | 32

2. Interrupting the Globalization of Indifference: Empire, Faithful Resistance, and Prophetic Pathos | 61

3. The Divine Favor of the Unworthy: When the Fatherless Son Meets the Black Messiah | 86

4. When *Ubuntu* Takes Flight: Justice, Politics, Reconciliation, and the Spirit of *Ubuntu* | 117

5. "The Righteousness of Our Strength": Reconciliation and the Historic Obligation of the Oppressed | 147

6. Deification, Demonization, and Dispossession: Mandela, Prime Evil, and the Hope That Will Not Go Away | 169

7. "A Hope Unprepared to Accept Things as They Are": Prophetic Theology—Speaking Truth from the Edge | 194

Bibliography | 227

Index | 235

Preface

> We must finally do away with theologically grounded restrictions in regard to action by the state—after all, it is only fear.
>
> —Dietrich Bonhoeffer, 1939

What has Soweto to do with Ferguson, or New York with Ramallah, or Baltimore with Cape Town? A lot, it seems. The cry for freedom and justice is heard everywhere. From the Arab Spring: *al-Sha'b Isqat al-Nizam!* (The People Demand the Overthrow of the Regime!) From South Africa: "Injustice Must Fall!" From occupied Jerusalem, "I am not leaving!" From the United States, "Black Lives Matter!" And from Palestine the simple, but utterly convincing truth—because it is prophetic, and one of the most audaciously hopeful and defiant cries I know—written on that infamous Israeli apartheid wall: "This Wall May Take Care of the Present but It Has *No Future*."[1] It is coming from different contexts, from different points across the globe, but it is one cry. What the people were shouting in Tahrir Square a few years ago captures exactly the cry of the new, militant youth everywhere else, from Hong Kong to Burundi to Uganda: *Huriyyah, Adalah Ijtima'iyah, Karamah!*—"Freedom, Social Justice, Dignity!" As in Egypt, that cry may have been stifled in all the brutal ways tyranny can devise, but it cannot be stilled. The world had heard, may try to ignore, deny, or viciously suppress,

---

1. I am grateful to my friend and colleague Dr. Stiaan van der Merwe who took the photograph of those impressive words on the wall while we were visiting Palestine in 2012 and graciously made it available to me. In South Africa, the "Injustice Must Fall" movement is a label that encapsulates the unfolding resistance across the country against the ongoing injustices as they are unmasked by the youth and initiated by the students at the University of Cape Town that started the "Rhodes Must Fall" movement, which for many continues to symbolize the new militant resistance movement as a whole.

but can no longer unhear the defiant, courageous, hopeful cry. Like William Cullen Bryant's truth crushed to earth, it shall rise again and again.

It is the cry itself, in the voices of the people, in the resilient hope of the people, in the persistent rejection of the empire's power over their lives, that constitutes at once the critique of empire and the resistance against empire. The cry ringing across the world is resistance against empire because it reveals truth. Mendacity is the life-blood of empires. Empires cannot live without it. It lies about itself, about the realities of oppression, domination and subjugation. It lies about the people: not just about what the people need, but about what the people deserve and are entitled to. It proclaims that whatever is good for the empire is good for the world. The cry for justice, freedom and dignity exposes the truth about the empire, but simultaneously it reveals the truth about the people: their outrage at injustice and their longings for justice; their outrage at oppression and their love for freedom; their outrage at exploitation and their desire for dignity; their outrage at the destruction of their lives and their strength in the indestructibility of their hope.

It is a cry against the consciously induced, politically manipulated fear that has become such a frightening reality in modern-day politics, fueled and carefully managed by shameless politics and its adherents in the mainstream mass media,[2] calculated to prevent the people from thinking for themselves about what is presented to them, the choices they make and the consequences of these, but also questioning the power of empire in fear of losing its "protection." The wave after wave of protests on the streets in the face of armies of occupation and police acting like armies of occupation; the "days of rage" against an empire whose power lies in the constant rage of domination, intimidation and threat of annihilation are so much more than "protest." They are, in innovative and persistent ways, revolutionary resistance against fear. The brutal retaliation we are seeing is not just an

---

2. See, e.g., Wodak, *The Politics of Fear*. In this excellent study Wodak's linguistic and political analysis gathers impressive evidence of the normalization of nationalistic, racist, patriarchal, and anti-Semitic rhetoric, all of them constituting the politics of fear that is entrenching social divides of nation, gender and body. Although she pays much-needed attention to the fear of the Other regarding Europe's immigrant communities ("The Politics of Exclusion"), and to the rise of antisemitism in Europe ("The Politics of Denialism"), the book would have gained even more credibility in my view if she had included a chapter on Israel's politics of fear regarding the legitimate and utterly urgent question of justice toward and the dignity of Palestinians, with perhaps just as much attention to what one might call "The politics of occupation and victimhood." For such a deliberate use of the politics of fear in Israel as justification for not just unending war but for the militarization of everyday life and normalization of military action at the slightest pretext, see the extraordinary study of Halper, *War Against the People*. For Wodak's discussion on the role of the media, see chapter 6.

effort to stamp out the resistance; it is a systematic attempt to destroy the courage and love of freedom that defy that fear.

This book is an effort to address what I consider to be a major challenge to faith communities and quite specifically to the church today: What is our response to the renewed struggles for justice, renewed nonviolent revolutions for peace, dignity and wholeness that are raging across the globe? These revolutions are mostly led, like the anti-apartheid struggle in South Africa in its final phases since 1976, by the youth. These young people are not all Christians, but many of them are, and even if they are not, it makes little difference. They are challenging the church, in ways that are both recognizable and completely new, to be an active presence in these struggles. They are doing this because they remember, or have been told of a time, that there was such a thing as "the prophetic church" participating in, even giving leadership in those struggles. Just as earlier, the church must know and understand that there is a struggle going on, choices must be made and neutrality is not possible.

The title of this book is drawn from the words of the nineteenth-century black Presbyterian minister, abolitionist and fighter for justice in the United States, Henry Highland Garnet, and in chapter 1, but throughout this work, we will explore what those words mean for us today, as this generation, in the sobering words of my friend and colleague from South Africa, Takatso Mofokeng, faces pharaohs "who look like us." The reference, obviously, is to the exodus story, and here "Pharaoh" stands for the oppressive forces of the empire subjecting the people of Israel to slavery and hardship. On the other side of the Red Sea—a fitting metaphor for the struggles for freedom and justice we have been fighting for so long—where we expected freedom, justice, and peace, we are discovering the same injustices as before, the same arrogant defiance of God and the people's hopes and dreams, the same oppression because our liberators have made common cause with global forces of oppression and are benefiting from these injustices, as the people continue to languish in poverty, misery and neglect, their hunger and thirst for justice and bread unfulfilled.

They, our new pharaohs, in the words of warning and admonition from the book of Deuteronomy, have committed a crucial transgression Yahweh was so insistent the kings of Israel shall not commit: Israel's kings shall not "return the people to Egypt." In Deuteronomy 17 it is the very first, and clearly the most decisive thing "the king shall not do." Returning the people to Egypt is returning them to slavery and a mindset of slavery as the price for acquiring "more horses." Horses, as instruments of war, are the expression of their belief in might as power, declaring their dependence on military strength rather than on Yahweh's steadfast love. They are subjecting themselves to the militaristic mindset of the empire, embracing the desires of the empire for domination and subjugation through violence and annihilation. They are tying the people's fate to that of the empire by turning their backs on Yahweh, putting their own faith in the empire's gods of war or pretending that Yahweh, like the gods of the other nations, is a god of war.

They are forgetting the reminder of Elisha as he mourns the departure of Elijah taken up in that chariot of fire, that it is precisely not military might, but the presence of prophetic faithfulness personified by Elijah that is "the chariots of Israel and its horsemen" (2 Kgs 2:12). In other words, they are following the ways of empire, putting their faith, like the empire, in weapons, war, and violence, instead of trusting in the faithfulness and steadfastness of God that bring justice, prosperity, and peace. Eager to please the empire, bask in its reflected glory, share in its ill-gained spoils, they are, "like [the kings of] the nations around them," selling out the liberty of the people in order to gain favor, social and economic patronage from the empire. This despite the emphatic, "You must never return that way again" (Deut 17:16), which in this context carries the same weight as "you shall not bow down before them."

The title of this volume is double-edged. It refers to the fact that "the pharaohs," the present powers of oppression and exploitation, indeed physically look like us. In our present situation we are fighting people whom we have honored as liberators and entrusted with political power for the sake of justice and dignity. For a generation or so perhaps, the Palestine Liberation Movement, with Yasser Arafat as their leader, might have held symbolic power that resonated with Palestinians' hope for freedom. For this generation, however, that hope has long dissipated. Palestinian academic and human rights activist Mazin Qumsiyeh laments "how the Palestinian leadership betrayed its people leaving young and old with a sense of orphaned leadership." Qumsiyeh states, "I worried not that the Palestinian cause will die . . . but that the selfishness, ego, and incompetence of self-declared leaders can only delay the inevitable freedom and dispirit a population otherwise willing and able to liberate itself."[3]

For South Africa and the United States, this situation is no less, perhaps even especially, poignant. In an extraordinary historic moment we have elected persons from within our midst who carried with them that once-unthinkable image: President of South Africa and President of the United States of America. But also, these two political figures carried with

---

3. See Mazin Qumsiyeh, "End of Time?" HumanRights Newsletter." April 28, 2016, https://sites.google.com/site/onedemocraticstatesite/archives/end-of-time-by-mazin-qumsiyeh.

them huge symbolic significance: the hope and dreams for the fulfilment of justice, peace, and dignity of millions, no matter their race, creed, or national origin, for a world less attuned to the clamor of war and more in tune with the music of peace.

In Pretoria, on that historic day in May 1994, Nelson Mandela was inaugurated as South Africa's first black, democratically elected president. It was one of those days of days.

> We have triumphed in the effort to implant hope in the breasts of the millions of our people. We enter into a covenant that we shall build the society in which all South Africans, both black and white, will be able to walk tall, without any fear in their hearts, assured of their inalienable right to human dignity—a rainbow nation at peace with itself and with the world.[4]

Our ears perked up when we heard the word "covenant," for in South Africa that is a loaded word, heavy with the burden of our colonialist past, tinged with a blasphemous sacramentalism, soaked in blood. Mandela did more than just juxtapose the covenant into which he has invited the people of South Africa with the covenant (the "vow") of white Afrikaner South Africa, made at the occasion of their war with and victory over the Zulu nation in the "Battle of Blood River" in 1838.

In democratic South Africa, on December 16, we celebrate a public holiday called the Day of Reconciliation. It replaced another holiday, actually a holy day, a civil-religious, sacrilegious, nationalistic fest from apartheid's history, called the Day of the Vow referred to above. It was the day on which white, apartheid South Africa, more specifically the Afrikaans-speaking white Christians, celebrated the military victory of the Boers over the Zulu nation, a gift from their powerful god, together with the right to claim the land as their own. After the victory over apartheid and the dawning of democracy, the day became Reconciliation Day—a deliberate, hopeful renaming—celebrating the decision that black South Africans would seek reconciliation rather than retribution, forgiveness rather than revenge, justice for the living rather than justice for the dead, when we had to decide on how to respond to 350 years of slavery, dehumanization, genocide and dispossession, and to the consequences of the crime against humanity called apartheid.

In his reflections on reconciliation as restoration, John De Gruchy has offered insightful comments on the two memorials at the scene of the Battle of Blood River, the one built to celebrate the Day of the Vow and the

---

4 See "Inaugural Speech, Pretoria [Mandela]–5/10/94," http://www.africa.upenn.edu/Articles_Gen/Inaugural_Speech_17984.html.

victory of the Voortrekkers, and the other, built by the ANC rulers in the province of KwaZulu-Natal in 1998, to keep alive the heroic story of the Zulu warriors. But it is clear that these two monuments do not symbolize reconciliation—they symbolize division. "Built on either side of the river, they reflect opposing powers and civilizations confronting one another across an unbridgeable chasm. In so many respects, South Africa remains as divided as ever . . . ."[5]

The people of South Africa did not ask for a tit-for-tat monument worshipping the past, glorifying the violence from Boer warriors and Zulu *impi's* alike, but not taking us any closer to true reconciliation. We expected justice. We took Mandela at his word that his covenant of reconciliation and peace was meant to be entirely different, entirely in contrast with that covenant with Baal that has held place of honor in South Africa for so long.

De Gruchy also comments on Mandela's use of the word "covenant" in that inaugural speech.[6] It is not the same as the theological understanding of covenant that has played such an important role in the history of certain expressions of Reformed theology, for instance, De Gruchy writes, but "there is an analogous relationship, for covenant implies a new commitment to each other that transcends simply agreeing to coexist." A covenantal relationship goes further than a social contract because it is concerned about reconciliation rather than mere co-existence: "It means recognizing the way in which power has been abused in serving self-interest and developing structures of inequality and injustice, and seeking ways to achieve equity rather than the protection of vested interests."[7]

For ordinary South Africans listening to Mandela on that day, these were portentous words, adding weight to the enormous authenticity and authority conferred upon Mandela by the people and which he carried with him on to that podium. In response, we offered forgiveness instead of revenge, healing instead of retribution, the inclusivity of a shared destiny with whites instead of a retrogressive exclusivity built on an unforgivable past. We have a right and the duty to hold those who claim Mandela's legacy accountable and insist upon the justice, dignity, and equity that covenant proclaims.

Similarly, on the campus of Egypt's Cairo University in 2009, when President Obama spoke so passionately to the world in general but to the Muslim world in particular, he still carried with him the powerful aura of truthful commitment to justice and world peace that marked his campaign

---

5. See De Gruchy, *Reconciliation*, 183–84.
6. Ibid., 185–87.
7. Ibid., 186.

for the presidency, and the people's faith in this commitment was not yet shattered by subsequent history. It was, by any measure, an extraordinary speech. That is the day he spoke of the needs and common aspirations we all share, regardless of race, religion, or station in life.

> These needs will be met only if we act boldly in the years ahead; and if we understand that the challenges we face are shared, and our failure to meet them will hurt us all. For we have learned from recent experience that when a financial system weakens in one country, prosperity is hurt everywhere. When a new flu infects one human being, we are all at risk. When one nation pursues a nuclear weapon, the risk of nuclear attack rises for all nations. When violent extremists operate in one stretch of mountains, people are endangered across an ocean. When innocents in Bosnia and Darfur are slaughtered, that is a stain on our collective conscience. That is what it means to share this world in the 21st century.[8]

Obama kept the same bold, hope-filled tune as he spoke of his intentions vis-a-vis the all-important issue of justice for Palestinians, and as no US president before him, he raised the hopes of Palestinians and all justice-loving people across the world. After the obligatory recognition of the relationship between the state of Israel and the United States, and the need for Israel's security, Obama went on to say,

> On the other hand, it is also undeniable that the Palestinian people—Muslims and Christians—have suffered in pursuit of a homeland. For more than 60 years they've endured the pain of dislocation. Many wait in refugee camps in the West Bank, Gaza, and neighboring lands for a life of peace and security that they have never been able to lead. They endure daily humiliations—large and small—that come with occupation. So let there be no doubt. The situation for the Palestinian people is intolerable. And Americans will not turn our backs on the legitimate Palestinian aspiration for dignity, opportunity, and a state of their own.[9]

We now know how consistently and carelessly Americans have continued to turn their backs on legitimate Palestinian aspirations since these words were spoken. Those of us who listened to these words as they resounded from Cairo to Palestine to Cape Town and believed them rejoiced.

---

8. See Barack Obama, "Remarks by the President at Cairo University," https://www.whitehouse.gov/the-press-office/remarks-president-cairo-university-6-04-09, 5.

9. Ibid., 8.

We accepted the sincerity of Obama's embrace of our holy scriptures: "The Holy Koran tells us . . . "; "The Talmud tells us . . . "; "the Holy Bible tells us . . . " We have the right, and the obligation, to continue to challenge these politicians, their politics, and the systems that stole their hearts, and to hold them accountable. We also have the obligation to put away the politics of sentiment and look the new pharaohs, whoever they may be, and however much they may look like us, squarely in the eye. Clear, critical appraisal of politics and our involvement in it must ensure that we do not repeat the mistakes of the past—looking to Mandela and Obama as our opportunity to make history rather than an opportunity to make history rhyme with freedom and justice. In the first instance we merely revel in the historic moment, proud of our share in creating it; in the second, resisting the temptations of sentimentality, we take a hand in history and make the moment a moment of historic agency.

In a stunningly clear, cogent, and courageous article, Aislinn Pulley, a leader of the Chicago Black Lives Matter movement, raises the voice of the radical youth and helps us in this. She explains why she has declined an invitation to the White House. In February 2016, the Obama administration invited civil rights activists and leaders from around the country to discuss a range of issues, including the administration's efforts on criminal justice reform and to celebrate Black History Month. Despite pressure from many quarters, including the pressure of who else was going, this young leader "respectfully declined" the invitation.[10] She expected "genuine exchange on matters facing millions of Black and Brown people in the United States." Instead, what was arranged was "basically an opportunity and a 90-second sound bite for the president. I could not, with any integrity, participate in such a sham."

This young leader not only shows amazing strength of character. She also offers us remarkable political insight into the workings of the politics of the pharaoh, where it is indeed all about sound bites and cooption while doing the bidding of the rich and powerful. She also knows how to hold politics accountable, while holding herself accountable to the revolutionary politics the people have embarked on. By not accepting the invitation and her very erudite reasoning on why she refused, she raises the bar for those who did go very high indeed. In more than one way this may turn out to be a Kairos moment for the ongoing struggle in the United States.

---

10. See Aislinn Pulley, "Black Struggle Is Not a Soundbite: Why I Refused to Meet with President Obama," February 18, 2016, http://www.truth-out.org/opinion/item/34889-black-struggle-is-not-a-soundbite. The list included an impressive array of "civil rights struggle heroes."

Aislinn Pulley understands the difference between a revolution and the politics of sentimental submission. So she insists that she is not ready to meekly accept the administration's definitions of criminality, justice and freedom. Her definition of criminality for example, includes mayor of Chicago Rahm Emmanuel's decisions "to close half the city's mental health-care centers," or "conducting the largest public school closure in US history." She defines as "criminal" the killings by police of black Chicagoans, the torture of "over 100 Black and Latino men" in places like Homan Square, the cover-ups, the lies, and the silences. For her, "criminal" is the endemic, systemic socio-economic injustices and the deliberate neglect that caused the people of Flint, Michigan, to drink poisoned water.

Then she speaks of the demands Black Lives Matter has put on the agenda. Striking here is that those demands not only include "domestic" issues: funds for public education, a living wage and free health care for all among them. Her mind is set on global justice and it is a ringing call:

> We demand the immediate closing of Guantanamo Bay and the return of the confiscated land to the people of Cuba. We demand the return of all troops in Iraq and Afghanistan. We demand an immediate end to all money going to Israel while the occupation of Palestine continues. We demand an immediate withdrawal of all US troops in Africa under US Africa command. We demand an end to the ongoing police violence against Indigenous people and that this colonized United States be returned to Native peoples. We demand the immediate halting of the deportation raids of undocumented people. We demand full reparations for all descendants of the trans-Atlantic slave trade.[11]

Not only is her voice clear and unambiguous, she shows more political wisdom, in my view, than any of the 2016 presidential candidates in the United States, and she rises far above the depressingly myopic, and unedifying, political discourse of the mainstream media and the presidential political machinery. She does this because she understands better the disastrous global impact of US imperial politics, the indivisibility of justice, the deadly foolishness of a foreign policy that is no more than a policy of global corporatist domination, endless war and devastating aggression. She understands the need for compassionate justice and peace at home and abroad as fundamental for both a responsible, responsive, participatory democracy, a stable, more just world, and the salvation of the soul of a nation.

But finally she understands better than most that the hope for real political change does not lie in the reckless politics of world domination

11. Ibid., 5.

and violence espoused by the White House and Capitol Hill—whoever sits there—but in the struggles of determined, hopeful people: "Finally, we assert that true revolutionary and systemic change will ultimately only be brought forth by ordinary working people, students and youth—organizing, marching and taking power from the corrupt elites." Here is the voice of the generation that finally understands Martin Luther King Jr.'s call for a revolution as a revolution of values. I can scarcely find better evidence of, and argument for, leadership by the youth of the current revolutions than this.

The subtitle reflects a belief that has grown within me from my earliest years of participation in struggles for justice, and has only been reinforced as the years go by. Aislinn Pulley's last sentence grasps it well. And for me, the single most important characteristic of peoples' struggles is their hopefulness. This is not to argue that this hope is not vulnerable, not always under attack, the target of the kind of scorn only the powerful, in their hubristic arrogance, can display. But this hope is resilient, not only because it is a "hope against hope" but because it is rooted in faith and the willingness to engage in sacrificial struggle for the sake of justice.

This hope is the hope of the *sizwe*, the Zulu word for "nation." But the word "nation" has strong connotations with "the state" as a political entity. And in a "nation state" the inhabitants of that state may well form "the nation." It is infused with nationalism. But nationalism, as manipulative a political reality as one can get, can also be manipulated. A people cognizant of their oppression and having taken the decision to struggle against their oppression and for freedom, justice, and dignity will resist that manipulation. For me "the people" means the people in resistance to oppression and exploitation, a people determined to claim and protect their human dignity. That is the sense in which I will use the word "people," as in the cry "The People Demand the Overthrow of the Regime!" or as in the South African "People's Congress" that met in Kliptown, near Johannesburg, in 1955, that same congress that produced the "Freedom Charter" as a "people's document," which we will consider in more detail below in the Introduction. The Introduction will hopefully make clear what I mean when I speak of a revolution carried by the people and driven by the hopes of the people.

One of the most important lessons we have learned about keeping hope alive and responding to her call, is that we should no longer mindlessly and uncritically invest our hope in those with political power, or those to whom we have entrusted our political power.[12] No, at a spiritual level we find our hope in our faith in Jesus of Nazareth in whom, as Matthew's Gospel teaches us, all those struggling for God's justice will find their hope. That hope we

12. I have offered my thoughts on this subject in a previous publication. See Boesak, *Dare We Speak of Hope?* For my argument why I refer to hope as feminine, see ch. 2.

invest in the determination of the people themselves, as agents of challenge and transformation, in the power of the people, as we will learn from M. M. Thomas in chapter 1, to be the bearer of dignity and the dreams for the shaping of a new society. I see the hopeful *sizwe* at work in the revolutionary movements all over the world. I will mention only three of many examples across the globe, and they come from occupied Palestine, occupied Jerusalem, and South Africa.

One of the most despicable ways in which the Israeli government is punishing those involved in the Palestinian struggle for dignity, freedom, and justice is through the withholding of the bodies of those called "terrorists" killed by Israeli forces, police or settlers. This policy and the policy to demolish their families' homes "constitute some of the most egregious human rights violations against Palestinians in Jerusalem," writes Palestinian writer and law graduate based in occupied Jerusalem, Budour Youssef Hassan.[13] And Israeli writer, activist and founder of the Gush Shalom peace movement, Uri Avnery calls it "the most atrocious and stupid measure . . . a supreme act of cruelty . . . I am almost too ashamed to bring this up."[14]

But these cruelties have mobilized the people. On December 1, Hassan tells us, youth held a concert at the Palestinian National Theatre—also known as El-Hakawati—in support of parents with children in prison and those waiting for the release of their children's bodies. The theatre's largest hall was filled to capacity; revenues were allocated to home reconstruction.

But there is ongoing direct action too. Back in March 2014 Palestinians formed a human chain and encircled the walls of Jerusalem's old city, with participants demanding the return of martyrs' bodies before the peaceful protest was violently dispersed by Israeli forces. But the struggle continues. These measures, Hassan continues to inform us, did not stop Hijazi Abu Sbeih and Samer Abu Eisbeh from setting up a protest tent in the yard of the International Committee of the Red Cross building in Jerusalem's Sheikh Jarrah neighborhood. "While the tent was initially erected to provide the two with shelter when they rejected Israel's order to banish them from Jerusalem, it was soon transformed into a vibrant space of civil disobedience."

For nearly two weeks, the tent brimmed with energy and revolutionary spirit free of factional divisions. Concerts were held there along with public lectures and discussions. More than just providing support for the two young protesters, those who attended were imbued with a rare sense of genuine, if short-lived, freedom. Here they were able to sing, raise their

13. See Bodour Youssef Hassan, "This Uprising Is about More than Knives," January 27, 2016, https://electronicintifada.net/content/uprising-about-more-knives/15416.

14. See Uri Avnery, "A Lady with a Smile," *Tikkun*, February 13, 2015, http://www.tikkun.org/nextgen/knesset-attempting-to-throw-out-its-arab-members-by-uri-avnery.

voices against the Israeli occupation, chanting "I am not leaving," immerse themselves in debate and organize. "Palestinians," Budour Youssef Hassan writes, underscoring my point about my faith in youth leadership, "are often asked about the alternative to their corrupt and failed leadership. Those who visited the tent could get a glimpse of what that could be like."

The protest tent, and Israel's arrest raid there, "did not capture the attention of international journalists, even though these nonviolent forms of resistance and Israel's crackdown on them are at the heart of Jerusalem's story." But the people's hope is not in the attention of international journalists with their agendas beholden to the empire. It is in their unshakable belief that their struggle will bring justice, dignity, and freedom, in the confidence in the righteousness of their strength, as we shall hear from Steve Biko in chapter 5, and it is in their faith in God as the God of justice.

From Palestine comes the story of the Christian family who refuses to give up their Bethlehem hill farm.[15] Watching as the Israeli settlements arose around them, enduring immense and growing pressure to move, the Nassar family has been battling to hold on to their ancestral land the family has owned for ninety-eight years. They are stubbornly committed to nonviolent resistance, firmly rooted in their Christian beliefs. On May 19, 2014, the family saw a bulldozer, guarded by Israeli soldiers, was at work uprooting their olive trees. The whole orchard, the best part of a decade's work, was gone.

In 1991 already the Israeli military authorities, in precise and frightening imitation of the South African apartheid authorities with their "Land Acts," "Group Areas Act," and forced removals, declared that more than 90 percent of the farm now belonged to the State of Israel. Since then it has only gotten worse. "They want us to give up hope and leave . . . they are trying to push us to violence or push us to leave," the family say, but are insistent that they will stay. So nobody can force them to leave, just as nobody will force them to imitate the violence and aggression of their oppressors. But more than that, says Amal, a daughter of the family, "nobody can force us to hate. We refuse to be enemies." That phrase, they told reporter Daniel Silas Adamson, painted on a stone at the entrance to the farm, was first used in 1916 by their father, Bishara Nassar. For the family, it still holds. Not only will they refuse to leave, says the son, Daher Nassar, speaking with defiant, indestructible hopefulness, "I will plant more trees, double trees."[16]

---

15. See Daniel Silas Adamson, "The Christian Family Refusing to Give Up Its Bethlehem Hill Farm," *BBC Magazine*, June 18, 2014, http://www.bbc.com/news/magazine-27883685.

16. Among the many moving stories of unflagging courage and defiant hopefulness is the story of resistance against the occupation in the Palestinian village of Nabi Saleh,

In March 2015, in the first fiery weeks of the student uprisings in South Africa, one of the first questions to be settled was the role of white students in the movement. At stake was not just the question of the nature of the struggle; at stake was also the character of the struggle. Would this struggle be a "black" struggle, shutting out whites because of their real or imagined inherent or inherited inability to join wholeheartedly in a struggle aimed at their real inherited white privilege? Or would this struggle be inclusive, drawing in white students in embodied solidarity,[17] thereby creating room for other, fundamental issues of justice, upholding its indivisibility, simultaneously giving real meaning to reconciliation, in defiance of what reconciliation has become in our politics?

In the midst of these battles, a young white student writes about the new militant movement, only just begun as the "Rhodes Must Fall" movement on the campus of the University of Cape Town.[18] Jessica Breakey

---

which continues in some form or another every week, effectively reversing the dynamics of power between the Israeli occupation forces and the villagers. Their weapon is not a gun or a bomb, but creative, nonviolent militancy. Apart from the weekly protest marches, "sometimes this weapon takes the form of a stone wall blocking the army's way; at other times, it comes in the form of a poem or piece of art. In all its iterations, however, it represents a constructive refusal to be subjugated—a refusal the world should finally take notice of and respect." See Zachary Faircloth "Lessons in Resistance from the Palestinian Village of Nabi Saleh," April 27, 2016, http://muftah.org/lessons-in-resistance-from-the-palestinian-village-of-nabi-saleh/#.V, 4/29/2016.

17. The term "embodied solidarity" was used by Larycia Hawkins, associate professor at Wheaton College, who after some months of strife, contention, and threats of dismissal had resigned from the faculty. Larycia Hawkins had been wearing a hijab in an act of courageous "embodied solidarity" with Muslims and as protest against Islamophobia. She had also stated that Muslims and Christians worship the same God, a statement the college administration found highly offensive, initiating disciplinary procedures. In a wave of support and admirable courage, evangelicals on the campus and across the country stood up in her defense. In an email, Dr. Peter Goodwin Heltzel described the students at Wheaton as "fierce, faith-rooted activists in this fight to abolish racism, sexism, and Islamophobia in evangelical colleges, congregations, and communities." To me it seems the signs of the hopeful *sizwe* are everywhere.

18. On the main campus of the university stood a towering statue of Cecil John Rhodes, the nineteenth-century personification of Britain's devastating imperial policies in Southern Africa. The statue became the focal point of growing awareness and anger in black students who saw the link between the glorification of South Africa's colonial past and their ongoing oppression in the country of their birth. They also saw the link between the imperialist oppression personified by Rhodes and the ongoing oppression of black people under the rule of a South African government subservient to the imperialist forces of the twenty-first century. A black student threw sewage on the Cecil John Rhodes statue, expressing that understanding and the anger felt by many and sparking the militant, nonviolent protest movement that quickly moved from the "Rhodes Must Fall" movement on the UCT campus to the "Injustice Must fall" movement engulfing the whole country. The Rhodes statue was taken down, and the students, youth and members of civil society are now concentrating

writes about the first act of protest at the statue by a black student and the reaction of a white student passing by. She sees this moment as "an act of contradictory beauty, a catalyst of a movement which has been brewing for years at this institution . . . "

She knows that this act is about resistance against the colonialism of the past that the statue personifies, but that it is also about ongoing oppression and white privilege. So she speaks with courage and candor, with honesty and integrity. "I cannot talk about white privilege as though I am an outsider. I cannot pretend I am not cloaked in freedom, opportunity and advantage. I cannot separate myself from this privilege that is so deeply embedded within everyone whose skin is a similar hue to mine." She talks about the tendency among many young whites to "distance ourselves from and refuse to see what is so clearly in front of us." Whites, she says, have given themselves permission "to ignore the hidden and unearned advantages that we willfully wrap ourselves in." She knows that this refusal to acknowledge this truth is "hindering the process of social transformation" in South Africa, and she pleads for "the moral responsibility to account for it, to be conscious of how we perpetuate it."

But then she goes further and puts both the black and white students to the test. "More than just accepting our privilege, it is time that we explore the idea of what it means to be a white ally." She means an ally of the movement against white privilege and white interests, against oppression and exploitation. Whites do have a place in this new revolution, she insists, but "we should be humble enough to ask where our place is, to pledge our solidarity and support but not to speak on behalf of black students, to not claim to represent their struggle and most importantly to know when we should be loud and when we should keep quiet." Because whites have been raised in positions of power, "we are not equal." It is for that equality that they must work together, and in order to do that, she says, "We must think deeper and do better. We *need* to think deeper and do better. It is our moral duty. It is also the least we can do."

As the revolution in South Africa unfolds, its striking characteristics are its inclusive nature, its persistent nonviolence, the strong presence of whites along with blacks, and the remarkable leadership of young female students.

---

on issues of systemic injustice still haunting the country and its people. What follows is taken from an article by a young white student, Jessica Breakey, and it is in her articulation of the issues at stake, her willingness to invite discussion, and her courage in stating her convictions so clearly in the face of opposition and sometimes derision from other students, white and black, that I see the beauty and the power of the hopeful *sizwe*. See Jessica Breakey, "White Students: Why We Need to Think Deeper and Do Better," March 24, 2015, http://www.bonfiire.com/cape-town/2015/03/white-students-why-we-need-to-think-deeper-and-do-better/.

This is what I mean by "the hopeful *sizwe*." And this hopeful *sizwe* will not go away.

❧ ❧ ❧

This book is an effort to grapple with some of the major issues as we are confronted with new and renewed struggles for justice, freedom, and human dignity raging across the world today. In many, if not all, of these revolutions young people and students have assumed roles of great responsibility and creative, steadfast, risk-laden leadership. These revolutions are taking place in new, and sometimes overwhelming, crisis situations, and these crises are occurring in what has been called our "post-apartheid," "post-racial" societies. In reality, these new uprisings tell us, it is very much a pre-freedom world. In the present situation of disillusionment, anger and growing mistrust it is almost inevitable that one of the first things to fall under suspicion and put under pressure is South Africa's choice for reconciliation, rather than continuation of the conflict. That is understandable, but I hope we will resist that temptation. In this work I plead for the fundamental rightness (and righteousness) of that decision. As I have argued before, it is not reconciliation that is to blame, but what South Africans have made of it, turning it into a political pietism that has failed to serve justice, dignity, and equity. This book continues the search for reconciliation that is radical, real, and revolutionary.[19]

The book engages not just "the issues" but enters into conversation with the people who raise them in specific contexts. So along the way we meet and engage Pope Francis, Archbishop Desmond Tutu, scholars from various disciplines, but especially the youth, students, workers, and community members, those engaged in the search for freedom, reconciliation and justice in South Africa and the rest of the world where the South African model is held up as exemplary. So in the course of our discussions we will consider reconciliation, justice, the African concept of *ubuntu* that played such a crucial and even controlling role in South Africa's reconciliation process, and matters of faith, politics and struggles for justice, and the role of persons of faith in those struggles. And we will consider if there are indeed lessons to be learned for ongoing struggles across the globe.

Over the years I have been constantly shaped by what I have experienced as a young person with other people in the struggle for justice in South Africa, and what I have learned from others. I continue to be impressed by what I am learning now from the new generation of young leaders and activists in ongoing struggles from South Africa to the US to Palestine. These

---

19. See Boesak and DeYoung, *Radical Reconciliation*.

three places of confrontation and hopeful struggle will be constant points of reference throughout this book. The young people have raised probing, uncomfortable, but utterly serious questions about our politics, our revered processes of reconciliation, about justice, our realities of oppression and our dreams of freedom. They are not afraid to challenge those we hold in high esteem and those processes that we have held up as salvific for our people. Their conversations with me, their public discourse, and their engagement with the fundamental issues of politics, justice, and reconciliation have been critical in the ongoing formation of my thinking. I will try to respond to the issues these young people themselves have put on the table, and I will treat them as inescapable challenges for the church in general and for prophetic theology in particular, as New Testament scholar Obery Hendricks puts it, to treat the needs of the people as holy before God.[20]

This book has been several years in the making, and it has matured as the encounters with many wonderful, engaged, justice seekers have grown, in South Africa of course, but also since my visit to Palestine and our sojourn in the United States since 2012. Some of what is presented here is based on sometimes exciting, sometimes difficult, but always deeply rewarding conversations with young people and communities in South Africa, the US and Palestine. These pages hopefully make clear how seriously I have taken those encounters. Some chapters have been presented as papers for discussion among colleagues, and their comments have been gratefully received. Other colleagues and friends have read several chapters. All of them, especially Dr. Curtiss Paul DeYoung, Dr. Fait Muedini, and Dr. Obery Hendricks, have honored me with critical comments that I have found very helpful indeed. I think the work is the better for it.

A book is a conversation with oneself, it is said, and in that sense this volume is also continuing my conversation with my last five publications since 2005. For those familiar with those works, it will also be clear how far I myself have traveled on this journey. A book is also a conversation with others and as such it is an invitation. With this book I hope to broaden that conversation and that it will allow still others to join us on that sometimes risky, sometimes treacherous, but always challenging and rewarding journey toward the fulfillment of justice, peace, and dignity for all God's children.

In my *Running with Horses: Reflections of an Accidental Politician* (2009), I reflected on what the African National Congress and its Alliance partners are proud to call "the National Democratic Revolution"—spelled with capitals, and which, at that time "seemed to have been captured" by then president Thabo Mbeki and his supporters within the ANC. In response to the debates raging between the (presumably "bourgeois") ANC and the "real left," this is what I said then:

20. See Hendricks Jr., *The Politics of Jesus*, 101–12.

> [I]n my view the real revolution still has to be fought. The revolution I speak of will not have the agenda of the left nor of the new bourgeois revolutionists, in whichever "camp" they might now find themselves. What we have seen in this first phase of our democracy has been the revolution of values, hopes, aspirations, and dreams that have all gone under in the wave upon wave of fake revolutionary fervour on behalf of class and group interests. The real revolution should have everything to do with those matters that should have been building blocks for our democracy but which now have become stumbling blocks: humanity, justice, peace, integrity, equity, reconciliation. The question then is not when the SACP [South African Communist Party] and COSATU [Congress of South African Trade Unions] will "recapture the socialist revolution" but rather, when will the people, in restoration of our spirituality of struggle and in the rightful claim upon our power, reclaim those values in the only revolution that will matter.[21]

It might very well be that we have arrived at that pivotal moment. It is now clear that the "revolution" has not been "re-captured" in the internal coup engineered by Jacob Zuma and his supporters nor in the all but disastrous way the ANC is now leading the country. It is now equally clear that whatever happened within the ANC and its change of leadership had nothing to do with revolutionary ideals of whatever ilk. What is clear is that for this generation South Africa, and the world for that matter, have entered a pivotal moment.

As always, my wife, Elna, and our daughters, Sarah and Andrea, deserve my deepest gratitude and highest praise for their patience, endurance, and constant encouragement. Their love has not only kept me strong; their active engagement, in their own ways, in the work for justice in the world, and their willingness to share their thoughts with me have opened doors for my mind to go through I did not even see. Learning from one's children is a truly awesome experience. What more could anyone wish for?

I am especially grateful to my editor, Dr. Charlie Collier, Jacob Martin, Calvin Jaffarian and the editorial team at Wipf and Stock for their help and encouragement. They have gone beyond the call of duty to make this project work.

Allan Aubrey Boesak

May 2017

---

21. See Boesak, *Running with Horses*, 329–37. The quote is on 329.

Acknowledgments

The following chapters were published previously and are now used here by permission in edited and expanded form:

Chapter 3, "The Divine Favor of the Unworthy: When the Fatherless Jesus Meets the Black Messiah," *Hervormde Teologiese Studies*, Volume 61, Art. # 933, DOI: 10:4102, 2011.

Chapter 6, "Deification, Demonization and Dispossession," *The International Journal of Public Theology*, Volume 8, No. 4, ISSN: 1872–5171.

Chapter 7, "A Hope Unprepared to Accept Things as They Are," *Nederduitse Teologiese Tydskrif*, Volume 55, Supplement 1 (2014).

"Poem for South African Women," by June Jordan, from *Directed by Desire: The Collected Poems of June Jordan*, Port Townsend, WA: Copper Canyon Press, 2005, copyright by the June M. Jordan Estate Trust. Used by permission.

INTRODUCTION

Seeing Satan Fall Like Lightning from Heaven

The New Militancy and the Hopeful Sizwe

> We are the ones we have been waiting for.
>
> —June Jordan, 1978

In the Presence of World Revolution

"We are," wrote M. M. Thomas—that remarkable and influential lay theologian from India—in a small monograph for the World Student Christian Federation (WSCF) somewhere in the 1950s, coauthored with J. D. McCaughey, "in the presence of a social revolution on an unprecedented, one might say, on a world scale."[1] The authors were reflecting on the social upheavals, revolutions for freedom and struggles for independence that swept the Global South at that time. They would not only speak of the places where violent insurrections were challenging the imperial, colonialist powers from Europe and the United States. Those revolutions would also include the nonviolent, militant struggles of the people of India, Northern Rhodesia (Zambia) and Tanzania against the British, that of the people of South Africa against the apartheid regime, and the nonviolent revolution for civil rights in the United States, for example.

The question here is threefold: first, what is the nature of this worldwide revolution, and second, can we as Christians see God's purposes at

---

1. See Thomas and McCaughey, *The Christian in the World Struggle*, 15.

work in this revolution? Third, should Christians join in this struggle for the sake of God's purposes, which M. M. Thomas identifies as justice, a new humanity, and the humanization of the world? This book is an attempt, in different ways, to respond to these questions, with its point of departure articulated by Thomas: God is involved in the struggles for justice for the sake of the humanization of the world, and Christians, "in the grip of this essential truth," cannot but "witness to it."[2] They cannot but join God in God's choices for justice, righteousness, and dignity. At this point of the twenty-first century, we are once again in the presence of revolution—great, sweeping upheavals set on establishing justice.

The revolutionary ferment sweeping the world of the first half of the twentieth century Thomas is speaking of was not about "furthering the aims of Communism" as so many would have it, far too easily dismissing the real causes of the revolutions and the genuine desires of the people engaged in them. It was also about more than just a demand for food: "The demand is for justice and not food," Thomas quotes independent India's first Prime Minister Jawaharlal Nehru, "and will not be satisfied with less than justice." In fact, Thomas states, introducing an even more compelling thought, "basic" to the revolution is "the new sense of dignity and historical mission" embraced by the people, "and the demand of the people is for *power as the bearer of dignity* and for significant and *responsible participation in society and social history*."[3]

This understanding of revolution is highly significant. This is not about "turning the tables" on oppressors and in the process exacting retribution for centuries of feudal or colonialist oppression. Neither is it a revolution to gain power *for the sake of having power*. It is wresting power not as instrument of political self-gratification, manipulation and destruction, but as bearer of the dignity of the people as they seek significant and responsible participation in society and history. It is not the power *over* others, but the power *shared with* others, to serve others in the pursuit of justice, dignity and wholeness as a common good in a qualitatively different society that is sought here.[4] That is a point of great political, social and psychological significance. One of the great and abiding questions, from those early days of freedom struggles to today, would be whether those engaged in these struggles sufficiently understood the nature of power, and sufficiently engaged the possibilities of creating a power dynamic entirely different than

---

2. Ibid., 39, 40.

3. Ibid., 19, emphasis original.

4. Already in my 1976 dissertation I emphasized this understanding of power. See Boesak, *Farewell to Innocence*, ch. 2.

the kind of power they were struggling against, a use of power that would be geared toward a humanizing struggle and as a result, a humanizing future.

The revolutions we are experiencing, the momentarily subdued, but nonetheless continuing struggles in the countries of the Arab Spring, carry the same theme—that of "delayed defiance," writes Iranian scholar Hamid Dabashi. As I see it, the same is true of the renewed struggles for justice in South Africa and the United States. "What we are witnessing unfold before our eyes... is the moment of a delayed defiance, a point of rebellion against domestic tyranny and globalized disempowerment alike, now jointly challenged beyond the entrapment of postcolonial ideologies." It is something new, still unfolding and open to the future. Significant in the new revolutions is the acute awareness that this is resistance against imperial power and might in all their global manifestations. One might consider it, Dabashi says, "a Palestinian intifada going global."[5]

The consequences are not trivial. What the world was seeing was in fact "a succession of vastly consequential and yet inconclusive social uprisings that required reconsideration of the very notion of 'revolution' as we have inherited and understood it so far."[6] Seeing unfolding events in Egypt, Syria, Yemen, Saudi Arabia, and Bahrain we now know with even more certainty than Dabashi did at the time of his writing, that these were not "conclusive revolutions as we have understood them in the exemplary models of the French, Russian, Chinese, Cuban, or Iranian revolutions of the last three centuries." Instead, we should reconsider our understanding of revolution:

> Revolution in the sense of a radical and sudden shift of political power with an accompanying social and economic restructuring of society—one defiant class violently and conclusively overcoming another—is not what we are witnessing here, or not quite yet. There is a deep-rooted economic and social malaise in all these societies.... No single angle of vision—economic, social, political, or cultural—would reveal the totality (and yet inconclusive disposition) of these massive social uprisings. Instead of denying these insurgencies the term "revolution," we are now forced to reconsider the concept and understand it anew.... The longer these revolutions take to unfold, the more enduring, grassroots-based, and definitive will be their emotive, symbolic, and institutional consequences.[7]

---

5. See Dabashi, *The Arab Spring*, 2, 3.
6. Ibid., 4.
7. Ibid., 5, 6.

But further, and this is the other great issue involved here, this is a revolution anchored in and embraced by the people. For Thomas the revolution is not in the hands of a small, revolutionary elite, the "vanguard" of the revolution, capable alone of changing society, marginalizing the people, the *lumpenproletariat* as Lenin, following Louis Blanqui, would have it, dooming them to be mere cannon fodder for the vanguardist fervor of this revolutionary elite, to be used and then discarded once the revolution is won.[8] Thomas places the power in the hands of the people as the heart and driving force of the revolution, claiming their right to participate with dignity and responsibility in the shaping of a new society. In the process they are also shaping a "new humanity," a term Thomas will come back to in later years, in his reflections on if, where, and how God is at work in the revolutions and upheavals in the world.[9]

So for Thomas, even though revolutions have their origin in a corrupt situation of injustice and oppression,[10] God is at work in the global struggles because despite the power of evil forces also at work in all revolutions, the revolution is fundamentally about social justice and the creation of a "new humanity." Despite the ways in which the revolution can be betrayed,[11] and despite the destructive presence of "false ideologies," the Christian ought to

---

8. It was the nineteenth-century French revolutionary thinker Louis Blanqui who first used the phrase "dictatorship of the proletariat" by which he meant for a small, conspiratorial elite to seize power in the name of the working class. Lenin successfully seized on this tactic and then, with a handful of subordinates, set out to dismantle autonomous soviets and workers' committees, carrying out "what became, in essence, a right-wing counterrevolution that introduced a system of repressive, centralized state capitalism and state terror." See Hedges, *Wages of Rebellion*, 14. Marx never embraced Lenin's call for this "revolutionary vanguard" but it has evolved into the principle of "democratic centralism" the African National Congress in South Africa is so loathe to disentangle itself from, causing such grave contradictions for itself and for politics in its rule in a participatory, democratic society. See Johnson, "Liberal or Liberation Framework?" I do not share Johnson's views on "liberation" and "liberal" as she applies them to the South African situation, but the point she makes is nonetheless valid.

9. See Thomas, "Issues Concerning the Life and Work of the Church in a Revolutionary World," 89–98. I have had cause to return, in different contexts, to these reflections and it is remarkable how relevant Thomas' thoughts have remained in the new manifestations of revolutions and world struggles for justice at different times and in different world contexts. See Boesak, *Farewell to Innocence*, 80–90; see also Boesak, *Kairos, Crisis, and Global Apartheid*, 19–25.

10. "Revolution is a malady," Thomas quotes Russian revolutionist and thinker Berdyaev: "it bears witness to the fact that there has been no creative power for the reformation of society, and that the forces of inertia have triumphed." See Thomas and McCaughey, *Christian in the World Struggle*, 33.

11. Ibid., 25–37. Thomas points to three "perils" through which the revolution can be betrayed: the peril of the technical betraying the social, of power becoming an end in itself, and the corruption inherent in every revolution.

be involved in those struggles because, taking their stand with the Church leaders of Asia, Thomas and McCaughey write,

> The Gospel proclaims that God's sovereignty includes all realms of life. Christ sitting at the right hand of God reigns and the church owes it to the world to remind it constantly that it lives under [God's] judgement and grace. It is not the challenge of any ideology but the knowledge of the love of God in Christ for [humankind] that is the basis of the Church's social and political concern.[12]

Just slightly more than a decade later, Martin Luther King Jr. would speak of the revolutionary impulses engulfing the world of the 1960s, seeing the connections between struggles, and it is as if he spoke prophetically of our times. "The deep rumbling of discontent that we hear today," he wrote, his thoughts going to the power of freedom songs, "is the thunder of disinherited masses rising from dungeons of oppression to the bright hills of freedom," and he heard "the rising masses" singing "in the words of our freedom song, 'Ain't nobody gonna turn us around.'" King's linking of the civil rights movement's freedom song to the freedom struggles elsewhere in the world is a powerful proclamation of his own understanding of the "inescapable network of mutuality" of global struggles for justice:

> All over the world like a fever, freedom is spreading in the widest liberation movement in history. The great masses of people are determined to end the exploitation of their races and lands. They are awake and moving toward their goal like a tidal wave. . . . For several centuries the direction of history flowed from the nations and societies of Western Europe out into the rest of the world in "conquests" of various sorts. That period, the era of colonialism, is at an end. East is moving West. The earth is being redistributed.[13]

That revolutionary movement is emphatically present in our day. This should not surprise anybody, King argued—and in my view this remains as true now as it was then—because "oppressed people cannot remain oppressed forever," and "the yearning for freedom eventually manifests itself." King sees not simply historical connection, but historical continuation in the "thrilling story" of the exodus when Moses stood before the Pharaoh crying, "Let my people go!"

---

12. Ibid., 14, referring to the Asian Church leaders' declaration from their Bangkok assembly, January 1950.

13. King, *Where Do We Go from Here*, 179–80.

This was an opening chapter in a continuing story. The present struggle in the United States is a later chapter in the same story. Something within has reminded the Negro of his birthright of freedom, and something without has reminded him that it can be gained. Consciously or unconsciously, he has been caught up by the spirit of the times, and with his black brothers of Africa and his brown and yellow brothers in Asia, South America and the Caribbean, the United States Negro is moving with a sense of great urgency toward the promised land of racial justice.[14]

Now, in the first decades of the twenty-first century, the prophetic insights of M. M. Thomas and Martin Luther King Jr. help us understand the new revolutions of our own day. They are as well, as Martin King called for, revolutions in search of a "radical overturning of values" of their societies, and as M. M. Thomas understood, a struggle for power "as the bearer of dignity" and for the right to participate in the shaping of their own history and destiny. Answering Martin King's call, these are struggles for understanding at last that it is about the confrontation with "the giant triplets" of racism, militarism and capitalism, as identified by King and that today, far from being just American—albeit largely and powerfully driven by the United States as still the most potent imperial power on earth—are without a doubt recognized as at the heart of global oppression, exploitation and imperial domination.

Cornel West, one of the very few truly organic intellectuals of our times, grasps perfectly what "this marvelous, new militancy" in Ferguson, Baltimore, New York, Oakland, Cleveland, and other places in the United States is all about. It is, he says, the outcome of "an analysis of capitalist wealth inequality, gender domination, homophobic degradation, and imperial occupation" which he correctly identifies as "all concrete forms of plunder," that requires "collective fightback, not just personal struggle." This is an astute and crucial distinction, for without this understanding one is not able to resist the dangers and temptations represented by black and white neoliberals who are ostensibly, but only partially and superficially, concerned, nonetheless remain paralyzed by their captivity to the establishment and in the final analysis—as West correctly points out—"become a distraction from the necessary courage and vision we need in our catastrophic times."[15]

---

14. Ibid.

15. Despite the sensationalized and somewhat misleading headline, and the equally sensational response of Michael Eric Dyson, Cornel West's argument is substantial and entirely convincing. See Michael Kassel, "Cornel West Delivers Blistering Take-down of Ta-Nehisi Coates—Michael Eric Dyson responds," July 16, 2015, http://observer.com/2015/07/cornel-west-delivers-blistering-takedown-of-ta-nehisi-coates.

The new, militant youth see and understand the connections: between globalized militarism and the militarized actions of police on their own streets in Oakland and Cape Town; between the devastation of capitalism in their neighborhoods, occupied Palestinian lands, black townships and the destruction of socio-economic inequalities on a global scale; between the unconquered and emboldened racism from mass incarceration to education to the Oscars, and to where the bombs fall and the drones strike. In doing so they understand, finally and fully, and better than the world around them has any inclination to, that Dr. King was right: it is their time to break the silence.

Turning their backs on half a century of deliberate domestication, calculated appropriation and crippling captivity to the "I Have a Dream" syndrome and the more recent but nonetheless powerful myth of "Madiba magic,"[16] the revolutionary youth are at last responding to the radical King.[17] They are doing what he pleaded for as he found the courage to break his own silence: they are looking at the world they have inherited, "questioning the fairness and justice of past and present policies" of Pharaohs on both sides of the blood-red waters of struggle.

As King increasingly did toward the end of his life, they understand the systemic nature of oppression and they are coming to see that "an edifice which produces beggars needs restructuring." With their embrace of King's embrace of "radical values" they too look "uneasily on the glaring contrast between poverty and wealth." With "righteous indignation" they look across the world and see individual capitalists as well as international corporations of the West and East "investing huge sums of money in Asia, Africa and South America, only to take the profits out with no concern for the social betterment of the countries" and with King, they are saying: "This is not just." They look at the alliance between the rich North and the "landed gentry" and local capitalist elites in the global South and they are saying, "This is not just." Their radicalized values are emboldening them to "lay hands on the world order and say of war: 'This way of settling differences is not just.'"[18]

And so with the hopeful determination that spurred on Martin Luther King Jr., they, too, say: "There is nothing, except a tragic death wish, to prevent us from reordering our priorities, so that the pursuit of peace will take preference over the pursuit of war. There is nothing to keep us from molding

---

16. An expression South Africans use to admiringly describe something that only the persuasive power of Mandela could accomplish or inspire others to achieve.

17. I am referring to the steady radicalization of Dr. King between 1964 and 1968, but especially in this context to one of his greatest and most radical speeches, "Beyond Vietnam," 201–17.

18. See Martin Luther King Jr., "Beyond Vietnam," 214.

a recalcitrant status quo with bruised hands until we have fashioned it into a brother- [and sister] hood."[19]

Seeing Satan Fall

As I, like millions across the globe, I suppose, sat glued to the television over the first months of 2011, watching events unfold in North Africa and the Middle East, my thoughts constantly returned to two biblical texts, one from the prophet Isaiah and the other from the Gospel of Luke. Isaiah prophesies, "[In a very little while] the meek shall obtain fresh joy in the LORD . . . for the tyrant shall be no more" (Isa 29:19-20), and Jesus says, "I have seen Satan fall like lightning from heaven" (Luke 10:18).

I have preached from these texts during our own liberation struggle in South Africa in the most difficult of times, while oppression and violence were our daily bread, while our people were bleeding and dying in the streets, and while, in the very apt Shakespearean expression, our country was becoming less and less our mother and more and more our grave.[20] It is, I am afraid, also the situation in which the people of the countries of the Arab Spring now find themselves, as imperialist forces from without and counterrevolutionary forces from within have hijacked the revolutions for justice and freedom from Tunisia to Libya, and from Egypt to Syria, and from Yemen to Saudi Arabia and Bahrain.[21] And in a violent twist of irony, now as well the people of the United States.

But these words from the Scriptures are not the siren songs of desperate optimism: they are rooted in the promises of God and the Lordship of Christ over every single inch of life, including our struggles for dignity and justice. They are anchored in the sacrificial commitment of the people to

---

19. Ibid., 215.

20. "Alas, poor country!" Ross laments in Shakespeare's *Macbeth*. "Almost afraid to know itself. It cannot be call'd our mother, but our grave, where nothing, but who knows nothing, is once seen to smile; where sighs, and groans, and shrieks that rend the air are made, not marked; where violent sorrow seems a modern ecstasy" (Act 4, scene 3).

21. See, e.g., Dabashi, *The Arab Spring*. His hopeful language of the "delayed defiance" that gave rise to the "discovering of a new world," the "liberation of geography" and a new "language of revolt," so vibrantly captured in the cry, "The People Demand the Overthrow of the Regime!" is now under severe pressure. What he foresaw as a terrible possibility has since come true, giving rise to the renewed struggles that are still unfolding. But it makes his grasp of the heart of the matter even more profound: "For Mohammed Bouazizi to remain the martyred witness of a revolution that will not replace one dictator with another, one false prophecy of freedom with another, there is only one logical and lasting measure: the people" (132).

the struggle for justice. They are fashioned by the imagination of the people toward freedom over against the turgid rigidity that is the mindset of oppression and false consciousness. They hold out the inextinguishable hope for a people in struggle whose faith is fundamental to that struggle. With Isaiah, they can sing of the tyrant whose days are numbered and with Jesus they have seen Satan fall like lightning from heaven. However, they see that only *because* they are in the struggle and they know that even if that participation calls for suffering and sacrifice, they will rejoice, "knowing that suffering produces endurance, and endurance produces character, and character produces hope, and hope does not disappoint..." (Rom 5:3–5).

Watching the scenes on television, I remembered our own struggle. I saw once again the ancient, grim resolve of Pharaohs of all times not to let the people go, set against the unstoppable determination of a people to be free. I saw the millions from Tunisia to Egypt to Libya and Yemen, from Jordan to Bahrain and Syria, wave after wave of human hunger and thirst after justice and righteousness, with every step and every day carving renewed hope out of utter despair. I saw strength emerging from a well that yesterday and the day before was dry and unyielding. People who had virtually given up on themselves and on ever gaining freedom seemed to gain new strength. I saw the determined, yet fragile, militant, nonviolent resistance despite unremitting pressure and almost unbearable provocation, and the contagiousness of courage. I saw the faces of the women, men and young people standing up for freedom and justice; and I saw the children on the shoulders of their parents, the woundable hope of a nation displayed in gap-tooth smiles and waving little hands.

But soon enough I also saw the face of naked despair as the fires of violence and attrition consumed the hopeful flame of nonviolent revolution, as violence sought, as it always seems to do, to brand every resistance to tyranny with its imitation of tyranny in seemingly endless efforts to exert control over the desires of people to free themselves from tyranny. Every struggle in every situation has its uniqueness, finds its own way in its own historical set of circumstances, and responds to each and every context in its own ways, according to its own impulses, hopes and dreams. There is, however, an underlying social, political and historical connectivity to all these struggles, past and present, and in our globalized world community, aided by the explosion of global communication, it is more so than ever.

Before the end of 2011 we had seen civil-servant protests in Botswana, a first in that country's history, and mass action in Malawi, with people directly linking their actions to the events further north. Doubtless there is a rising tide of rebellion against injustice, and it is global. We are indeed in the presence of world revolution. The regional and global consequences of the Arab Spring are yet to be fathomed, let alone assayed, writes Hamid Dabashi,

> As is evident from Greece, Spain and the UK, the unrest is not limited to the Arab or to the Muslim world. The sense of dissatisfaction extends well into the Mediterranean, from labour migrations to a variety of economic woes demanding "austerity measures." From Senegal through to Zimbabwe and Djibouti. As the initial interaction spread . . . it became clear that this was a full-fledged dialectic between the national and the transnational.[22]

This raises compelling questions for all countries where tyranny still holds sway or is being reasserted, where the people are deprived of their basic rights; where, like in the United States, democracy has turned into plutocratic oligarchies;[23] or where, as in South Africa and India, liberation movements turned into governments have forgotten or forsaken the ideals of the struggle for freedom. For these nations in North Africa and the Middle East, it seems to me, a *kairos* moment has indeed come, as the Palestinians recently again made crystal clear.[24]

These revolutions, including the revolution that ended formal and legal apartheid in South Africa, have not yet run their course. What we are witnessing is "the unfolding of an open-ended revolt, the conjugation of a

22. Ibid., 24. Dabashi speaks of a "transnational will to resist tyranny" that comes to the fore as counter-revolutionary forces, from the United States, Saudi Arabia, and Israel to "outdated outfits" like the ruling regime in Iran and Hezbollah, go to mind-numbing lengths to try to contain this revolution. As we witness the relentless war of the US-Saudi led coalition against Yemen, an essentially defenseless country against overwhelming might, we have to conclude that Dabashi is right.

23. A study titled "Testing Theories of American Politics: Elites, Interest Groups, and Average Citizens," undertaken by scholars at Princeton and Northwestern University, and using extensive data collected between 1981 and 2002, concluded that the United States is an oligarchy, dominated by its economic elite. "The central point that emerges from our research is that economic elites and organized groups representing business interests have substantial independent impacts on US government policy, while mass-based interest groups and average citizens have little or no independent influence." The researchers come to the conclusion that "democracy by coincidence," in which ordinary citizens get what they want from government only when they happen to agree with elites or interest groups that are really calling the shots, is not what will satisfy average citizens who, even though they have the vote, cannot compete with the overriding influence of the wealthy, powerful elites who have most impact on government and policy decisions. See Gilens and Page, "Testing Theories of American Politics." For a sobering, perhaps frightening look at the disastrous impact of money on American politics and its democratic processes, see Mayer, *Dark Money*.

24. See the Palestinian Kairos Document, http://www.*kairos*palestine.ps/index.php/about-us/*kairos*-palestine-document.

new revolutionary language and practice, predicated on a reading of reality that is an *opera aperta*—an 'open work' . . . a self-propelling hermeneutics that mobilizes a constellation of suggestions yet to be fully assayed."[25] But they will continue, because they are grounded in the will for genuine freedom and justice anchored in the hearts of the people, who themselves, as Thomas saw so clearly and prophetically, are demanding power "as the bearer of dignity and for significant and responsible participation in society and social history."

When, for example, we think of South Africa's struggle for freedom, its democratic transition and the ongoing struggles for justice and dignity, think not first of the Constitution with its values shaped by *ubuntu*; or of the democratic institutions put in place as guardians of the Constitution. Think of the people. Think not first of the body of laws and policies and statutes. Think of the people; their struggles, their joys, their tears, their cries, their ideals and their hopes, their courage. Without them there would have been no struggle. Without them there would have been no victory over apartheid. Without them there would be no dreams of a different society and a different world. Without them there would be no hope.

It is always the people, the *sizwe*, the struggling *sizwe*, the sacrificial *sizwe*, the hopeful *sizwe* that make the difference. They, through the darkest days, believed and knew with Isaiah that it would be only a little while, and the tyrant would be no more. They believed with Jesus as he assured the seventy upon their return from their mission where they saw "even the demons" submitting to them, that even though there were to be extraordinarily difficult times ahead, ultimate victory is assured, because he had already "seen Satan fall like lightning from heaven."

It is important not to romanticize this. Luke's account of "the sending of the seventy" cannot be separated from Matthew's "mission of the twelve" (Matt 10:5–42). Matthew devotes virtually a whole chapter to this subject, and it makes for sober, and sobering, reading. There, the emphasis is not on the final victory, but on the challenges and sacrifices awaiting the disciples as they go about preaching the coming of the reign of God. In Matthew Jesus's words are somber, if not dark. There, the "demons" are named, and in being named they are unexpectedly, and frighteningly, close to home. There, the disciples are sent out as "sheep among the wolves," warned that they would be "dragged before governors and kings because of me."

Governors and kings are one thing. They are the representatives of earthly powers, bent on holding on to that power with violent, cold-blooded

---

25. See Dabashi, *Arab Spring*, 230. See also Boesak, *Kairos, Crisis, and Global Apartheid*, 19–20.

viciousness. But what if the oppressed themselves are captivated by those powers, and overcome by desires for personal gain, are no longer capable of truth and faithful resistance against Satan as Jesus was in the wilderness? When they cannot withstand the temptations dangled before their eyes: of self-obsessed instant gratification, control over others and the security for oneself that power over others brings (turning stones to bread); of the invincibility and the self-delusion about the availability of God and control over God that power secures ("throw yourself down"); and of promises to fulfill dreams of empire, to "rule the kingdoms of the world" if only one would "bow down and worship"?

Then it is quite another thing: brother will betray brother; children will rise against parents "and have them put to death." There "persecution" rather than victory is the certainty, and it is not triumphant anticipation but "endurance to the end" that is the watchword. There the joyful "how much more!" of God's loving care and compassion regarding the followers of Jesus, just three chapters previous (7:11), becomes the startling and malignant "how much more!" of their portion of suffering and pain of 10:24–25. This is all because of Jesus, and because a "disciple is not above the teacher." Hence the repeated: "Do not be afraid of them."

Jesus was not speaking on behalf of the rich and the powerful in the palace and the Temple. Reveling in their power and the security of their privileged position, they had no need of assurances from this rebel leader of the rabble of Galilee. He, a true prophet from among the people, spoke on their behalf, the powerless but hopeful ones, and he is not promising them unfettered power and uncontested victory over the demonic forces. Satan's fall is not the inevitable outcome of an eschatological grand finale. Here it is spoken as prophetic truth in the face of imperial realities of oppression, disempowerment, and endless violence. It is Jesus' assurance that the struggle for the reign of God with its values of compassion, truth, justice, peace, and servanthood will overcome the reign of the Roman Empire with its inevitabilities of violence and war, domination and subjugation, alienation and dehumanization. This cannot happen without struggle and sacrifice. Certainly there will be victory. But it will be costly. Seeing Satan fall is not the guarantee of a smooth, untroubled walk to freedom—it is the assurance of hopeful struggle, and here the hope is not the anxious cravings of needful bravado but the assurance of the presence of the Living One who "counts even the hair on your head" (10:30). And in the end, the Apostle Paul will tell the church, it is not the followers of Jesus in their own power and triumphant might, but rather "the God of peace" who will "trample Satan under your feet" (Rom 16:20).

Secret Talks, Sacrificial Struggles, and the "End Game"

In South Africa, the dominant narrative about our struggle, our victory over apartheid and our transition to democracy is more and more a determined effort to turn it into a story about backdoor deals, secret pre-negotiation talks, and elite pacts, completely negating the struggle as the struggle of the people. This is a crucial point we should ponder more than we are clearly doing. Contrary to this imperial myth, the so-called endgame of our struggle for freedom was not played out in the secret deals, pre-negotiation settlements, and elite conspiratorial pacts concocted by the political aristocracies from both sides, as for example political philosopher and political broker as the astute representative of the white establishment, Willie Esterhuyse, would have it.[26]

In this version, the "end of apartheid" was brought about by the few— the elite, secret pre-negotiators who made the deals acceptable to the white elites that would predetermine the parameters of the "real" negotiations at Kempton Park as well as the future of democratic South Africa. These pre-negotiated deals, presented as the necessary prerequisites for South Africa's reconciliation process, would prove to be devastating to the need for justice, which in my view is the more necessary requirement for a durable, sustainable, and cohesive process of reconciliation and reconstruction, and there were those who warned that this would be so.[27]

Typically though in Esterhuyse's view, the failures presently crippling South Africa's democratic development are not ascribed to the disasters that elite compacts, excluding the vast majority of the people, and predicated on

---

26. See Esterhuyse, *End Game, Secret Talks and the End of Apartheid*. The somewhat presumptuous claim, apparent in the title—"the end of apartheid"—already reveals the confidence in the dominant narrative, despite the historical evidence.

27. See, e.g., Terreblanche, *Verdeelde Land,* who speaks of these secret talks as "a secret elite conspiracy" entirely to the benefit of the white elite and the new black political aristocracy roped into the deal (92–94). "The 'great prize' for the ANC political elite at the secret negotiations was that they, and they alone, would be declared previously disadvantaged individuals (PDI's) who would qualify to become political representatives with lucrative salaries or would become the beneficiaries of (BEE) Black Economic Empowerment and Affirmative Action contracts . . . The 'great prize' to which American pressure groups that participated at the secret negotiations aspired to was to convince the ANC to accept the ideologies of neoliberal globalism and market fundamentalism, so that South Africa could become a neo-colonial satellite of the American-led neoliberal empire"; see Terreblanche, *Lost in Transformation*, 72–73. The secret pre-negotiations are confirmed by others, see, e.g., Sparks, *Tomorrow is Another Country,* and Bond, *Elite Transition.* Sparks accepts the legitimacy of these secret talks; Bond, like Terreblanche, is far more critical. See also my critique in chapter 4 below.

compromises that serve the interests of the old white elite and the new black aristocracy, were bound to bring. Esterhuyse finds the fault elsewhere: with, amongst other factors, the failure of the Government of National Unity and the Truth and Reconciliation Commission.[28] That the reconciliation process did not live up to expectations, built as it was on the shaky and artificial foundations of a reconciliation process devoid of a commitment to the restoration of social justice, rights and human dignity, and upon an Act of Parliament that put severe, and deliberate, limitations on its effectiveness, cannot be a surprise. In my view, the problem was not, as Esterhuyse argues, that "ethnic, socioeconomic, political, and structural violence has taken on too much of an intertwined, endemic and systemic character over time."[29]

Esterhuyse writes as if systemic, endemic violence is a phenomenon of the last twenty years, because somehow the careful plans hatched in the secret deals were not allowed to come to fruition. The problem is that the violence Esterhuyse complains about had been "intertwined, systemic, and endemic" for decades, centuries, in fact. The further problem is that the elite pacts were not designed, and had no intention, to confront the systemic and structural socio-economic injustices that are the indisputable legacies of South Africa's colonialist and apartheid past. Rather they strengthened them and lured the new black elite into accepting them, to the detriment of the vast majority of South Africa's people. Neither did the elite pacts consider the systemic violence inescapably inherent to apartheid and hence to any "modification" of it as a central problematic, and consequently, neither did the TRC. One of the great miscalculations of the TRC, as Ugandan political scientist Mahmood Mamdani has conclusively argued, is that it considered only *physical* violence as "a human rights crime."[30] The systemic violence of apartheid as expressed, for instance, in the forced removals, social engineering, the myriad discriminatory laws and practices, or the apartheid education systems for blacks, was not at all taken into account.

For Esterhuyse, the fact that the TRC "afforded people to tell their stories" was a good thing, but the fact that the TRC "could not bring about sustainable reconciliation and peace" created a problem.[31] In truth, victims of apartheid crimes may certainly have found therapeutic value in "telling their stories" and even sometimes confronting their tormentors with the truth of their experiences. But "telling their stories" in those public amnesty hearings remained just that: there was no guarantee of remorse, repentance

28. Esterhuyse, *End Game*, 302–18.
29. Ibid., 303.
30. See Mamdani, "Beyond Kempton Park." I return to this issue below.
31. Esterhuyse, *End Game*, 311.

or restitution in response to the (re)telling of those wrenchingly painful experiences. "Telling their stories" could never be a substitute for the radical, systemic distributive justice the people deserve and without which reconciliation would never be complete, sustainable, and durable. What is also not taken into account here is the fact that offering a platform for "telling their stories" does not necessarily include the element of a shift of power and power relations so vital for true reconciliation and the restoration of justice, dignity, rights, and community.

Within the context of truth-telling, a real shift of power requires at least the showing of genuine remorse, asking for forgiveness; and the repentance *that results in the undoing of injustice and the doing of systemic justice toward the transformation of society*. And it is in the systemic undoing of injustice and the doing of justice that the poor and oppressed will be truly empowered. The "space" that was created for the telling of stories was not only space for revealing the truth, or as much of it as could be found. It was also space for remorse, repentance, and forgiveness; for the beginning of systemic processes toward holistic justice, and therefore space for the beginning of healing. And it is here where the TRC had the opportunity to turn political theater—however dramatic it might have been—into a moment of redemption for the victim, the perpetrator, and for the whole of South African society. This is where, reminding ourselves of Mahmood Mamdani's critique, the fragmented elitist drama could have become the beginning of the politics of holistic justice. I am of the view that the TRC, in the virtual reinterpretation of its mandate on this point under the leadership of Archbishop Tutu, should have been far more deliberate on the issue of social, distributive, holistic justice, and I make that point in chapter 4 below.

It would be closer to the truth if Esterhuyse would have tried to acknowledge that the TRC's failure in this regard is due to at least two factors in my view: the TRC, as an *outcome* of Esterhuyse's much vaunted secret pact, could not be expected to bring the "sustainable reconciliation and peace" Esterhuyse now expects it to have accomplished. Secondly, as I will argue below, if the TRC had remained steadfast to the mandate it had given itself without government permission, namely to interpret reconciliation on the basis of the Christian gospel, it would have been able to challenge the limited mandate from parliament more effectively. Here I am not so much talking of the amnesty process, but of social justice, active, *distributive justice* as inseparable from reconciliation.

More importantly however, secret talks that lead to elite pacts guaranteed to serve the interests of the few, excluding the people, ignoring their struggles, hopes and sacrifices, are doomed to failure. It is not much different from—albeit a more respectable, sophisticated version of it—the old

Leninist "revolutionary vanguard" theory we have spoken of before. The elites might have devised clever ways of securing power and keeping it in the hands of a few for as long as it lasts, but those caught up in such fraudulent pacts cannot act for justice and truth no matter how much, like the African National Congress, they claim to do so. They merely prolong, or inherit already irredeemable untruths and petrified injustices. They will not find the courage to join the struggle for justice because it will be directed against them, the new pharaohs on the other side of the blood-red waters. And in their resistance against justice for the sake of the preservation of injustice and privilege they will, as Martin Luther King Jr. saw so clearly, "surely be dragged down the long, dark, shameful corridors of time reserved for those who possess power without compassion, might without morality, and strength without sight."[32]

The truth is that, despite the dominant narrative, the "end game" that brought an end to apartheid was not played out through those secret talks in the castles and manor houses of Switzerland and the United Kingdom, between those who from the lofty heights of white South African supremacy and privilege and from within the disconnected world of exile politics sought to direct South Africa's politics, divorced as they were from the deepest dynamics of the internal resistance. It was played out in the streets of struggle, sacrifice, and hopeful determination. In my view, this is the fundamental current that runs through every phase of the struggle. Even just a glimpse at history confirms this.

Shadows of the Light[33]

In the decade of apartheid rule following the election victory of the National Party in 1948, the people understood that the struggle had just entered a new phase; that the long, long, road had just become longer, that racial hatred had just been legally permanentized, officially legitimized, and politically institutionalized. But that also meant that the call for freedom had become clearer, more urgent, more compelling. They abandoned what Nelson Mandela called "constitutional protest" and in 1952 opted for nonviolent revolutionary resistance, engaging the oppressor in the persistent mass actions of civil disobedience that became known as the Defiance Campaign in ways that changed the rules of that engagement completely. They stepped away from the strategy of petitions and appeals to successive white minority

---

32. King, "Time to Break Silence," 217.
33. This is taken from the title of an earlier work. See Boesak, *Shadows of the Light*.

regimes and from the belief that the oppressor would feel any obligation to respond with political responsibility and sensitivity for justice.

They decided they could no longer protest against apartheid in statements and appeals while obeying apartheid laws that called into question the very validity of those appeals. They decided that obeying apartheid laws was in fact not a sign of civil politics but complicity in their own oppression and lending legitimacy to laws that destroyed their humanity. They now understood that openly challenging the oppressor in the streets with actions of mass civil disobedience was in fact the dignity they owed themselves and the generations to come. So instead of depending on the persuasive powers in letters and petitions directed at the white government or the Crown of England penned by the leadership, they called upon the courage and determination of the people to be free. The people took to the streets.

It is always the people, the determined people, the hopeful *sizwe*. They understood that the struggle was far from over, and that yet more, and new sacrifices would be called for. They understood that the oppressor would not relinquish power without a struggle; they knew that the road to freedom would always be via the cross, but that they could not allow their dreams to be reshaped by the tyranny of racist oppression. They flooded the streets in that historic, decisive Defiance Campaign of militant, nonviolent mass actions of civil disobedience; they filled the air with songs of struggle, and they spoke through Albert John Mvumbi Luthuli, that remarkable Christian leader of the struggle in the middle of the twentieth century:

> The task is not yet finished and South Africa is not yet a home for all her sons and daughters. Such a home we wish to ensure. From the beginning our history has been one of ascending unities, the breaking of tribal, racial, and creedal barriers. The past cannot hope to have a life sustained by itself, wrenched from the whole. There remains before us the building of a new land, a home for [all] who are black, white, brown, from the ruins of the old narrow groups, a synthesis of the rich cultural strains which we have inherited.[34]

The people have heard and understood Albert Luthuli as he told us in that same passage cited above that "somewhere ahead there beckons a civilization, a culture, which will take its place in the parade of God's history beside other great human syntheses. . . . It will not necessarily be all black; but it will be African."[35] So South Africans today continue to fight for that nonracial, inclusive, profoundly African society even in the face

---

34. Luthuli, *Let My People Go!* 229–30.
35. Ibid., 230.

of continued racism, narrow ethnic nationalisms, a new black nativism and revived tribalism that can only lead to disaster if left unchecked. These were Luthuli's words, but they would have remained the musings of a lonely prophet had they not been embraced, given life and a future by a hopeful, determined people.

The hope I am speaking of is not the optimism of wishing-well politics. It is grounded in the history of struggle. The year 2015 marked the sixtieth anniversary of one of the most remarkable political moments in South African history. In Kliptown, on June 25, 1955, the people came together in a gathering called "The Congress of the People." This meeting brought together more than three thousand delegates from civil society and political formations, from every religious community, from across the country, white and black, to write and adopt the Freedom Charter, one of the most important political documents of the twentieth century.[36] The Congress, as well as the historic document that was its handiwork, express in a most profound way the resilient, uplifting hope of the people set against the dismal, hopeless politics of apartheid.

Apartheid, having become the official policy of the land in 1948, was just beginning to tighten its grip on every aspect of life in South Africa. From the start this process would be relentless. At Kliptown the people responded, with righteous anger but not with hatred; with utter disdain for legalized racism but with no thought of racism in return; with unequivocal rejection of the society that was being forced into shape but with an unerring eye on the alternative society they dreamed of and worked for. So, against all the realities of apartheid, against the distorted imaginings of white superiority and black inferiority; and in the face of white dispossession of their land, their dreams, *and* of their future, they spoke through the Freedom Charter:

> South Africa belongs to all who live in it, black and white, and that no government can justly claim authority unless it is based on the will of all the people . . . that our country will never be prosperous or free until all our people live in brotherhood . . . without distinction of colour, sex or belief . . . And therefore we, the People of South Africa declare . . .

This was a moment of amazing political insight, but even more: it was a moment of untrammeled, defiant hope. The Freedom Charter is an irrevocable exposure of the evil of apartheid. Every phrase is a devastating critique of the political, sociological, and moral suppositions of apartheid; every

---

36. The text of the Freedom Charter can be found at http//:www.historicalpapers.wits.ac.za/inv_pdfo/AD1137/AD1137-Ea6-1-001-jepg.pdf.

sentence is a ringing condemnation of the political, social, and economic intentions of apartheid; every word is a resounding declaration of resistance against the politics of apartheid. In one single paragraph the fundamental truths about genuine democracy are held up as a scorching judgment of apartheid South Africa:

- It exposes and rejects the foundational distortions and fallacies of apartheid: "South Africa belongs to all who live in it . . ."
- It stipulates the basic requirement for legitimate governmental authority: there is no true government without the consent of the governed.
- It spells out the difference between naked power and legitimized authority.
- It unmasks apartheid's political heresies by holding on to the belief in the strength of a common humanity responsive to, responsible for, and accountable to one another, and to the belief in the power and necessity of a nonracial, inclusive democracy based on equality and reconciled diversity.

That is why the Charter is such a credible example of what M. M. Thomas meant when he spoke of the power of the people as the bearer of dignity and for significant participation in the shaping of their own history.

In its judgment on apartheid and its claim on the altogether different vision of the future, the Charter did one other, profound thing. It wrested power from the hands of the powerful oppressor and placed it firmly in the hands of the powerless people, thereby empowering the people beyond measure. Apartheid may have shaped the past; it may have a stranglehold on the present; but it shall have no right to fashion the future. That right belongs to the people.

In claiming that right the Charter, in ways we may not yet have fully understood or appreciated, gave the people the power and authority of authentic speech. It is speech vested in the will of the people, a will to freedom now being asserted over against the willful arbitrariness of apartheid. The emperors of ancient Rome, in the reported words from Nero, proclaimed, "All is mine to decree." Those were decrees backed by the merciless violence of the empire, always against the interests of the people, disdainful of the hopes of the people, destructive of the life of the people. These were decrees announced in the arrogant assurance that the people could not withstand them, change them, or rise up in resistance against them. These were decrees that always benefited the rich and powerful, the privileged inner circles of imperial patronage.

In like fashion, against the will of the people, against the common good, and against the yearnings of the future, the architects and builders of apartheid decreed its laws, its crimes, and its inhumanity. Now, through the Charter, the people assert their will, and the people *declare*. And it is a declaration of the will to hope, life, and freedom. That is the power of transformed and transformative speech. It is the language of revolt, the grammar of hope, creating space for the politics of freedom—completely undermining the certitudes of apartheid by making them a site of struggle and creative contestation.[37]

The oligarchs of darkness *decree*, but the people *declare*. The potentates of apartheid *decree*, but the people *declare*. The purveyors of oppression, their hearts anchored in violence, *decree*, but the people, their hearts emboldened by hope, *declare*. This was a moment of startling political insight, of awesome courage, of audacious hope, not denying the manifested realities of apartheid, but nullifying their validity over their lives. Apartheid decreed the intentions of capitalist enslavement; the will of the people declared freedom. Apartheid decreed the power of arrogant racial domination and social engineering; the people declared the authority of equality, diversity and inclusivity. Apartheid decreed the supremacy of injustice, the people declared the invincibility of justice.

It was a moment that shifted the power from those sitting on the thrones of racist presumption to the people walking in the shadows of the light: in the shadow of painful struggle, but in the light of confident solidarity; in the shadow of sacrificial suffering but in the light of contagious courage; in the shadow of constant contestation and temptations of betrayal, but in the light of unstoppable freedom. This is the hopeful politics the people have bestowed as a gift to every generation, and this is the politics that should inspire us now, at this moment of new and renewed struggles. There might be shadows, but they are shadows because of the light.

"We Are the Ones We Have Been Waiting For"

The year 2016 marks sixty years since the epoch-making women's march to the Union Buildings in Pretoria against one of the most hated pieces of legislation, the infamous Pass Laws. At the heart of these laws was not only the severe restriction of movement by black South Africans, but the denial of their citizenship of the land of their birth. The women's march was an event with highly important political implications.

---

37. See Boesak, *Dare We Speak of Hope?*

In that march the women did more than just sing that rightly acclaimed and universally loved freedom song, *Strijdom, wathint' abafazi, wathint' imbokodo! Uzokofa!* ("Strijdom, you have touched a woman, you have struck a rock—you will be crushed!"). They not only claimed their right to protest against the inhuman pass laws of the apartheid regime; they also claimed their rightful place in the struggle as simultaneously their march established telling critique of the entrenched patriarchy of the liberation movements. This is of great significance, moreover, because it signals a profound shift of power relationships within the movement itself. The eloquent and courageous young women of the Arab Spring, the Black Lives Matter movement, the Palestinian intifadas, the Jerusalem intifada, and the Injustice Must Fall movement are all, in their own ways, heirs to this singular moment of historic transformation.

South Africa's freedom and its transition were made possible by struggle, but more so by sacrifice; by suffering but more so by resilience; by pain but more so by joyful determination; by political understanding but more so by audacious hope; by visionary leadership but more so by the courageous, determined people. They gave life to African American poet June Jordan's wonderful poem in honor of the Women's March, "Poem for South African Women." The poem ends with these words: "We are the ones we have been waiting for."[38]

The last verse of that powerful poem reads as follows:

And who will join this standing up

and the ones who stood without sweet company

will sing and sing

back into the mountains and

if necessary

even under the sea

we are the ones we have been waiting for

June Jordan's powerful line "we are the ones we have been waiting for" is an acknowledgment and celebration of the people, their power, their capacity for initiative and leadership, their capacity for grasping the vision of the revolution, making it their own and running with it, determined to see it become reality. "We are the ones" means we are no longer waiting for some

38. See June Jordan's classic and moving poem, "Poem for South African Women," written in commemoration of the Women's March, August 9, 1956, and presented at the United Nations on August 9, 1978. Available at http://www.junejordan.net/poem-for-south-african-women.html.

external power like the permission of the men, or Lenin's "revolutionary vanguard" that would, all of them, first manipulate the women's desire for freedom, use their power, then deny their agency in the revolution and in the shaping of their own history.

"We are the ones" taking a hand in history, shaping history with a different kind of power, the women are saying. This truth echoes strongly in the dynamics of the new militancy we are witnesses of today. In Chicago's Black Lives Matter movement, writes Salim Muwakkil, "Black women are so prominent in the movement's leadership, the era might also be characterized as a matriarchal moment."[39] At the heart of it is "a 30-year-old radical black queer feminist who is [Mayor] Rahm Emmanuel's worst nightmare." And the connections with South Africa are real, radical, and poignant. "At the end of my very first year," says Charlene Carruthers, "I had the opportunity to study in South Africa."

> We were there 10 years after the end of apartheid. Going to South Africa was perhaps the closest I could get to what it could look like if I was around in America in 1978. I was 18 and coming from a city that is still very segregated. That trip expanded my consciousness around what it meant to be Black on a global level or outside of Chicago, really, and got me interested in politics . . . We do this work through what we call a 'Black queer feminist lens' because we believe that in order to achieve liberation for all Black folks we have to be radically inclusive . . . [40]

This is the hopeful power of the powerless that shattered and overcame apartheid's politics of despair.

The foundations for South Africa's transition into democracy and for a humane, responsive, and compassionate society lie in the remarkable ways the struggle for freedom was waged and the consistency with which the ideals for an open, inclusive, nonracial, participatory democracy were upheld, cherished, and nurtured despite the harshest forms of oppression, the most cynical political manipulation by the apartheid regime as well as the African National Congress' political aristocracy, and the most relentless violence.

Even when, as the very last possible response to the intransigence of white power and privilege and the unremitting violence of a racist, minority regime, they were forced to adopt a military strategy, the aim was not

---

39. See Salim Muwakkil, "The 30 Year Old Radical Black Queer Feminist who is Rahm Emanuel's Worst Nightmare," February 1, 2016, http://readersupportednews.org/news-section2/318-66/34941-the-30-year-old-radical-black-queer-feminist-whos-rahm-emanuels-worst-nightmare.

40. Ibid.

to drive white people into the sea. It was not to sow as much death and destruction as possible. It was not even to conquer. It was to uphold and realize the dream of a nonracial, open, democratic society.[41] So they spoke through Nelson Mandela as he, on behalf of all of them, stood in the dock facing the apartheid court:

> The time comes in the life of any nation when there remain only two choices—submit or fight. That time has now come to South Africa . . . We shall not submit . . . I have fought against white domination and I have fought against black domination. I have cherished the ideal of a democratic and free society in which all persons live together in harmony and with equal opportunities. It is an ideal which I hope to live for and to achieve. But if needs be, it is an ideal for which I am prepared to die.[42]

In the dominant narrative, in a deliberate attempt to alienate Mandela from his people and dispossess the people of their role in the struggle, Mandela is presented as speaking only in his own behalf. In truth, while Mandela may have spoken in the first person as "the first accused," he was in fact speaking on behalf of all the accused, and by the same token on behalf of all the people who had taken the risks with those about to be sentenced. Mandela did no more than articulate their fight, their hopes and dreams, their determination to die if necessary as they had shown throughout the struggle. If he had spoken just for himself, the speech would have been unbearably self-centered, no more than empty braggadocio. To make it so is to dishonor both the leader and the people. But because he spoke for the people it was filled with the authority of authentic heroism, the heroism of a people convicted by their right to freedom.

"This then," Mandela told the court, "is what the ANC is fighting. Their struggle is a truly national one. *It is a struggle of the African people, inspired by their own suffering and their own experience.* It is a struggle for the right to live."[43] It is always about the *sizwe*. And when that generation was exiled, banned, and imprisoned; when all political activity was suppressed, driven underground, and declared illegal; when apartheid thought it had broken the back of the resistance, it was the children who in 1976 picked up the staff and held it high, a beacon for the masses to see and follow, a staff pointing at a promised land not yet seen but always dreamed of and believed in.

---

41. See the discussion in Boesak, *Kairos, Crisis, and Global Apartheid*, 180–92.

42. See http//:www.anc.org.za/content/nelson-mandelas-statement-dock-rivonia-trial, "Mandela's Statement from the Dock."

43. Ibid., my emphasis.

In 1983, when a new generation came together in what would become South Africa's largest, nonracial, nonviolent social-resistance movement, one that would break down the last bastions of apartheid, we understood that it is of crucial importance to allow ourselves not just to be *beckoned* by the ideals of the struggle, but to let those ideals *infuse* the struggle, lead and give shape to the struggle, so that we should not only follow those ideals but embrace them *as we struggled*:

> We must not allow our anger over apartheid to become the basis for blind hatred of *all* whites. Let us not build our struggle upon hatred; let us not hope for revenge. Let us, even now, seek to lay the foundations for reconciliation between whites and blacks in this country by working together, praying together, struggling together for justice. . . . [For] in the final analysis, judgment will be made not in terms of whiteness or blackness whatever the ideological content of those words may be today, but in terms of the persistent faithfulness to which we are called in this struggle.[44]

In doing this, young South Africans more than thirty years ago were not only holding the struggle to its own inner core promises of nobility, it deliberately created room for authentic reconciliation without which no revolution is complete. These are the wellsprings of South Africa's struggle for freedom and its transition to democracy. It was because of this that when the time came, we made the kind of choices that stunned the world and caused many to speak of the "miracle" of our transition. And in truth, it was not completely far-fetched. We struggled against all odds for over three centuries and we won. We were locked in battle with truly demonic forces and we never gave up. We stood alone in the world for so long but we endured. We were traumatized by indescribable violence and dehumanization but when the time came for fundamental choices we chose the open hand reaching for a shared future, not the closed fist grimly gripping the past. We chose solidarity with and justice for the living rather than revenge for the dead. We chose reconciliation over retribution, the risk of forgiveness over the triumph of justified condemnation.

We chose the political justice of Kempton Park over the criminal justice of Nuremberg. We set aside justifiable victor's justice, did not claim the power of well-deserved victim's justice, but chose for the vulnerability of survivor's justice. In doing this we went further than most have seen or recognized: we did not say that all *black* South Africans were survivors. We called *all* South Africans survivors: we all survived this horror called

---

44. See Boesak, "Peace in Our Day," 155–63.

apartheid. And at the deepest heart of *that* lies *ubuntu*: the understanding that my humanity is inextricably bound with your humanity; that I am only what I am when you are what you are meant to be; that in hurting or despising or dehumanizing me you are hurting, despising and dehumanizing yourself; that in my embracing and forgiving you I restore your humanity and mine and restore the community that was lost because of what you have done. This is a generosity of spirit that is stunning in its depth and its width. This is a spirituality that has far-reaching and radical political implications.

This is not the work of one person, not even of one such as Nelson Mandela, extraordinary human being that he was. This was the work of the faithful, sacrificial, hopeful *sizwe*, and, we shall argue in this work, the only response to this unbelievable magnanimity, this indescribable forgiveness, this unimaginable trust, is the reciprocity of justice. The fact that South Africa's youth are once again in the streets, continuing the struggle in search for that justice and true freedom in the face of the betrayal of their liberation movement, resisting a new pharaoh "who looks like us," is a sign of their refusal to abandon the fierce and audacious hope that they have inherited from previous generations. Their disappointment has not driven them to despair. It has rekindled their resolve, and their hope has given them strength to continue to believe in the political necessity and the salvific power of genuine reconciliation.

It is true that words such as *reconciliation* and *forgiveness* taken from the Bible and made applicable to politics can become powerful means of radical transformation. But as we discovered in South Africa, they can also become no more than political pietism—in other words, not as a critique of the political process, but turned into a handmaiden of it and subservient to the demands of expediency, divorced from those realities that make true reconciliation possible, durable and sustainable: confrontation with evil rather than papering over the cracks; repentance, remorse, forgiveness, restitution, and the reciprocity of social, distributive justice as the only response to the scale and depth of political, communal, and personal forgiveness white South Africans were offered by blacks in our reconciliation efforts.[45]

Christians, driven and captivated by the disturbing presence of the "essential truth" will be compelled to ask: what *kind* of freedom, what *kind* of equality in what *kind* of society are we speaking of? What kind of justice is being called for? If we are speaking of diversity, is that a *reconciled* diversity? Christians will insist upon laws that do not merely frame legality, but respond to morality; on a legal system that will protect, guard and promote the rights of the most vulnerable, rather than just be responsive to the

---

45. See Boesak and DeYoung, *Radical Reconciliation*.

whims and wishes of the rich and powerful. The legal system that prevailed in apartheid South Africa, and some of the shocking decisions emanating from the courts in the United States, even though both pretended and still purport to be societies with respect for the rule of law, and the shocking way even international law is driven, fashioned and paralyzed by the politics of power have at least taught us that much.

Such resistance requires understanding, courage, the willingness to suffer, and pathos. The pathos of the revolution is most naturally for the cause of the revolution. The pathos of the Christian is for the spirituality of the struggle, for the realization of the dreams, hopes and aspirations of the people, for the dignity of their sacrifices, for the redemption of their future and for their unhindered participation in the shaping of history. It is for the subversion of the prevailing order until it conforms to the norms of the kingdom of God: justice, peace, wholeness, humanity, inclusion, and dignity. Our pathos is not just for the revolution, it is for the prevention of an incomplete revolution. If the justice that embraces all, is compassionate and indivisible is not sought and done; if patriarchy finds refuge but women's dignity and rights are not regarded, promoted and protected in our public, sacred and private spaces; if our children cannot rejoice in a hopeful future; if we pontificate on the cause of the revolution but do not revere the sanctity of the earth, of our land, our rivers and seas and the air; if power is not the bearer of dignity for the people and the agent for significant and responsible participation in their own society and social history, the revolution remains incomplete.

In the parable of the Good Samaritan, I have proposed elsewhere,[46] Jesus makes the Samaritan stop not just to bind the wounds of the man lying in the road. Jesus makes him stop "to challenge and break the cycle of violence; the violence of the bandits who kill in the name of the struggle, and the violence of the passers-by who benefit from the oppression and the very violence they pretend not to see; who turn the other way, claiming the neutrality of religious non-involvement." Jesus does not reject the struggle against oppression; he turns the revolution in a fundamentally different direction. "He reminds the revolution of the power of love, a love that is revolutionary because it is humanizing . . . " This is what radical love means and Martin Luther King Jr. understood so well: it is not just for the success of the revolution, it is for what one could call the *ubuntufication* of the revolution. It is not just about winning a revolution and overturning an evil, unjust order. It is about preserving the humanity of the revolutionary

---

46. See Boesak, *Kairos, Crisis, and Global Apartheid*, 195–96.

while restoring the humanity of the oppressor, seeking the creation of a new humanity, a humanized society.

Kairos Palestine: Following the Ways of Love, Peace, and Justice

This, the stubborn search for the *ubuntufication* of the Palestinian struggle, is what makes the Palestinian Kairos Document so persuasive. Palestinian theologian Mitri Raheb has provided impressive context in a small, but important book. The way to understand the horrors of Israeli oppression and occupation, the indifference of most of the world, and the Palestinian struggle—the pain and suffering of it, the vision of justice and peace that drives it, the flame of hope at the heart of it—is to understand that from the very beginning, this was resistance against empire.[47] This resistance against empire is also the framework within which best to understand the *kairos* document that comes from Palestine. The Palestinians call their document "A Word of Faith, Hope and Love from the Heart of Palestinian Suffering."[48] Speaking of faith and hope is fairly general in other Kairos Documents, but the strong emphasis on love in *Kairos Palestine* is unique, and seeing the context, extraordinary. But it is as if the Palestinians were determined to take M. M. Thomas, Martin Luther King Jr., and Albert Luthuli seriously and apply their belief in the power of love as a key to the Christian's participation in struggles for justice and peace to a situation as devastatingly difficult, complex, and challenging as one dares to imagine.

For *Kairos Palestine* love is not a sentimentalized, spiritualized concept that seeks to lift us up above the realities of occupation, war, oppression, and suffering that are the burdens of their daily lives. They do not make it easy for themselves either. Love includes love for both friends and enemies.

---

47. See Raheb, *Faith in the Face of Empire*. Raheb writes, "The emergence of five regional powers around the first millennia BC and the development of those powers later into formidable empires have shaped the fate of Palestine throughout the last twenty-five hundred years as an occupied territory and a battlefield for competing empires. The occupation of Palestine by Israel today is thus another link in a long chain of uninterrupted occupation. Such occupation is the defining feature of our history, beginning with the Assyrians (722BC), the Babylonians (587 BC), and the Persians (538 BC), followed by the Greeks (333 BC), the Romans (63 BC), the Byzantines (326), the Arabs (637), the Tartars (1040), the Crusaders (1099), the Ayyubids (1187), the Tartars (1244), the Mamluks (1291), the Mongols (1401), the Ottomans (1516), the British (1917), and the Israelis (1948/67) to name just the major occupiers" (4).

48. See Kairos Palestine, "A Moment of Truth: A Word of Faith, Hope and Love from the Heart of Palestinian Suffering," 2009, http://www.*kairos*palestine.ps/index.php/about-us/*kairos*-palestine-document.

"Love is seeing the face of God in every human being. Every person is my brother and my sister." But love is also the gift of discernment. Seeing God in the face of the other does not mean accepting evil or aggression on their part. "Rather, this love seeks to correct the evil and stop the aggression." So it is an active, combative love; a love that is not afraid to ask the deeper, more difficult, painful, confrontational questions. Nor is it afraid of taking the risks of faith and hope.

Love uncovers and speaks the truth: "The aggression against the Palestinian people *which is the occupation,* is an evil that must be resisted." Love calls evil by its name, and by naming it, it demystifies it, brings it into the open, in a way that the Western mass media almost never does. In doing so, love exposes the embedded biases and presumptions of the mass media, the cowardice of politicians and political institutions, and the hypocrisy of the bulk of the international community who cannot seem able to hold the government of the State of Israel accountable for its oppression of Palestinians and its blatant disregard for international law. This love comes from the powerless, but in exposing and challenging evil it wrests power from the hands of the powerful and places it in the hands of the powerless, breaking the hold of fear in the minds of the oppressed, which always feeds on the denial of their own reality.

Kairos Palestine insists that love is resistance. This is the way it expresses itself in situations of oppression, domination and dehumanization. A love that denies the reality of evil cannot but deny the truth that love is resistance to that evil, in the process denying its deepest character and the deepest truth about itself. *Kairos Palestine* goes further. The occupation is "a sin and an evil" that must not only be resisted, it "must be removed." Resistance for its own sake can easily become frustrated futility, a mechanical response to oppression dictated by the oppressor without insight and without hope that the situation could ever be changed. When resistance is coupled with the will to remove the evil, resistance becomes meaningful, shapes the imagination, and opens up new possibilities for creative resistance without which no struggle can survive. Christian love does not coerce into resistance, however—it "invites" it. We join the struggle not because we are driven by historical determination, by blind hatred, reckless lust for heroism, or by ideological pressures. We join the struggle because we are beckoned by love.

But how does love resist and remove evil? "Love puts an end to evil by walking in the ways of justice." This is the compelling logic of the essential truth in the Palestinian struggle: love resists by walking in the ways of justice. Hence *Kairos Palestine* rejects violence: the violence of the Israeli state and the violent response of desperate Palestinians who believe that violence is the only language the occupier understands. But they forget that the language of violence is incessantly, unceasingly spoken by the occupier with the very intention that it will become the only language the oppressed will ever know how to speak. As long as that is the case, the oppressor's inability to speak in another language except the language of intimidation, threat, oppression and excessive violent force will never be unmasked. Therein lies much of the oppressor's strength. Violence to maintain oppression is ultimately futile and self-defeating. The oppressor knows this. But as long as the occupier can call forth an anticipated, almost programmed violent response from the occupied, the belief in what is essentially a futility is strengthened. Only the oppressor can benefit from that. Changing the language of response to oppression empowers the oppressed, weakens the grip of violence, places the initiative in the hands of the powerless. "The ways of force must give way to the ways of justice."

Because love is an obligation for the Christian, *Kairos Palestine* argues, resistance is an obligation, a right and a duty. But the logic of combative, resistant love leads to creative resistance, to finding ways "to engage the humanity of the enemy." That is not wishful thinking: it is the surest way for the oppressed not to lose their own humanity in a struggle where one of the chief aims of the oppressor is the dehumanization of the oppressed. Resistance in love will take the form of the ways of peace: it will break the cycles of violence and terror, thereby breaking the hold of violence on the lives of both oppressor and oppressed. The ways of peace will continue to disrupt the myths of peace through "peace talks" that have no meaning, "peace maps" that lead only to self-justification, "peace enforcement" through intimidation, threats, and endless war. The ways of peace expose "peaceful co-existence" through apartheid and walls of separation; they expose the violence of war as well as of political pietism and cooptation.

The ways of peace will break the cycles of inertia in the world-wide church to move them from statements to action and will break the cycles of indifference in the international community, exposing their complicity in and tolerance of an evil through which they seek to salve their consciences. That is why the boycott, divestment and sanctions movement is so important as an act of love: it is not coercion, but in the words of *Kairos Palestine*, an invitation to join the Palestinians in a struggle to right an injustice *they* did not create, to end a war *they* did not initiate, and to bring peace to a region and a people the world had purposely and willfully abandoned, because that world had itself left the ways of peace for the false peace of a conscienceless conscience, for the unfulfilled peace of a hardened heart.

"Through our love," *Kairos Palestine* declares, "we will overcome injustices and establish foundations for a new society, both for us and our opponents. Our future and their future are one. The choice is between the cycle of violence that destroys us both and the peace that will benefit both." And in yet another reminder of the essential truth of their nonviolent revolution, the Palestinian Christians express their hope that "we will see here a 'new land' and a 'new human being,'" a land truly holy because it stands where God stands, a people truly new because they are sanctified by hope, faith, and love. That indeed, is a word of faith, hope, and love from the heart of suffering.

In a report on what is now more and more seen as a "third intifada," also called the "Jerusalem intifada," a journalist from *The Guardian* interviews young people, students, and older Palestinians on the ongoing struggles.[49] The video shows once again how important it is to look at the issues through the eyes of those who are "at the heart of suffering." The steadfast commitment of the students is not altogether unexpected. What is striking is the attitude of the older generation. Standing in her shop, the journalist asks a middle-class businesswoman whether she agrees with what is going on, and whether the uprisings are not too much of a risk for her business. Clearly the expectation here was a response at least more cautious, or hesitant, keeping in mind the "normal" interests of a businessperson in such circumstances. But the woman answers, "You are speaking of business. We are speaking of souls that are lost, about the lives of our children. . . . We give birth to our children in order to give them a good life." A "good life" here does not mean a life of plenty, prosperity and a false peace bought through submission to Israeli tyranny. It means life in dignity, freedom and true peace. Life without the terrors of the occupation. Life with hope and meaning. This hope is life-giving, but it is—and this is as important—death-defying.

These are the voices of the determined, hopeful *sizwe*. It is they who make me believe that despite all its awesome power, despite the relentless viciousness of the violence, and despite the arrogance of the Israeli state because it feels secure in the uncritical support of world powers, the occupation will be ended, that wall, more and more the solidification of all the tyranny of oppression and the horrors of occupation in Palestine and in Jerusalem, will come down, and the Palestinian people shall be free. Indeed, the words of our prophetic graffiti artist remain: "This Wall May Take Care of the Present, but It Has *No* Future." They, like Jesus, have seen Satan fall like lightning from heaven, and they, like Isaiah, know that despite the present and the realities of the politics of oppression, occupation and indifference, "it is only a little while, and the tyrant shall be no more."

---

49. See "Is This the Third Intifada?" October 18, 2015, www.theguardian.com/world/video/2015/oct/18/israel-palestine-this-third-intifada-video.

It is not only time to break the silence. We can no longer deny for our times what Martin Luther King Jr. knew to be true of his time: "These are revolutionary times." He went on to say, expressing his own steadfast belief in the power of the hopeful *sizwe*, "The shirtless and barefoot people of the land" are "rising up as never before," and our call is to side with them in their resistance against injustice everywhere. "Our only hope is to recapture the revolutionary spirit and go out into a sometimes hostile world declaring eternal hostility to poverty, racism, and militarism."[50] While doing this we shall have to remember that the words of Hamid Dabashi about Tunisia and the Arab Spring are essential for every situation where the new militancy is embraced:

> For Mohammed Bouazizi to remain the martyred witness of a revolution that will not replace one dictator with another, one false prophecy of freedom with another, there is only one logical and lasting measure: the people.[51]

Walking in the ways of justice is walking by faith, not by sight. It is a way fraught with risk, unrequited longing, and relentless sacrifice. But behind and within the revolutions of our day, says Thomas, and in spite of everything, the Christian sees by faith the righteous hand of God. And it is this essential truth that grips and compels those who in faith and hope join struggles for justice and peace.

"Even in the worst human situation God's creative and redeeming will is active, waiting to be grasped by faith, seeking to bring [humankind] into responsible relation to [God] and to one another. It is by faith we walk and witness in the sphere of politics, as in every other sphere: our hope for politics is that at the Last Day this will be revealed as the true, inner meaning of the struggle of our own and every other day."[52]

---

50. King, "Time to Break Silence," 216.
51. Dabashi, *Arab Spring*, 132.
52. Thomas and McCaughey, *Christian in the World Struggle*, 40.

CHAPTER I

Pharaohs on Both Sides of the Blood-Red Waters

Why We Cry, How We Cry, and Who Can Cry

What do we do when the Pharaoh looks like us?

—Takatso Mofokeng, 2015

"Why We Cry, How We Cry, and Who Can Cry"

In the summer of 2015 Jamye Wooten, one of the young, articulate leaders of the #BaltimoreUprising and Baltimore United for Change (BUC)[1] spoke at the Duke University Summer Institute for Reconciliation.[2] Wooten puts three questions at the center of his talk: "Why We Cry, How We Cry, and Who Can Cry?" What we see on the streets and university campuses is a "cry." Wooten explains: "Why We Cry" deals with the systemic and

---

1. BUC is a coalition of organizations and activists with a long track record of working for social justice in Baltimore. They intend to use the tools available to them—social media, nonviolent protests, etc.—"to lead us to an Ella Baker moment and movement . . . to holistic community development where the end goal is not reform or rights, but power." See Jamye Wooten, "DeRay: Who Sent You and Who Do You Serve?" February 8, 2016, www.http://kineticslive.com/deray-who-sent-you-and-who-do-you-serve?

2. Jamye Wooten, "Who Has the Right to Be Violent?" November 12, 2015, http://www.thebtscenter.org/who-has-the-right-to-be-violent. Jamye Wooten is the name that is consistently encountered in this chapter, not to give the impression that he is the only person from the struggle movements who speaks out—that much will be clear in this book—but because I engage him quite specifically in this presentation at Duke University and I consider his views an important representation of more widely held views in the movement.

structural violence in Baltimore City—the years of neglect, disinvestment and underdevelopment. "How We Cry" addresses the uprising against those ongoing injustices and the community's response to state violence and systemic and structural violence. "Who Can Cry?" raises the question of whether oppressed groups are allowed to express their pain publicly. "Do blacks or the most marginalized in our society have the right to express frustration, anger, and outrage?" Wooten asks.

But before we can fully respond to these important questions I propose that we consider the broader, more historical backdrop to Wooten's address. I refer to black theologian Marvin McMickle's now famous question in his slim but important book of the same title: "Where have all the prophets gone?"[3] It is exactly the question being asked by young people like Jamye Wooten involved in the new struggles for justice today, and not only in the United States. It is of course in the first instance a question about the existence or non-existence of the prophetic church. It is also a question about what happened under the watch of the former anti-apartheid, civil rights struggle activists for the last quarter of a century or more. It is a question about struggles for justice and dignity, prophetic truthfulness and faithfulness, about power and powerlessness, complicity and resistance. As Jamye Wooten spoke about the uprisings in the streets, we, looking back over the last fifty years or so, had been celebrating all sorts of triumphant anniversaries.

It is seventy years after Gandhi led the Indian masses in the Salt March and the sixtieth year of the Women's March against the Pass Laws on Pretoria as well as the historic Peoples' Congress in Kliptown, near Johannesburg, the meeting that gave birth to the Freedom Charter, discussed in the Introduction. It is just more than sixty years since the Defiance Campaign, the mass actions of civil disobedience in South Africa that changed not only the character of the anti-apartheid struggle but also the course of our history; sixty years since 17 year-old Claudette Colvin's brave defiance, followed six months later by Rosa Parks' decision to sit down on that Montgomery bus and the start of the Civil Rights Movement in the United States. We celebrated fifty years of the Civil Rights Act, the March on Washington, the Letter

---

3. See McMickle, *Where Have All the Prophets Gone?* McMickle's concern is "the need to restore prophetic preaching to a place of urgency in the life of the American church," to identify and combat the obstructions in the way of such prophetic preaching: "A narrow definition of justice that does not extend beyond abortion and same-sex marriage, the emergence of an oxymoron called patriot pastors, the focus on praise and worship that does not result in any duty and discipleship, and, finally, the vile messages of prosperity that seem to have overtaken the pulpits and the airwaves used by televangelists across the country" (vii).

from a Birmingham Jail, just over twenty years of South African democracy, and twenty-five years of the release of Nelson Mandela.

There are also those moments of excruciating trauma that will forever be remembered: almost on to seventy years after what the Palestinians call the "Nakba," when they were violently driven from their ancestral lands and homes by the Zionist government of the new nation of Israel, in collusion with the vile politics of Britain and France, still not allowed to return; fifty-five years after the Sharpeville Massacre when the police opened fire on nonviolent protesters in South Africa, killed sixty-nine persons and wounded more than 180. It is thirty years after the massacre at Uitenhage in the Eastern Cape when on March 21, 1985, Archbishop Tutu and I preached at the funeral of twenty-seven victims of apartheid police brutality.

It is fifty years after the assassination of Malcolm X and almost as many after the death of Chief Albert John Mvumbe Luthuli, the man who gave such courageous and insightful Christian leadership to the struggle as president of the African National Congress, the historic liberation movement of South Africa. Almost five decades ago Martin Luther King Jr. was murdered. It is forty years since sixteen-year-old Hector Petersen and another young student, Hastings Ndlovu, seventeen, were shot down on the first day in the first wave of the Soweto uprisings that marked the penultimate phase in the anti-apartheid revolution inspired and led by the youth. Almost as long ago the South African police murdered Steve Biko, the bright young mind who shaped and led South Africa's Black Consciousness movement in the early seventies, dead even before he reached his prime. All this and much more besides have been woven into the fabric of our being and have become the very fiber of our lives, our struggles for justice, our dreams of dignity and hopes of freedom. These moments, in their different ways, all tell us about the road traveled by oppressed people in their quest for justice, freedom, and dignity.

So the cry Jamye Wooten draws our attention to is not a cry out of nowhere, as it were, without reason, rationale or historical context. Neither is it a cry of sentimental helplessness to which society can respond with its customary condescension and then move on as if nothing had happened. It is a cry of disappointment and frustration, of anguish and anger, of defiance and resistance. Marvin McMickle's troublesome question is exactly the question being asked by young people involved in the new struggles for justice today.

This cry is a cry of grief for the situation in which the people find themselves, and the cry is the announcement that the situation can no longer be tolerated. The cry is raised as critique against the empire and its workings of oppression. Just as in the exodus story the history of liberation begins with the "cry" and "groaning" of the people of Israel, reminding God of God's covenant, this cry calls upon God to remember the covenant and to "know" the people's condition. Moreover, Hebrew Bible scholar Walter Brueggemann makes the crucial point that the real criticism of the empire begins in the capacity to grieve because that is the most visceral announcement that things are not right. "Only in the empire," Brueggemann goes on to say, "are we pressed and invited to pretend that things are all right . . . As long as the empire can keep the pretense alive that things are all right, there will be no grieving and no serious criticism."[4]

Notice Brueggemann's choice of words, and one can sense the ever-present threat of the violence that is the empire's life-blood: the empire "presses"—forces, coerces, pressures. But it also "invites"—manipulating our fears, anxieties and desires, luring and deluding us with promises it never intends to keep, is not even capable of keeping. It is an invitation that contaminates the mind even as it tempts the heart, for it is all pretense. The crucial thing the empire can never do is *listen*, for listening requires a response. For that, as ancient Israel finally learns in the exodus story and the prophets never tire of telling them, we have to direct our cry to the One who hears. Without the courage to cry out real criticism of the empire cannot begin, and without serious criticism liberative action cannot take place.

The cry that is ringing out across the world is therefore not a plea *to* the empire, but instead a serious criticism *against* the empire that is keeping millions in captivity; against the minions of empire in our most intimate midst; against what Wooten calls the "preacher pacifiers" of the empire that pretend that there is nothing wrong, that the "freedom" of the people as defined by the empire is indeed freedom and not new, sometimes harsh, sometimes subtle forms of enslavement. It is a criticism against the way things are, and against the determination of the empire to keep things the way they are.

> It makes clear that things are not as they should be, not as they were promised, and not as they must be and will be. Bringing hurt to public expression is an important first step in the dismantling criticism that permits a new reality, theological and social, to emerge.[5]

The young activists of the Black Lives Matter movement intuitively understand Brueggemann's theological point, underscoring his implied

---

4. See Brueggemann, *The Prophetic Imagination*, 11.
5. Ibid., 12.

political point, very well indeed. Activist Jamell Spann describes what he calls "respectable politics":

> [R]espectable politics are a type of political viewpoint that seeks change, power, or recognition through appeasing . . . the system rather than opposing it on just about every level, like I feel it should be. And you can't gain your freedom or you can't gain more power by appealing to . . . to the humanity of a social construct that proves to you it has none. You can't appeal to the better side of a person who has no better side, honestly.⁶

For these reasons the cry is not a cry of resignation, but "a militant sense of being wronged with the powerful expectation that it will be heard and answered."⁷ Hence the renewed struggles for justice. This renewed engagement with issues of justice and renewed struggles for justice has also called renewed attention to the role of the church in such struggles. It has also raised questions about whether the church is ready and willing to accept a renewed call for prophetic involvement, if not prophetic leadership, in such struggles.

It is not cynicism but bitter experience that has made a new generation realize that the assertion, almost axiomatic in the United States, "Justice for All," should not be the mindless mantra it has become. Much like post-1994 South Africa's oft-stated characterization of its democracy—"nonracial, nonsexist, participatory"—it should not be uttered with a period at the end, and certainly not with anything as emphatic as an exclamation mark. It is not a triumphant proclamation, as if these claims were in fact a reality in the lives of all, or even the majority of the peoples of these two countries. It is more the expression of a desire for things yet to come, a longing for a God-given right yet to be recognized and realized. It is also the acknowledgment that, despite the centuries of pain and suffering and determined struggle, this struggle for justice is far from over and—one should hope—the acknowledgment of the incontrovertible truth that without struggle and pain, sacrifice and hopeful endurance, systemic transformation and redeemed politics, justice will not become reality.

That justice, which has always been our hope, even if it is a hope against hope, is not the justice that so many pretend will trickle down in reluctant drips from miserly clouds in a time of drought. We are speaking of the justice that rolls down like waters and the righteousness that surges like a mighty stream. It is rooted in the biblical prophetic tradition where justice, hope, and judgment are not separated. John Calvin is correct when

---

6. See Francis, *Ferguson and Faith*, 71.
7. Brueggemann, *Prophetic Imagination*, 12.

he reads these famous words from the prophet Amos as more than just the fulfillment of God's desire for justice for all God's children. It is also God's judgment in defense of the weak and the wronged. Justice, Calvin says, shall be a "violent stream"; it shall "*run down* as violent *waters*, as an impetuous *stream*. Judgment shall 'rush upon you and overwhelm you.'"[8] Justice for the poor and oppressed is also judgment on the oppressor for actively pursuing injustice, heeding neither the cry of the oppressed nor the demands of a just God. It is vital to keep these two elements together.

The present, global revolutionary fervor of the younger generation recognizes the fundamental, painful truth of it: that justice is still elusive, and the struggle for it still isn't over. After all these years of resistance, after all the pain and suffering and death, we are still climbing that mountain, still reaching for the mountain top. We may have heard of the Promised Land, but we still can't see it and we know we have not reached it. The contexts in which we raise the question about justice today—the challenges for the prophetic church in all the places where the dust of struggle refuses to settle—make it undeniably clear: there still is a crisis, and it is greater than ever before.

The Crisis and the Cry

The cry that is the primal critique of empire always arises from within an acute and unbearable crisis. But here is the first lesson we have learned about the crises we are facing. It is the poor and the oppressed, the wronged and the destitute, who know that there is a crisis. They do not have the luxury to deny it, for their whole lives constitute one, perpetual crisis. For the rich and the powerful there is no crisis, because first, they, with their greed, rapaciousness, and violence are the cause of the crisis; and second, because they always benefit from the crises that crush the poor. They deny the existence of the crisis, because it is not in their interest to acknowledge it, the pain and suffering it is causing, the contradictions it represents in their politics and, if they claim to be believers, in their faith. Neither are they inclined to recognize the terrible judgment it invites on societies that make injustice and inequality their foundation.

Let me cite a recent, historic example from our South African experience. In May 1976, a month before the Soweto uprisings, Desmond Tutu, then Dean of the Johannesburg Cathedral, wrote a letter to the then Prime Minister of apartheid South Africa, John Vorster. The letter is the work of a gentle, soft-spoken Tutu, pleading with the government, appealing to

---

8. See Calvin, *Commentaries*, commentary on Amos 5:24, emphasis original.

Vorster's human side. Yet the letter is written with a sense of great urgency. It warned of a crisis which, unless attended to urgently, could turn into disaster. It spoke of the anger in the black communities in Soweto that could engulf the whole country, offering advice, a sensible path forward, and prayers and prophetic witness.

The Prime Minister dismissed the letter with disdain, thereby dismissing the advice and the warning. A month later, with Soweto in flames and the blood of innocent children on the streets and the revolt spreading rapidly across the country, John Vorster would still mindlessly repeat his infamous mantra: "There is no crisis."

The powerful, ensconced in their power, acknowledge no crisis. Doing so would require the need for introspection, remorse, conversion, and fundamental transformation. As long as they feel secure in the protection that oppression brings, and as long as their privileged positions are not threatened, as long as they believe their wealth remains undiminished, there is no crisis. As long as they believe the oppressed can be controlled and their demands suppressed, managed or ignored, there is no crisis. They do not see the crisis because it is a crisis they created and forced upon others for their own profit. It is the oppressed and the powerless who experience perpetual crisis. And because the Prime Minister, his government and most of white South Africa did not feel the effects of the crisis they did not care. It falls to the oppressed themselves to cry out against injustice and take the crisis to the doorstep of the powerful, so that it can no longer be denied.

From the United States, multibillionaire Stephen A. Schwarzman presents an even more recent and almost perfect example of my present argument. Schwarzman says he is puzzled by the amount of discontent apparently felt by other Americans these days.[9] Speaking at the World Economic Forum in Davos, Switzerland, in January 2016, he asks, "What is the vein that is being tapped into across parties, that has made people so unhappy ... What is everyone protesting about?" For Schwarzman, it seems, the unhappiness is caused by the US's presidential politics, especially democratic socialist Bernie Sanders, whom he finds "almost more stunning than what is happening on the Republican side."

Throughout the interview, Boardman writes, Schwarzman remains "publicly oblivious to politicians who support illegal wars and call for more, to Americans who fight and die in illegal wars that also promote terrorist responses, or to the way America treats its veterans, whether wounded, homeless or damaged in invisible ways (like the country)." Schwarzman can

---

9. See William Boardman, "Wall Street Worldview: Why Are People Upset?" February 2, 2016, http://readersupportednews.org/opinion2/277-75/34964-wall-street-worldview-why-are-people-upset.

identify three reasons for what he sees as instability in the world: the economic slowdown in the US and China; the geopolitical situation, which for him means immigration, ISIS, Pakistan, Iran, and North Korea's hydrogen bomb; and third, "unsettled markets." Not a word about endless war, the urgent need for peace, or the truly unsettling socioeconomic inequality gap. "With nothing to say at Davos about war or torture or drone executions or the predatory American military presence in more than 100 countries around the world, Schwarzman suggested that the country is in 'some kind of odd protest moment.'" For the comfortable, the rich and powerful, the global crisis is no more than an "odd protest moment."

However, and this is the second lesson I am trying to emphasize here: being confronted with such intense crises raises yet another, deeper, most important question, namely, is the church able to see in the crisis what the Bible calls the *kairos*? In October 2015 over a weekend in Ferguson, Missouri, called by St. John's UCC's "Beloved Community," the Black Lives Matter movement and other religious and grass-roots activist organizations, a colleague and I participated in worship, discussion sessions, and workshops. We were talking about the meaning of what we call "radical reconciliation" and what that would mean in the efforts toward the restoration of justice, dignity, and trust in St. Louis and the state of Missouri. The presenter of the Ferguson Report, Bethany Johnson-Javois, a young woman and a prime example of the level of excellence displayed by the leadership there,[10] began by explaining why this moment in history is a *kairos* moment for Ferguson, the state of Missouri, and the people of the United States. She raised the question about the church's readiness for this *kairos* moment, and she was exactly right.

We live our lives by chronological time, "clock-time." It is the succession of moments by which we count our days. Kairos, however, is God's time, the given time; the time by which we make our days count. Kairos is the time in which momentous things are about to happen, a moment in

---

10. See *Forward through Ferguson: A Path toward Racial Equity*. The printed report is offered as a companion to the report online: forwardthroughferguson.org, which contains not just facts and figures but more importantly the stories of the people of Ferguson, exposing the reader directly to the pain, suffering, and hopeful struggles that contextualize the hard facts and point to the real meaning of a commitment to engage in "a process of reconciliation, healing and change." Significantly, "Radical Reconciliation" was the banner under which the weekend of workshops, discussions and worship was called, the title of a book I coauthored with Dr. Curtiss Paul DeYoung. See Boesak and DeYoung, *Radical Reconciliation*. The thrust of our argument in the book is that if reconciliation in politics, personal relationships, community, and society is to be truly durable and sustainable, it should conform to the norms of the gospel: radical, revolutionary and transformational.

which the signs of the times in which we live could, by the grace of God, be discerned, understood and acted upon. To embrace that moment is to find salvation, to miss the moment means disaster.[11] So the question from the youth is: can the prophetic church discern the *kairos* as a moment of truth, a time in which God challenges us and calls us to discernment, repentance, conversion, and commitment in order to bring justice to God's suffering children and transform the world?

In the Gospel of Mark it is Jesus himself who announces his work on earth as the coming of the *kairos*. "The time has come," Jesus says, "the kingdom of God is near. Repent, and hear the good news" (Mark 1:4). As Jesus speaks, first-century Palestine is an occupied country, under the heel of the Roman Empire. In the palace in Jerusalem sits Herod Antipas, a fearsome, bloodthirsty, heartless tyrant put there by Rome. In the temple the religious elites are ruling with punctilious attention to the paying of taxes and tithes of "mint, and dill and cumin," but with scant regard for the needs of the people, what Jesus calls the heart of the Law: mercy, compassion, and justice (Matt 23:23). It was a time of crisis in all sorts of ways but fundamentally ignored because for the Romans, as for the imperial powers of our time, the lives of the poor, the oppressed and the vulnerable did not matter.

The Romans called political pronouncements from Caesar "good news," gospel, in Greek, *euangelion*.[12] But those pronouncements proclaimed Rome's untrammeled and unchallenged power, confirmed the people's subjugation and Rome's triumphant domination. They proclaimed new forms of exploitation, further securing the enrichment of the rich and the impoverishment of the poor. They were announcements of death, destruction, and annihilation. Those words were deeply comforting to the powerful and to those who benefited from their collaboration with Rome's power. It was "good news", *euangelion,* because it reaffirmed the status quo and their position of power. But to the powerless, exploited masses they were destructive, life-threatening, death-dealing pronouncements.

Into this crisis, this situation of hopelessness and fear, comes Jesus, proclaiming *his* good news that the *kairos* had come; the kingdom of God was at hand. Surrounded by Roman garrisons, with Herod on the throne, the Temple turned from a house of prayer into a den of thieves, and the people in the wilderness of despair, Jesus comes to proclaim that the *kairos* has come. The gates of righteousness have been opened wide, and the righteous—the faithful coworkers of God, those who believe the good news, the

---

11. See Boesak, *Kairos, Crisis and Global Apartheid,* "Introduction" and ch. 1.

12. See Elliot, "The Apostle Paul and Empire," 98. It was used most famously to celebrate the "good news" of Augustus's ascent to power.

tried and tested who follow Jesus in faithful and costly discipleship—shall enter (Ps 118:19). The moment has come to challenge, and stand up against, the reign of Caesar, which was a rule of violence and war and conquest; of domination and subjugation, of terror and suffering and humiliation. Over against this reign of terror stands the kingdom of God: a reign of peace and justice, of mercy and compassion and inclusion. This was true *good news*, hope-giving, life-affirming, prophetic *euangelion*, exposing the lies of Rome as the customary, arrogant, imperial mendacity that this time shall not remain unchallenged. Here the challenge is immediate: in the very word Jesus snatches out of the mouth of Caesar to announce the coming of God's reign.

A "Subversive Memory"

This is the good news the new nonviolent revolutions driven by the youth are calling for and need to hear. During the decades of the civil rights and anti-apartheid struggles the prophetic church in South Africa and the United States understood both the crisis and the *kairos*. Marvin McMickle's question is not conjuring up a nostalgic but fictional moment from the past. It is a yearning for what once really was the reality. He wants to *reclaim* the prophetic tradition of the church. I will return to the concept of "the prophetic church" below. For now it is sufficient to describe this church as the church, never fully reflected in the institutional church, but in the prophetic witness and faithful resistance of the multitude of Christians whose faith led them to political activism, the church driven by a radical gospel of compassionate justice, hope and liberation.

There was a time in our very recent history when the world could not but recognize the disturbing, challenging presence of the prophetic church and acknowledge the truth of God's words to Ezekiel: "Whether they hear or refuse to hear (for they are a rebellious people), they shall know that there has been a prophet among them" (Ezek 2:8). The question now is: is the church ready to fulfil that role again? If the answer is yes, it will be like it always was: the prophetic church, the remnant who, those outside the camp of institutionality and acceptability, as surely an offense to the powers that be as they are an embarrassment to the church beholden to the powerful. Even so, those who will not shrink away from this call will find that they are not alone but side by side with those, as Yahweh reassured Eljiah, "who did not bow the knee to Baal and every mouth that has not kissed him" (1 Kgs 19:18).

That prophetic church discerned the signs of the times and saw in the crisis the *kairos*, the moment of truth. But it was not just the truth about the situation in which we found ourselves, one of racist oppression and degradation, of economic exploitation and political subjugation. Simultaneously, it was also the truth revealed about the church, our complacency, our complicity and our resignation to our oppression. It was the truth about our abundance of self-righteousness and our paucity of prophetic courage; our ceaseless sermonizing and our impoverished wisdom. So for the prophetic church the *kairos* moment was turned into a self-critical moment, a moment of repentance, conversion, and commitment.

But the *kairos* is not only a challenge, as the South African *Kairos Document* reminds us. It is also a moment of grace.[13] So, through the grace of God we became the prophetic church, never fully reflected in the institutional church. It was not the church of the cautious, balanced ecclesiastical hierarchical elites, but it was the church of the people—the struggling, protesting, suffering, people; the faithful, hopeful *sizwe*. This is precisely the church called to account and into renewed action by the youth today.

It was important not only to see and understand the nature of the crisis our people were facing. The crucial question was whether we understood that the crisis also presented us with the *kairos*; whether we knew that God's time had come. The question was whether we could hear the voice of God in the cries for justice and freedom that emanated from the hearts of the poor and the oppressed. It was our *kairos*, our moment of decision and commitment.

We saw then, in the words of the Black Lives Matter movement today, what theology, conversion and commitment looked like: in the spirituality of struggle, in the prayers of hope and fierce determination, in the marching feet of thousands upon thousands, turning streets of submission into sites of struggle and alleys of fear into highways of freedom.

Despite the threats and intimidation, despite the dogs and water hoses and guns; despite imprisonment, the bombings and the killings, we held high the name of Jesus, believed the promises of the God of justice and claimed our freedom, our rights and our dignity. Cities on a map were turned into citadels of confrontation. Names on sign boards became shrines of freedom: Selma and Montgomery, Soweto and Mitchell's Plain, Bethlehem and Ramalla. A letter from a Birmingham jail became a twentieth-century Pauline Epistle to the church of Jesus Christ across the world.

---

13. The South African 1985 Kairos Document is a document written by groups of Christians spread across the country and was a radical Christian response to the apartheid situation in general but especially to the state of emergency and its consequences for the oppressed communities. It was not so much addressed to the apartheid government as to the oppressed and to the church in South Africa. Hence the subtitle, "A Challenge to the Church." It can be accessed at http://www.sahistory.org.za/archive/challenge-church-comment-political-crisis-south-africa-*kairos*-document-1985.

The prophetic church saw and understood the crisis. We knew there was a struggle for justice going on, and where there is a struggle there is suffering, and where there is a struggle there is hope, kept alive by the sacrifices of the people. We understood then that neutrality was no longer possible, because it means taking the side of the oppressor without taking responsibility for it. Neutrality means standing on the sidelines, hiding from the confrontation and the pain, but benefiting from the wounds of others when the struggle is over. Neutrality means seeing the crisis but not knowing the *kairos*—that God's time had come; not hearing the call, that our time had come for conversion and action.

But because repentance, conversion, and commitment are inseparable as faith and costly discipleship are inseparable; and because repentance and conversion mean turning *away* and turning *toward*, *kairos* moments of theological understanding and faith discernment always turn into moments of prophetic truthfulness, of political commitment towards acts of justice. It is a sign of great hope that we see the start of the awakening of the prophetic church in places where the cry is most clearly heard and seen.[14]

This is what the cry of the youth is calling us to. We know that although the struggle against formalized, legalized apartheid has come to an end, the struggle for justice is not over and the fight against global apartheid[15] is just beginning, and in particularly frightening ways has draped its suffocating cloak over Palestine.

We now realize that all the talk of our so-called post-racial, post-apartheid societies is a sham; that the professed satisfaction with our personal gains does not allow us the denial of the disastrous gap between rich and poor; that our claim on and pride in our personal status of private privilege disconnected from the realities of the vast majority of our people do not really hide the deeper truth that black lives, as well as poor peoples' lives and women's lives, LGBTQI+ lives and Palestinian lives, still don't matter. Our earlier response to the *kairos* call of God is a dangerous memory because it is subversive of subterfuge, self-delusion and political pietism. With Marvin McMickle, we have to confess that as a church, we have largely lost the courage our calling demands, and in too many ways betrayed both the message of the radical Jesus and the faith, hope and endurance of the people.

---

14. We are seeing this in the courageous and faithful participation of some church leadership in Baltimore, Ferguson, and elsewhere where a new and blessedly consistent prophetic presence is being experienced; see, for example, the testimonies gathered in Francis, *Ferguson and Faith*, especially chapter 6.

15. For the use of this term, see the introduction to Boesak, *Kairos, Crisis and Global Apartheid*.

But calling all this to mind is not meant as some kind of Christian, socio-masochistic castigation or self-glorifying recall of our struggles, sufferings, and triumphs.[16] Neither is it offered to shore up our flagging credibility in lieu of actual vigilance, critical and self-critical engagement over the past few decades. It is what German theologian Johann Baptist Metz called "a dangerous memory."[17]

But it is probably good to remind ourselves that when Metz first used the phrase in the original German edition of his book, he spoke of the *"memoria subversiva,"* not just the "dangerous" but "the *subversive* memory of Christ." By that he meant that the way we remember Christ in our lives and witness must be the way Christ lived and worked: in setting the power of love against the loveless powers, challenging the forces of evil, subverting their authority and breaking their hold over the lives of God's children. This is the reason why the powers resisted him, persecuted him, and crucified him, condemning him to the death of rebels, revolutionaries and runaway slaves, those who constituted a clear and realistic threat to the empire.

The memory of the suffering of Christ, Metz also insists, is embedded in the dangerous history of suffering in the world, against which Christ in his life, death, and resurrection rose up in revolt. That is the sense in which this memory is "dangerous". It is dangerous because it is subversive of systems and structures, of power and privilege, of grand myths and dominant narratives, and of the enslaving, intoxicating power of violence. It is dangerous because it calls for a response to the suffering of humanity under the heel of the powers of oppression, degradation and dehumanization.

Is there reason to believe that the prophetic church, the church of the subversive memory of Christ, is present in the situations of conflict and confrontation, of pressure and promise? In my visits to those places in the United States and South Africa, I have seen firsthand the beacon of hope that prophetic church is becoming, and for Ferguson, Leah Gunning Francis has documented this in a powerful way, and the ongoing work of the Samuel DeWitt Proctor Conference, where Jeremiah A. Wright and Iva Carruthers are giving such remarkable leadership. In South Africa it is still a small flame, and in Palestine as well as those places around the globe where they are growing, the Kairos movements continue to remind the church of its prophetic calling.[18]

16. See Klapwijk, *Sociaal Masochisme en Christelijk Ethos*.

17. See his seminal work where he develops this still startling thought, *Faith in History and Society*.

18. See Francis, *Ferguson and Faith*. For the inspiring work of the Samuel DeWitt Proctor Conference see their website, www.sdpconference.info. Every year the Proctor conference brings together more than seven hundred persons from across the

But something extraordinary happens when we allow the subversive memory to work its way. In Ferguson, for example, Alexis Templeton, Jamell Spann, Brittany Ferrell, and the other young leaders of the Black Lives Matter movement did not have much reason to be drawn to the church, or to trust the clergy who were courageous and faithful enough to respond to their prophetic call, step out into the streets with the protesting masses and join the struggle in the name of a radical, revolutionary Jesus.

Perhaps it is best to allow one of the youth leaders of Ferguson to speak. The Bible does not just say love thy neighbor, says Alexis Templeton. It tells you what love is, so that you know exactly how to identify it and what love definition you need to live by. That, she says, is precisely what the prophetic clergy of Ferguson are doing:

> They come out, and they do exactly what the Bible says without doing exactly what the Bible says. They're fluid in their spirituality, and they're fluid in their reading of this Book. And actually the more you are fluid with it . . . the better your understanding of it. You're moving. You're just letting the Word push you. You're letting it come out of you. That's what you're supposed to do. And that's what the Starsky [Wilsons], and Traci Blackmons and your [Osagyefo] Sekous . . . your Mike Kinmans—that's what they have gotten up and done, and this has taught me that this is what the church is supposed to be. They have taught me to believe in God, and that's real. It was all in their walk . . . They allowed the Godlike features of the people to show them, in a better sense, what God is and what God is about and what God did with what God wants.[19]

A powerful testimony, that: clergy, theologians, and preachers humble enough, courageous enough, trusting God enough to step down from their pulpits, out of their ecclesial isolation, opening themselves enough to the power of the Spirit and the tumult of the streets, allowing the Godlike features of the people, the protesting, faithful, hopeful *sizwe* to show them, "in a better sense", what God is. Knowing, understanding and confessing that this is where God is to be found: in the outrage against injustice, in the faithful resistance against injustice, and in the hopeful struggle for justice. And in knowing this, to discover what God [is doing] with what [and who] God wants. And it is in their joining of the struggle, says Alexis, putting

---

generations in an ongoing and tireless effort to reclaim the prophetic tradition of the Black Church in the United States. For the hopeful resurrection of the prophetic church in South Africa, see www.*kairos*southernafrica.org.

19. Francis, *Ferguson and Faith*, 64.

their calling and their bodies on the line, that they taught her to believe in God. "It was in their walk." Is this, finally and ultimately, what the prophetic looks like?

But the point is that Alexis Templeton and the others met the prophetic clergy not in the safety of their sanctuaries, but on the streets of protest and danger; marching with them, facing the terrifying might of the police with them, willing to go to jail with them, for the sake of justice inspired by the revolutionary Jesus. So in response to Marvin McMickle's question, "Are all the prophets gone?" we can now, with gratitude to God say, "Not altogether." One can only hope and pray, while strengthening one's commitment and resolve, that the promise of prophetic faithfulness seen here will grow and come to fulfillment, for the sake of the church as well as of the world.

Pharaohs on Both Sides of the Blood-Red Waters

When Jamye Wooten spoke at Duke University, he addressed a crisis caused by incessant, systemic violence, white supremacy, domination, discrimination, exploitation and the perpetuation of impoverishment set against the extreme, but undeserved wealth of few. But he also addressed a crisis caused by complacency, fear and the inability to resist the lures, pressures and invitations of empire. He and his generation are children of post-civil-rights-struggle America who have discovered that the civil rights struggle did not produce the post-racial and pro-justice society as America claimed in the first heady years of the Obama era. He grew up with Martin Luther King Jr's words about a Promised Land and black liberation theology's exodus theology as essential parts of his political, social, and theological formation.

But Wooten spoke not only in the broader historical context discussed above. His words should be read against the even deeper historical backdrop of an epoch-making address by a truly worthy ancestor of the black freedom struggle in America. In 1843, that intrepid black Presbyterian minister, Henry Highland Garnet, in an address to the National Negro Convention held in Buffalo, New York, spoke a truth that the prophetic church today would do well to take as seriously as it was meant to be taken then, now almost 175 years ago. Garnet addressed a number of extremely important issues, both for his day and ours, and we will return to an effort of some deeper understanding of his words.

The crucial point Garnet makes is in this sentence: "It is impossible to make a grand exodus from the land of bondage. The Pharaohs are on both sides of the blood-red waters!"[20] This is precisely what the new revolutionary generation is discovering and this is what they believe they are fighting. In different words, but carrying the same meaning, they are asking the question my friend and fellow South African theologian Takatso Mofokeng raised in a discussion in Pretoria mid-2015 regarding the situation in South Africa: "What do we do when the pharaoh looks like us?" They are not wrong.

However, Garnet's address became immediately controversial mostly because of its call to violent resistance against slavery.[21] Consequently, the speech is most remembered for that call upon the readiness to take up arms: "Rather die freemen, than live to be slaves." And for the fiery exhortation: "Neither God, nor angels, or just men, command you to suffer for a single moment. Therefore it is your solemn and imperative duty to use every means, both moral, intellectual, and physical that promises success." And for the sober and disturbing conclusion: "There is not much hope of redemption without the shedding of blood."

As the struggles for justice and the brutal responses of oppressors continue across the world, these are words that many will surely continue to ponder, as Jamye Wooten and his generation are doing when, following the words, "Why we cry" and "how we cry," he asks the question, "Who has the right to be violent?" They will also have to consider, as Wooten also does, the meaning of the appalling hypocrisy of a society that cannot wait for the first stone to be thrown, the first window to be broken, to cry "violence!" while the teargas, batons, dogs and guns of the police or the army are always a "response" to the protest, as if the protest in itself is the originator of violence or a violation of a preexisting peace. Or worse: as if the situation of oppression and humiliation, land theft and violent oppression is not only not to be understood as violence, but to be meekly accepted as normal; just the way things are.

Here of course it is well to remember that in a very real sense, the Black Lives Matter movement, unlike the actions and "occupations" of armed, white militia groups for example, is always a threat because it addresses, in very real ways, the heart of the empire as Martin Luther King Jr. had defined it so long ago: its triple evils of militarism, racism, and capitalism. In

20. See Garnet, "An Address to the Slaves of the United States," 115–21.

21. Garnet wrote in the preface to its publication in 1843 (in an edition with David Walker's *Appeal*), "The document elicited more discussion than any other paper that was ever brought before that, or any other deliberative body of colored persons, and their friends." Opposed by Frederick Douglass, the call "failed by one vote to be adopted by the convention, which still advocated 'moral suasion' over political, even military, action." See Mullane, *Danger Water*, 114. Emphases and capitals are in the original.

South Africa the problem is returning with a great sense of urgency and in Palestine it is the tragic reality of everyday life where the violence of Israeli soldiers in tanks and wielding assault rifles is countered by a teenager with a stone, a knife, or a catapult.

Every generation, in every new struggle and every new context, will be called upon to consider what response to make to the call of freedom and justice, and every generation will have to take into account their own set of historical circumstances in considering the choice between violence and nonviolence. Those involved in struggles for justice and dignity have had cause to return to this burning and ever crucial question time and again.[22] My consistent testimony has been that persistent, militant, nonviolent strategies of struggle are far more likely to succeed, and since it calls for the humanizing of the struggle and of one's enemy it leaves room for real and radical reconciliation without which no revolution is complete. It is my firm conviction that it is this fundamental determination that has saved South Africa from the ravages and soul-destroying catastrophes of a bloody civil war.[23] One continues to hope fervently that the strength that is in nonviolent

---

22. See Luthuli, *Let My People Go!* King, *Where Do We Go from Here*, especially 56–69; Boesak, *Running with Horses*, especially 109–17; Boesak, *Dare We Speak of Hope?* 117–22; Boesak, *Kairos, Crisis, and Global Apartheid*, 180–92; also Cortright, *Gandhi and Beyond*.

23. In his highly engaging and well-written study, *Wages of Revolution*, 89–105, journalist and cultural critic Chris Hedges writes of the "conversion" of the African National Congress in South Africa, from the violent method of struggle to nonviolence. His source is Ronnie Kasrils, a respected member of the ANC leadership for decades. "By the 1980s, Mandela and the ANC leadership had recognized that as the struggle against apartheid evolved, it was the strikes and boycotts, along with the organizing work by nonviolent groups such as the United Democratic Front (UDF) the ANC's political wing, that were the best instruments for crippling the apartheid regime." I have great respect for both Ronnie Kasrils and Chris Hedges, but this statement is astonishingly a-historical. I called for the formation of the UDF and remained its most known voice until its disbandment by the ANC in 1991. Through the 1980s serious tensions had arisen with the ANC in exile, some of its members in the leadership of the UDF and persons of the internal resistance like me on the question of violence and nonviolence and later on the issue of the choice and level of international sanctions. The ANC wanted sanctions to remain at the same early 1980s level. In 1989, at the meeting of Commonwealth Heads of State in Kuala Lumpur, I argued strenuously for stronger, more specific financial sanctions on the regime. I argued that the demise of P. W. Botha and the takeover by F. W. De Klerk was a sign of weakness to be exploited and called for a strengthening of sanctions, especially financial sanctions. The ANC, represented at the gathering by former president Thabo Mbeki, had a different opinion. The ANC remained involved in and committed to violent strategies such as "Operation Vula" until the early 1990s, even while pre-negotiation talks with the white regime were ongoing, (see *Running with Horses*, 184–85). The UDF, reclaiming the traditions of the ANC in the Defiance Campaign of the 1950s, committed itself to militant, nonviolent methods of struggle. It is only afterwards that the ANC could no longer ignore the role and

militancy will resist and overcome the urge to imitate the worst in the oppressor and open the way toward meaningful transformation of society, and as long as the revolutions we are seeing stay so determinedly nonviolent that hope will remain alive.

It is not an easy or comfortable question to be sure, but it is an unavoidable one. It is never raised in the proper, civil conversations of the establishment or of the church and in the mass media almost always within the context of an unbearable hypocrisy. But it is called attention to by those in the struggle because they experience the violence of the establishment in ways too many to describe and they experience it in the response of the powerful to their cry for justice, as they experience it in the feigned neutrality of Wooten's "preacher pacifiers." This new struggle generation do not call for violence, and neither do they seek to justify the counter-violence provoked by the anger of the establishment that is inevitably forced into every struggle, since it is entirely impossible for the oppressor to surrender power and privilege without unleashing all the fury of the violence at their disposal. That much we have always known.

The question being raised is this: do those whose power, position, and privilege are guaranteed and safeguarded by violence in all its forms have a right to dictate to those struggling for justice what forms their resistance should take? It is a fundamental issue, since it rhymes with the question: do those who are depriving us of our freedom have a right to define for us what freedom means? Do those who feed daily at the trough of injustice

---

efficacy of nonviolence. I, for one, had known for a long time that purely on a practical basis, (the moral issues completely aside), the "ANC's tiny rebel bands were increasingly ineffectual" as Hedges states on 99; see Boesak, *Running with Horses* 110–17. As an organization, the ANC had never admitted to that. It still clings to the tradition of the romanticization of the violent struggle and uncritical veneration of its military wing, *Mkhonto we Sizwe* acting as if it was military struggle that finally brought down apartheid. The ongoing use of "noncooperation" that "brought the economic engines of the country to a halt," plus the growing effectiveness of the international campaign for boycotts, divestment and sanctions, especially financial sanctions towards the end of the 1980s, were specific strategies employed by the highly motivated, hope-filled and sacrificial people at the heart of the internal struggle. For some insight into this, see *Running with Horses*, Part Three. The claim that the UDF was the ANC's "political wing" is simply not true. The UDF considered itself accountable to the ANC as the historical and recognized liberation movement of the country, just as it considered itself accountable to the people of South Africa, the religious and civil society organizations that comprised the UDF, and the prophetic church that in many ways gave leadership to the struggle. Accountability did not by any means mean blind loyalty, and unavoidable tensions arose. We did not always see eye to eye. By 1991 the UDF was seen as enough of a threat to the ANC that the ANC had to use its historical status and political power to shut it down and subsequently claim all the work done by the UDF as essentially only at the ANC's behest and on instructions of its leadership in exile.

have a right to define justice for those in the struggle for justice? Within this context Wooten's question is not first about the justification of violence—in fact, he argues that whatever black people do in resistance to domination and oppression is branded as violence almost as a matter of course, whereas even violent protest by armed, white American militia groups, is not.[24] The issue is about the failure to understand the causes of violence. In this he falls back on Martin Luther King Jr., confident that the voice of this matchless prophet for justice and nonviolence speaks for his generation as well, since King knew, as this generation knows, that racism, injustice, and oppression "are still deeply rooted in America":

> I will continue to say that riots are socially destructive and self-defeating. I'm still convinced that nonviolence is the most potent weapon available to oppressed people in their struggle for freedom and justice . . . But at the same time, it is necessary for me to be as vigorous in condemning the conditions which cause persons to feel that they must engage in riotous activities as it is for me to condemn riots. America must see that riots do not develop out of thin air. . . . In the final analysis, a riot is the language of the unheard. And what is it that America has failed to hear? It has failed to hear that the plight of the negro poor has worsened over the last few years. It has failed to hear that the promises of freedom and justice have not been met. And it has failed to hear that large segments of white society are more concerned about tranquility and the status quo than about justice, equality and humanity.[25]

In other words, the conversation about (let alone the condemnation of) violence cannot begin unless it starts with the recognition and condemnation of the causes of that particular kind of violence, and unless it is willing to let go of the hypocrisy surrounding violence in public discourse

---

24. Recent events as I write seem to amply vindicate Wooten. Commenting on the armed takeover of a federal wildlife preserve facility in Oregon by armed white militia groups, journalist Carminah Townes writes, "News outlets have referred to Bundy's men as peaceful protesters, whereas Black Lives Matter activists have been called 'terrorists' and a 'grave threat' to police officers by Fox News and CNN analysts. Similarly Oregon's police's desire for a 'peaceful resolution' has been contrasted to the instantaneous police killings of unarmed black people, including Tamir Rice and Laquan McDonald." Clearly the "threat" police perceive in even a twelve-year old black boy is far greater than in grown, armed, white men with fascist tendencies. See http://reader-supportednews.org/news-section2/318-66/34450-here's-what-happened-when-black-people-tried-armed-occupation.

25. Martin Luther King Jr., "The Other America," speech at Stanford University, April 14, 1967, http://www.crmvet.org/docs/otheram.htm; also, in a slightly different version, in King, *The Radical King*, 235–44.

in society and in the church. Martin King discussed this matter in an address titled "The Other America." I agree absolutely with King, and so do the youth of America and South Africa, judged by their stubborn pursuit of nonviolent resistance; but unless the cry is heard and the hypocrisy surrounding the question of violence is changed, that "other" America and "other" South Africa will not be born. Meanwhile, the call for freedom will not be stilled, and in the face of mindless state brutality the question "Who Can Cry"—who, in other words, has the right to determine oppressed people's response to violence—will not be stifled. That question needs a response at a completely different level.

In his 2015 address Wooten raises the issue of physical violence—the unbelievable and intolerable (and still-rising!) numbers of persons of color shot to death by the police, security guards, and white vigilantes all over the United States, one every twenty-eight hours, according to research by the Malcolm X Grassroots Movement[26]—and the violence employed by a relentlessly militarized police force against peaceful protesters. But it is instructive to note that Wooten, like the prophets of the Hebrew Bible is not fooled into thinking that "violence" means physical violence alone. For him the violence of systemic injustices and structural abuse, oppression and dehumanization, is equally clear. So is the violence of a justice system that exonerates the killers of black people almost as a matter of course, or when eventually charged treats them entirely differently.[27]

It is, moreover, the violence of the confidence of privilege and power, with devastating honesty described by journalist Charles Pierce as he reflects on the mind of Officer Jason Van Dyke of the Chicago police force

---

26. See the study "Operation Ghetto Storm," 2012 Annual Report, on the extrajudicial killing of 313 black people by police, security guards and vigilantes, www.mxgm.org. This does not take into account the fact that in 2015, 550 people died in Texas jails alone while in custody at city, county, or state jails according to data from the state attorney generals office. Most of these inmates would be persons of color. See Jessica Hamilton, "550 People Die in Texas Jails in 2015 Alone," November 20, 2015, http://readersupportednews.org/news-section2/318-66/33590-550-people-died-in-texas-jails-in-2015.

27. See Todd Oppenheim, "Another Baltimore Injustice," November 28, 2015, http://mobile.nytimes.com/2015/11/29/opinion/another-baltimore-injustice.html. Oppenheim explains how, despite the remarkable fact that the officers involved in the death of Freddie Gray were actually charged, the court has given extraordinary treatment to the accused officers from their arrest to their impending trials in ways never considered for other, poorer, unprivileged accused. He gives some pertinent examples and concludes, "The irony is that a lack of fairness in the criminal justice system is part of what Baltimore's unrest is all about." Oppenheim's "lack of fairness" is the "structural violence" Wooten is pointing out. What actually becomes of the case against the officers remains to be seen.

as he emptied his gun into Laquan McDonald, shooting the black teenager sixteen times:

> [It is] the confidence that comes with being licensed to carry a gun as a defense against your fellow citizens. The confidence that comes with the knowledge that almost every powerful institution in your city will come to your aid if every powerless individual in the city is outraged by what you have done. The confidence that comes with knowing that the tapes will always be taken care of, the autopsy buried, and the official story spread far and wide before the truth ever is known, assuming that it ever is. The confidence that comes with being a white police officer in a major city in a terrified country.[28]

The violence Jamye Wooten so powerfully exposes is the violence of the double standard-hypocrisy of those in power, condemning the protests against injustice in the streets while they daily indulge in the obliteration of countless victims of their greed, lust for power, and world domination. Simultaneously he is showing that he understands perfectly the presence of the Pharaoh on the other side of the blood-red waters:

> Less than a week before President Obama contended that "there was no excuse for the violence in Baltimore," an April *New York Times* article quoted him as saying, in defense of his military drone strikes, "Let's kill the people who are trying to kill us." Similarly, when Israel led a 51-day military offensive in the summer of 2014 that resulted in the deaths of over 2,300 Palestinians, Obama claimed that Israel had "a right to defend itself."[29]

But like Aislinn Pulley in Chicago, Jamye Wooten, speaking for the young generation, does something more. He illustrates the remarkable political maturity of the youth movement in the United States to think globally, sorely lacking in the public discourse led by the politicians, in the mainstream mass media and in the churches in general, as he connects their own struggles to the global struggles for justice and freedom. He consciously links the struggle of the Palestinian people, led by the Palestinian youth, to the struggles against the violence of the state, led by the youth, in the United States:

---

28. See Charles Pierce, "Shoot the Kid 16 Times," Reader Supported News, November 30, 2015, http://readersupportednews.org/opinion2/277-75/33773-focus-shoot-the-kid-16-times.

29. Wooten, "Who Has the Right," 3.

Given the situation in Israel, we can see that extrajudicial killings in which the state serves as judge, jury and executioner of black and brown people are not simply a domestic issue. Since 2004 the US has conducted over 400 drone strikes, killing more than 2,400 civilians in Pakistan. Three hundred seventy of the strikes have been conducted under the Obama administration, and it is estimated that those particular attacks have injured up to 1,700 citizens, and killed as many as 1,000 more—including 200 children.[30]

Jamye Wooten protests against the violence of silence in the face of all these atrocities. When he speaks of "years of neglect," he is speaking of the relentless workings of the structures and systems of white supremacy. He is also speaking of the many almost-privileged blacks, as Martin Luther King Jr. already understood years ago, who have seen all this happening and escalating and were too self-satisfied, self-absorbed, and self-protective of their newly-acquired middle-class status to see that what was really occurring was not genuine progress, and certainly not liberation, but gentrified stagnation.[31] Martin Luther King Jr. correctly identified and applauded the freedom-infused drive of the youth of the sixties when they resisted and threw off the middle-class values so many tried to instill in them:

> It was precisely when young Negroes threw off their middle-class values that they made a historic social contribution. They abandoned those values when they put careers and wealth in a secondary role. When they cheerfully became jailbirds and

---

30. Ibid., 4.

31. Martin Luther King Jr. minced no words as he spoke of the disappointment of youth in the sixties: "It is disappointment with the Christian church that appears to be more white than Christian, and with many white clergymen who prefer to remain silent behind the security of stained-glass windows. It is disappointment with some Negro clergymen who are more concerned about the size of the wheel base on their automobiles than about the quality of their service to the Negro community. It is disappointment with the Negro middle class that has sailed or struggled out of the muddy ponds into relatively fresh-flowing waters of the mainstream and in the process has forgotten the stench of the backwaters where their brothers are still drowning." King, *Where Do We Go from Here*, 36–37. In his turn, Wooten criticizes "preacher pacifiers" who get roped in regularly by those in power to defend the establishment and justify its violence against the protesters, but themselves have not taken a stand for justice in any way that would endanger their cozy relationship with those in power. From Cleveland, yet another young clergywoman/activist, Rev. Waltrina Middleton, would make the same point in an email to friends: "What's even more appalling is knowing [state prosecutor McGinty, responsible for not even charging the police officer who killed 12-year old Tamir Rice] is protected by a Black mayor, a Black police Chief, and Black clergy . . ." She has a right to be angry at such betrayal.

troublemakers, when they took off their Brooks Brothers attire and put on overalls to work in the isolated rural South, they inspired and challenged white youth to emulate them.[32]

This, it seems to me, is exactly what the youth in the United States, South Africa, and Palestine are doing in their resistance to post-civil rights, post-racial, post-apartheid and post-peace road maps pressures to conform, accept, resign, and comply.

However, the controversy caused by Garnet's call to violent resistance should not distract us from an essential truth Garnet wanted his people to understand that day. Garnet's address invites us to think about three issues, not always as well-remembered and oft-quoted as the call to arms. But they are, in my view, as relevant today as they were then, and we should heed them more today than ever before.

First is his insistence that there can be no negotiation about one's freedom, with slave-owners or any other oppressor: "[G]o to your lordly enslavers and tell them plainly, that you *are determined to be free* . . . Tell them in language which they cannot misunderstand, of the exceeding sinfulness of slavery, and of a future judgment, and of the righteous retributions of an indignant God. Inform them that all you desire is FREEDOM, and that nothing else will suffice."

What every oppressor, then and now, must understand, is that the oppressed are determined to be free. They must be told in language that cannot be misunderstood, that God is a God of justice, and freedom, and judgment, and that freedom is what is desired: there is no substitute. The demand is for freedom not as defined by the oppressor—a "freedom" that requires the permission of and the limitations set by the oppressor. This is a lesson post-1994 South Africans, and young post-2008 black Americans have been learning through painful experience. The words, "nothing else will suffice," are a reminder that appeals to "gradualism", tinkering with "reforms" or adjustments to the system of oppression will not be acceptable; that the endurance of the oppressed is not to be confused with endless patience or with acceptance of a calendar for freedom set by slave owners. Slavery is evil and as such cannot be reformed or modified, it can only be irrevocably eradicated.

Here Garnet raises another truth we have always known but constantly have to be reminded of, even though Martin Luther King Jr. and Albert Luthuli, Malcolm X and Nelson Mandela never tired of telling us so: power is never willingly given up by the oppressor—it has to be wrested from their hands by the oppressed; freedom is never handed to the oppressed on a

---

32. King, *The Trumpet of Conscience*, 46–47.

silver platter—it is the gift of struggle and sacrifice. Frederick Douglass said it with unmistakable clarity:

> If there is no struggle, there is no progress. Those who profess to favor freedom and yet deprecate agitation are men who want crops without plowing up the ground; they want rain without thunder and lightning. They want the ocean without the awful roar of its many waters. The struggle may be a moral one, or it may be a physical one, and it may be both moral and physical, but it must be a struggle. Power concedes nothing without a demand. It never did and it never will. . . . The limits of tyrants are prescribed by the endurance of those whom they oppress.[33]

We should note, in parenthesis, that in uttering these words Douglass sounds much more radical than the Douglass who so vehemently resisted Henry Garnet 14 years before as we have seen above, and it demonstrates just how complex and inescapable these issues become when struggles for freedom meet relentless violent resistance from those bent on continued oppression and loathe to give up positions of power.

With Douglass' words ringing in our ears, Albert Luthuli's warning takes on an even more prophetic tone. "The road to freedom," are Albert Luthuli's immortal words, "is always via the CROSS."[34] It is noteworthy, though, that for Luthuli this is not a call for violence. For him this means our readiness to be nailed to that cross, like Jesus, absorbing the violence of the empire, its substitutes and its henchmen, taking upon oneself the pain and suffering of one's people, yet triumphing over evil and nullifying the power of violence to stop the triumph of freedom and justice. In 1961, when the ANC took their decision in favor of violent struggle, Mandela and Luthuli were on opposite sides of this debate. Mandela established *Mkhonto we Sizwe*; Luthuli remained steadfast in his choice for nonviolence. It speaks volumes for the rightness and wisdom of this choice that Nelson Mandela,

---

33. See Frederick Douglass, "If There Is No Struggle, There Is No Progress," a "West India Emancipation" speech delivered at Canandaigua, New York, August 3, 1857, http://www.blackpast.org/1857-frederick-douglass-if-there-is-no-struggle-there-no-progress. My thanks and appreciation go to Ms. Lisa Holland of CTS library and Ms. Sherry Utterback of the Indianapolis Central Library for their help.

34. Luthuli, *Let My People Go*, 232–36. Martin Luther King Jr.: "Lamentably, it is a historical fact that privileged groups seldom give up their privileges voluntarily . . . Freedom is never given voluntarily by the oppressor; it must be demanded by the oppressed." See "Letter from Birmingham Jail." See also Nelson Mandela, Statement from the Dock, http://www.anc.org.za/show.php?id=3430.

thirty years later, was the one to plead for forgiveness and reconciliation instead of ongoing violence and revenge.[35]

Garnet's second point is theological, simultaneously raising the question of human dignity: slavery (in all its forms, from the past as well as in the present) is an intolerable assault upon the dignity of black personhood. In a powerful reminder of the outrage of John Calvin on the question of tyranny and submission to it, Garnet says, "To such degradation it is sinful in the extreme for you to make voluntary submission."[36] Where in the first instance the sinfulness of oppression rests on the oppressor, now the burden of sinfulness is placed on the oppressed if they accept such oppression without resistance. There is no excuse for acceptance of the indignity of oppression for it "hurls defiance" in the face of God. This, Garnet argues, is sinful "in the extreme."

Furthermore, the condition of oppression, the harshness of the oppressor's rule, the difficult circumstances for resistance, the nebulous evil embedded in systemic injustice, the fear of the oppressor's retribution— none of this relieves the oppressed from claiming their God-given rights, since resistance to evil is the *duty* of the believer. In this Garnett is clear: "The forlorn condition in which you are placed does not destroy your moral obligation to God." And again, "Your condition does not absolve you from your moral obligation." The moral obligation "to God" is inseparable from the moral obligation to freedom and to one's own dignity. And while this reasoning brings Garnet to the conclusion that violence as a strategy for freedom struggles is not only acceptable but in all probability unavoidable, this same passion should drive those who believe in militant, nonviolent action for justice.[37]

Third is the sobering warning that "the Pharaohs are on both sides of the blood-red waters." On that day Garnet meant to say that fleeing across borders would not help. Whether to British territories or Mexico, the reach of slavery was everywhere: "The propagators of American slavery are spending their blood and treasure, that they may plant the black flag in the heart of Mexico . . . " That was true: the United States was not just annexing

---

35. For a more detailed discussion, see Boesak, *Kairos, Crisis and Global Apartheid*, 180–92.

36. See John Calvin's *Commentary* on Isaiah 14:7–8; see also my detailed discussion on this in Boesak, *Kairos, Crisis, and Global Apartheid*, 58, 59.

37. I used the same reasoning in 1979, in an open letter to the South African Minister of Justice, in defending the decisions of the South African Council of Churches to call for, participate in and lead actions of civil disobedience on a massive scale. See Boesak, "Divine Obedience," in *Black and Reformed*, 32–41. See for numerous references to the arguments made by John Calvin on this matter, see Boesak, *Kairos, Crisis and Global Apartheid*, ch. 2, esp. 50–64.

through brutal war Florida and New Mexico, Arizona and California, it had indeed plans to overrun Mexico itself, and it *would* have taken slavery with it.[38] There would be no respite for Africans anywhere.

These are the lessons to be taken to heart in the new situations of struggle we are facing. But how should we understand these words today? The goal today is not to physically try to outrun slavery—for the reach of empire is indeed global, but to claim authentic freedom, human rights and human dignity in the lands of our birth, in the places these were once denied us and that we have won through painful struggle, blood and sacrifice, or in the places where these are still denied us; to fight every new form of slavery wherever it is to be found.

On the other side of these initial struggles there was indeed the expectation of the fruits of sacrifice: the right to vote and to have a meaningful say in the affairs of our nations. The right not to go hungry; the right to a decent livelihood and decent education; the right to shelter and care; the right to defend these rights when they are threatened, to secure an ever better future for the generations to come.

These are rights previous generations have fought for and have won. How is it then, this generation has the right to ask, that fifty years after the signing of the Civil Rights Act, these very same civil rights are under threat as never before? In the United States there are renewed battles for the right to vote, as if the work of Fannie Lou Hamer and those who gave so much of themselves during those early voter registration campaigns counts for nothing. The disinvestment and neglect Wooten highlights that have brought socio-economic distress and social disintegration have their correlation in other, even darker realities: the US, jurist and pastor Wendell Griffin points out, currently devotes more of its budget to national defense and homeland security than on educating children, fighting disease, feeding the hungry and alleviating poverty. In 2013, before the current escalation of the war in Iraq, a study by a team of academicians tallied the cost of the war at $1.7 trillion, a figure that did not include $490 billion owed Iraqi war veterans for disability benefits. The study projected that expenses related to the war in Iraq could grow to more than $6 trillion over the next four decades.[39] This is not counting the ongoing, and expanding, war in Afghanistan, Syria, or Yemen.

Wendell Griffin, one of the rare prophetic figures in the church in the tradition of Jeremiah A. Wright, sums up precisely why young people in the United States are on the streets today, letting their cry of anguish,

---

38. See Zinn, *A People's History of the United States*, 149–69.
39. See Griffin, *The Fierce Urgency of Prophetic Hope*, 61.

anger, and disappointment ring out. Plainly, he says, the United States has not become more informed or more responsive to racial injustice since Dr. King died. "We have simply militarized the injustice in brazen ways." He calls the shallow, platitudinal embraces of Martin Luther King Jr. by political, commercial, and opportunistic religious leaders while disregarding his warnings and call for repentance "pimping" King's moral authority for their own benefit. Such contradictory behavior he calls "the re-assassination of Dr. King."[40]

Griffin mentions drone warfare, a militarized law enforcement culture, fiscal policies that promote the interests of corporates over the needy, the failure to attack the root causes of systemic poverty and promote the glaring income inequality gap. Like Marvin McMickle, he severely critiques the promoters of the prosperity gospel who "murder King's righteous indignation against injustice" and those who use religion as a weapon to deny civil rights to LGBTQI+ persons, the poor, immigrants, women, or "otherwise vulnerable" people. "We have," Griffin writes, "not weakened the giant triplets of racism, militarism, and materialism [as pointed out by King]. We have nourished, bred, and multiplied them."[41]

Young people, as Wooten has demonstrated, understand this perfectly well. So despite using our collective political power and using our right to vote—having put in power persons from within our midst, notably Nelson Mandela and Barack Obama, who spoke to us of hope and change and a better life for all; persons who we thought understood our struggles and our pain, our hopes and aspirations, in whom we have vested all our longings for justice and freedom—the sorrow songs have not yet ended. It is still necessary to raise the cry. Henry Highland Garnet was right: there are Pharaohs on both sides of the blood-red waters. In the war zones of Palestine sorrow still drenches our lives like Rachel's tears; in the hunger zones of South Africa's squatter camps, the children are still given stones for bread; and in the struggle zones of America's cities, freedom is strangled to death as Martin Luther King's dream, as he himself testified, is turned into a nightmare.[42] The children of this generation have now decided they must face and confront that nightmare.

In the United States as in South Africa, white supremacy is still foundational to our racialized societies and an honest discussion about race and white privilege is still violently provocative, entirely inadequate and

---

40. Ibid., 8.

41. Ibid., 9.

42. See "A Christmas Sermon on Peace," in King, *The Trumpet of Conscience*, 69–80. The rhythmic, rhetorically strong, and deeply moving passage "I watched that dream turn into a nightmare" is on 78–79.

hopelessly sunk in a quagmire of denialism. Today, the gap between rich and poor in both societies is wider than ever. Since 1994, South Africa has become one of the most unequal societies on earth. What is euphemistically called "income inequality"—as if this is all about "income" and not about voracious greed, exploitation, and manipulation—is in fact an unprecedented, sustained wave of hostility and aggression by the rich against the poor.

Mass incarceration is not just the "new Jim Crow," as Michelle Alexander has correctly described it. It is also a vast, oppressive, exploitative, and growing industrial complex. A young African American person walking down the street is nothing in the eyes of the powerful. But once in prison she or he becomes a valuable profit-making commodity, worth $30–$40,000 per year in revenues for the private prison system that by 2011 has grown into a $34.4 billion industry. At the beginning of 2016 it stood at a staggering $80 billion.[43]

There are Pharaohs on both sides of the blood-red waters of the civil rights struggle and the anti-apartheid struggle, and they look like us. In Palestine, in the words of father Jamal Khader of the Latin Patriarchy in his 2015 meditation on Christmas in Bethlehem, it seems that people have lost "all hope in a future of peace."[44] The struggles are ongoing; they are far from over.

Reclaiming the prophetic tradition of the church would mean discerning the *kairos* moment, repenting of our silence, our complicity, and our cowardice; turning anew to the God of our liberation, embracing once again the hopes of our people in our preaching and in our public witness. We must repent of our sentimentalized politics and recognize that a black face in high office is no automatic guarantee of justice for the poor and oppressed. We must understand much better than we do the seductive power of power and that it is not so much a question of *who* is in power but what they *do* with their power when in power. Suspending, even better, *abandoning* the credulous politics so harmful to the people and our witness, we must examine whose interests they serve while in power.

---

43. See Samuel DeWitt Procter Conference, *Bearing Witness*, 48. The $34.4 billion represents a growth of 9.1% from 2000–2011. See also Chris Hedges, "The Business of Mass Incarceration," July 28, 2013, http://truthdig.com/report/item/the_business_of_mass_incarceration_20130728. See also Eric Markowitz, *International Business Times*, January 25, 2015, http://readersupportednews.org/news-section2/318-66/34818-the-big-money-in-US-prisons. For a systematic treatment of the issue see Michelle Alexander's brilliant and groundbreaking work, *The New Jim Crow*.

44. See John De Gruchy, "Christmas Celebration as Protest," December 10, 2015, https://kairossouthernafrica.wordpress.com/2015/12/10/christmas-as-protest-john-de-gruchy/.

More and more, young South Africans seem to be doing just that. When South African president Jacob Zuma tells South Africans that "the ANC (African National Congress) comes first and the country second" it is not just a gross and utterly dangerous reversal of priorities, a display of the hubristic arrogance of power the ANC has so quickly acquired. What Zuma has in mind is the ANC he represents, argues young intellectual Motime Letsoalo, and that is an ANC that has hopelessly lost its way. It is the tribalized, narrow-minded ANC of which the province of KwaZulu-Natal has become the new stronghold. But this trend, "rooted in tragic ignorance and bigotry" has "reduced the ANC to a corrupt, tribalist, visionless party" which no longer offers the political home young people like Letsoala seek.[45] That is a call for fundamental change.

When Jamye Wooten has the courage to lift up the cry, to expose, and link domestic injustices, foreign policy disasters and unsustainable contradictions that flourish under a black president, that is extraordinary political discernment. When Sarah Boesak writes of the struggles for justice in South Africa on her Facebook page that they are "the great inheritance of South Africa; to know that we should be better, to demand that we can be better, and to fight so that we are better," this shows inspired determination. These young people know that the issues are fundamental, systemic, transcending race, beyond the confines of the politics of sentiment, and global. They also understand that they are face to face with the pharaoh on what was supposed to be the freedom-side of the blood-red waters. They are the new voices and the new face of the defiant, courageous, hopeful *sizwe*.

---

45. See Matome Letsoala, "Is Tribalism on the Rise under Jacob Zuma?" http://voices.news24.com/matome-letsoalo/2015/11/is-tribalism-on-the-rise-under-jacob-zuma/; Sarah Boesak, "Kill the Demon Today, Face the Devil Tomorrow," November 6, 2015.

CHAPTER 2

Interrupting the Globalization of Indifference

Empire, Faithful Resistance, and Prophetic Pathos

We must not be afraid to say it.

—POPE FRANCIS, 2015

The Desolate and Anguished Heart

"The joy of the Gospel fills the hearts and lives of all who encounter Jesus." These are the opening words of Pope Francis' courageous and inspiring Apostolic Exhortation of early 2015, *Evangelii Gaudium*.[1] This joy is a gift of grace and mercy, but it is fragile, the pope goes on to say, "confronted with a great danger in today's world, pervaded as it is by consumerism." That danger is "the desolation and anguish born of a complacent yet covetous heart, the feverish pursuit of frivolous pleasures, and a blunted conscience." Those very first words are a simple, but strong, unapologetic statement of faith. No one should be in doubt about the fundamental connectedness between faith in Jesus Christ, the joy the encounter with Jesus brings, and the things that endanger this joy.

It is also a sentence that combines deep pastoral concern with prophetic truth telling. The pope eschews euphemisms and the use of the word "consumerism" is not random. Embedded in the extraordinary global power of what is called "the prosperity gospel", it has indeed become "the gospel

---

1. Pope Francis, *Apostolic Exhortation Evangelii Gaudium*, para. 1–2, 3.

of consumerism." It is at the heart of today's global, neoliberal capitalism, central to what the pope calls "an economy of exclusion."

The pope seems to have his finger on the pulse. In 2007, South African theologian Ernst Conradie, together with a group of postgraduate students at the University of the Western Cape just outside of Cape Town, did a survey of the literature on Christianity and consumerism, trying to understand how "the ideology of consumerism shapes the lives of those in the lower middle-class in South Africa."[2] On the basis of that survey they identified the following points of entry for a critique of consumerism:

- "The consumer society is not sustainable": the consumer society stimulates a continuously expanding economy that is not sustainable on a finite planet in the long run;
- "Consumerism exacerbates injustices": the pervasive influence of consumerism amongst the rich and the poor is tragic because it reinforces economic inequalities;
- "The affluent have become the victims of their own desires": this sociological and psychological critique reveals that consumerism has severe impact on the health and lifestyles of the affluent themselves;
- "Consumerism undermines virtue and breeds vices": consumerism stimulates the worst in human beings: greed (avarice), hoarding, envy, covetousness, pleasure-seeking, and pride. In response, the virtues of wisdom, simplicity, frugality and care are typically retrieved;
- "The consumer society encourages commercialized cultural and religious practices": commercialization leads to shallow engagement with almost everything, including, for example, human sexuality, education and employment. Such commercialization also has a pervasive influence on ecclesial practices. And finally,
- "Consumerism amounts to idolatry": consumerism challenges almost every single aspect of the Christian faith.

In the circles of prophetic Reformed theology, theological critique has deepened from a critique on race and religion, apartheid and the theology of apartheid, to a critique on socio-economic injustices, greed and consumerism, globalism and global neoliberal capitalism. Hence the question of "idolatry" and "status confessionis."[3] Likewise, and ecumenically, the *kairos*

---

2. Conradie, "Globalisation, Consumerism, and the Call for a Status Confessionis," 53–76.

3. See Conradie, "Consumerism," 53–54. In 1982, the World Alliance of Reformed Churches (WARC, since 2011 the World Communion of Reformed Churches, WCRC),

document produced by Christians from nine countries in the Global South in 1989, South Africa, Namibia, the Philippines, South Korea, El Salvador, Nicaragua and Guatemala, offers incisive critique of the legacy of imperialism, colonialism and racism, and issues a strong call for conversion to those Christians who side with money, power, privilege, and pleasure. It unequivocally speaks of consumerism as "idolatry."

> In our countries, the worship of money, power, privilege and pleasure has certainly replaced the worship of God. This form of idolatry has been organized into a system in which consumerist materialism has been enthroned as a god. Idolatry makes things, especially money and property, more important than people. It is anti-people.[4]

Going wider still, and from a Buddhist perspective, underscoring the interfaith consensus on this matter, David Loy writes that "the market is already the most successful religion of all time, winning more converts more quickly than any previous belief system or value system in human history."[5] The pope seems to have grasped that crucial shift.

George F. Will, the influential conservative American columnist, derisively denounces the pope as one who "comes trailing clouds of sanctimony," embracing "fashionable," but "demonstrably false and deeply reactionary ideas" with the "indiscriminate zeal of a new convert." This pope may be "flamboyant" but he fails to understand the "spontaneous creativity of an open society in which people and their desires are not problems but celebrated as one of the [American] nation's premises."[6]

---

at the urging of South African black Reformed Christians, declared the situation of apartheid and its theological justification by the white Dutch Reformed Churches a *status confessionis*, a "state of confession", in other words a situation where, in the judgement of the Church, the integrity of the gospel of Jesus Christ is at stake. The WARC declared apartheid a "heresy" and suspended the membership of the two white Dutch Reformed Churches. In the following years a call went out, again strongly driven by black Reformed Christians from Southern Africa, to consider the situation of global apartheid, the injustices and social inequalities caused by global neoliberal capitalism as well as the threat to the Earth as a situation warranting the consideration of another *status confessionis*. Subsequently, in 2004, the *Accra Confession* was adopted. For the full text of the *Accra Confession*, see http://wcrc.ch/accra/the-accra-confession.

4. See "The Road to Damascus: Kairos and Conversion", in Gary S. Leonard (compiler and editor), *Kairos, the Moment of Truth, the Kairos Documents*, Ujamaa Centre for Biblical and Theological Community Development and research (2010), http//:ujamaa. ukzn.ac.za/Libraries/manuals/The_Kairos_Documents.sflb.ashx.

5. See Conradie, "Consumerism", 60, citing David R. Loy, "The Religion of the Market", *Journal of the American Academy of Religion*, 65/2, 1997, 275–90.

6. See George F. Will, "Pope Francis's Fact-Free Flamboyance," *Washington Post*, September 18, 2015; https://www.washingtonpost.com/opinions/pope-franciss-fact

Nonetheless, the pope defines those unfettered and celebrated desires as coming from a "desolate and anguished heart." To me it seems that the pope has understood the heart of the matter. That heart is desolate because it has lost the joy of the Gospel, does not respond to the love of Jesus Christ, has disdained the enrichment of human solidarity, and lost itself in the pampering of its own desires. It has hardened itself against the cries of the poor, the weak and the vulnerable, in so doing hardening itself against the pathos of God.

That heart is anguished because it resists what it knows Yahweh requires: to love mercy, to do kindness and to walk humbly with one's God. It is anguished because its endless, feverish pursuit of "frivolous pleasures" is an empty endeavor, alienating itself from the suffering and needs of others, caught up in the self-centeredness of instant gratification. That heart is complacent, bloated with self-satisfaction, yet it is covetous, restless with greed, in the unyielding grip of always wanting more, relentlessly pursuing that at the expense of others. Since it cannot *please* God, that heart seeks to *placate* God by "tithing mint, dill, and cumin," but constantly misses what Jesus insists are "the weightier matters of the Law: justice, mercy and faith" (Matt 23:23). That heart can find neither joy nor rest, so it deceives itself with the false and restless comfort of a "blunted conscience."

This blunted conscience is the exact opposite of what I have elsewhere called the "tender conscience" and described in this way:

> This [tender] conscience is a consciousness of the closeness of the other and of God. It means not only sharing the pain of the other, but also sharing the rage of God against injustice and inhumanity. [It is] a reasonable account of the hope that is within us. It allows the powerless to call us to account on account of that hope, for us as well as for them, and it allows the powerless to present us with the authority with which that hope endows them . . . People have *authority* even when they have no power

---

-free-flamboyance/2015/09/18/7D711750-5d6a-11e5-8e9e-dce8a2a2a679_story.html?utm_term=.b38cc4475f30. Other critics of the pope abound. The Heritage Foundation warned that the pope has "aligned himself with the far-left and has embraced an ideology that would make people poorer and less free." *First Things,* a Catholic publication, has called Francis "an ideologue and a meddlesome egoist." American Cardinal Raymond Leo Burke has suggested it might be necessary "to resist the pope's doctrinal shifts." "The church should not be thinking about markets at all", is the opinion of Rev. Robert Sirico, head of the Acton Institute, a conservative think tank. "Its job is to guide people's spirits, not their purchases." See Amanda Erikson, "Some American Catholics Really Dislike Pope Francis. Here's Why," *Washington Post,* http://www.washingtonpost.com/sf/local/2015/09/18/francis-is-a-global-sensation-but-to-certain-traditional-catholics-his-message-rings-hollow/?utm_term=.5ee01ef92993. September 18, 2015.

because of the incarnation of God and the hope for the promises of God that God has awakened, and kept alive, within them.⁷

Whenever our interior life becomes caught up in its own interests and concerns, writes Pope Francis, "there is no more room for others, no place for the poor. God's voice is no longer heard, the quiet cry of his love is no longer felt, and the desire for doing good fades."⁸ This is what Francis calls "indifference." Here it is still very personal, but the pope knows and will argue that this is the disturbing trend that has come with the global hegemony of imperial culture and the globalization of neoliberal capitalism. He will speak of "an economy of exclusion" and of growing and devastating inequalities, of the threat to human dignity, and the destruction of our common home, the Earth.

This situation is beyond oppression, exploitation, or disenfranchisement, Francis writes. It is about exclusion, for people might still be considered part of society, albeit its "underside." But they are no longer part of it: people no longer count; they are outcasts, "leftovers."⁹ I am sure the pope cannot mean that there is no such thing as "exploitation" or "oppression" anymore. The ruthless exploitation of the poor, especially women and children, as a source of cheap or forced labor, together with political oppression and suppression of their rights, is still one of the harshest (and growing) realities of global neoliberal capitalism. The scandalous treatment of workers—men women, and children—in the sweatshop clothing factories of Bangladesh by the great designer brands of the world is but one example of this. The sheer scale of deliberate disenfranchisement of African Americans and other people of color in the last decade or so through mass incarceration, the ceaseless overturning and rewriting of voting laws in several states and what Americans call "gerrymandering" of voting districts is not only a real danger to American democracy; it is an assault on human dignity with a casualness that stuns the mind.

Exclusion is of course not new. In the 1970s I had occasion to work with Father Cosmas Desmond, a Catholic priest who devoted his life to mission work in the then Bantustan called the Ciskei in South Africa. His book *The Discarded People* was one of the most horrific, and one of the most accurate, descriptions of hopelessness, suffering, hunger, disease, and death in those concentration camps the apartheid government called "homelands."¹⁰

---

7. See Boesak, *The Tenderness of Conscience*, 223.
8. *Evangelii Gaudium*, para. 53, 46.
9. Ibid., para. 53, 46.
10. Cosmas, *The Discarded People*.

I went there with him and after all these years am still haunted by what I saw. So black South Africans know what it means to be "excluded."

Elaine Storkey describes a new totalitarian world view as pervasive and hegemonic as any previous ideology and ironically, yet devastatingly effective in the postmodern context of Western societies:

> Effectively a new organizing principle has moved into place in the West that acts in the same totalitarian way as statism did in a previous era, and this in cultures described as post-modern and skeptical about "grand narratives." It is the principle of consumerism . . . It is a new grand narrative, communicated through indoctrination, traveling through the home and heart, and shaping the whole direction of societal living. With economic totalitarianism, the meaning of the economic and all other areas of life is geared toward consumption . . . Blessed are they who buy cars, perfume, holidays, furniture. The message is confirmed by luscious music, promised intimacy, smiling faces, and studios that construct and reconstruct heaven.[11]

What Storkey has observed in so-called postmodern societies in the Global North is now true of growing sections of the Global South as well, wherever global imperialism finds willing substitutes. To sustain enthusiasm for such a way of life, such normalized and unquestioned idolatry, for such systems of exclusion and dehumanization across the world, for the infliction of such suffering upon God's children on a global scale, requires, Francis argues, a "globalization of indifference."

> Almost without being aware of it, we end up being incapable of feeling compassion at the outcry of the poor, weeping for other people's pain, and feeling a need to help them, as though this was someone else's responsibility and not our own. The culture of prosperity deadens us. We are thrilled if the market offers us something new to purchase. In the meantime all those lives stunted for lack of opportunity seem a mere spectacle; they fail to move us.[12]

Twenty-one years ago theologian and social activist Jim Wallis already saw that which is alarming the pope today. He agonizes about the state of politics in the United States and despairs at what he sees.

---

11. Conradie, "Globalisation, Consumerism, and the Call for *Status Confessionis*," 59, quoting Storkey, "Sphere Sovereignty and the Anglo-American Tradition," 201–2.

12. *Evangelii Gaudium*, para. 54, 46, 47.

Our most basic virtues of civility, responsibility, justice and integrity seem to be collapsing. We appear to be losing the ethics derived from personal commitment, social purpose and spiritual meaning. The triumph of materialism is hardly questioned now . . . We are divided along the lines of race, ethnicity, class, gender, religion, culture and tribe . . . Our intuition tells us the depth of the crisis we face demands more than politics as usual. An illness of the spirit has spread across the land . . . [13]

This "illness of the spirit" is not just visible in the United States. It is global. Observing the world as we know it today, Wallis did not know how true and relevant his words would remain. Today half the world is having to live with the terror of an endless war on terror, inflicted upon millions of innocents by imperial powers and their lackeys in the Middle East and the Global South, the matching brutality of stateless groups now operating from West Africa to Afghanistan. The millions of displaced persons and refugees and the terrible fate of their children—the inevitable, if unacknowledged, result of war for profit and vainglorious but utterly destructive attempts at "regime change"—remains a shocking and humbling sight.

These are the victims of what journalist Naomi Klein, in a splendid work,[14] calls "disaster capitalism"; "shock and awe" economic strategies. They are the victims of a slew of international trade agreements beneficial only to international corporations, and policies of "structural adjustment" former World Bank Vice-President for Africa Edward Jaycox has called "a systematic destructive force in Africa."[15] There is no doubt that Wallis has been vindicated. These policies, however, all deliberately designed to benefit and protect the wealth and power of the rich North, are now affecting those countries of the North in not altogether unexpected, but nonetheless disturbing ways.

Racism, xenophobia, and a violent, virulent form of homophobia are running rampant, undisguised and unapologetically, across Africa, including South Africa, and many countries across the globe. In the United States, state-sanctioned, racialized violence against unarmed persons of color continues unabated. We stand aghast at the shameful spectacle of the inhumane treatment of refugees in the hands of people smugglers on the Mediterranean Sea, and at the borders of many European countries. Yet, in the reckless pursuit of profits for the few, the headlong plunge into incomprehensible policies that lead to ecological destruction, yet more "solutions" based on

13. Wallis, *The Soul of Politics*, xv.
14. Klein, *The Shock Doctrine*.
15. See Keet, "Systematic Destruction, 10–11.

repeatedly-failed military strategies, and yet more steps in the disastrous exclusion of the vast majority of the people of the globe, the madness continues. It is what the pope names as "the globalization of indifference."

The pope recognizes the challenges: an economy of exclusion, the fear and desperation of the majority of God's people across the world, the vast and growing gap between the rich and the poor caused by skewed and unjust economic systems held up by a "crude and naïve" trust in the "sacralized" workings of the prevailing economic system "where the powerful feed on the powerless."[16] Like the Kairos theologians of almost thirty years ago did in *The Road to Damascus*, Pope Francis decries the "the new idolatry of money": "The golden calf has returned in a new and ruthless guise in the idolatry of money and the dictatorship of an imperial economy."[17]

Human beings are reduced to one single need: consumption, and the root causes of the inequalities and imbalances are "ideologies which defend the absolute autonomy of the marketplace and financial speculation."[18] The thirst for power and possessions knows no limits, devours everything which stands in the way of increased profits. Whatever is fragile, like the environment, is "defenseless before the interests of a deified market, which becomes the only rule."[19]

All this constitutes a deep human crisis, which the pope interprets as a result of the "rejection of ethics and a rejection of God."[20] For the pope, God is rejected because God is "outside of the categories of the marketplace . . . [As a result], God can only be seen as uncontrollable, unmanageable, even dangerous, since [God] calls human beings to full realization and to freedom from all forms of enslavement."[21] Just over 15 years ago, German theologian Jürgen Moltmann understood what this means: the crisis we are facing is much more than a human crisis, he argues, but he takes it one step further.

> Our social and political frigidity towards the disadvantaged, the poor and the humiliated is an expression of our frigidity towards God. The cynicism of modern political and economic manipulators is an expression of our contempt for God. We have lost God, and God has left us, so we are bothered, neither by the

---

16. Ibid., para. 54, 46.
17. Ibid., para. 55, 47.
18. Ibid., para. 56, 47.
19. Ibid., para. 56, 48.
20. Ibid., para. 57, 48.
21. Ibid., para. 57, 48.

suffering of others *which we have caused*, nor by the debts we are leaving behind for the coming generations.[22]

Elsewhere[23] I have made an effort to respond to Moltmann's valuable insights in this way: in our inner life as in our political responsibility in the public square, we need to rediscover God. And we cannot discover God in the images we tend to find ourselves reflected in. God is not the mirror of our own deepest desires. Neither can we discover God as a distant stranger, a neutral Observer of human actions and therefore of human suffering and misery, aloof from and untouched by human pain. God is not the Silent Observer who leaves us to our own devices in order to preserve the maturity of our mind, to respect the integrity of our human reason—postmodernism's reward for our "independence" from God. We need to discover God in the consequences of our decisions and choices. We must learn, in the words of Moltmann, to discover and "revere God in the victims of our own violence," as the victims of human greed for world domination.[24]

It is not in withdrawing into ourselves that we find God. It is in reaching out in solidarity and empathy to the wounded other, seeking with them the comforting reality of God's compassionate justice, that God reveals Godself to us. Therein lies the tenderness of conscience I am pleading for. It is not simply an "inner voice" which leads us to deeds of charity. It is the presence of love that demands justice, that cannot rejoice in the lie and that creates havoc within ourselves until justice is done. It is the piety that is subversive towards acceptance of complacency within and tolerance of wrongs without.

To Stand Where God Stands

I have engaged Pope Francis quite extensively because I have deep appreciation for his prophetic stance on the questions of socio-economic justice, inequality, human dignity, and his critique of globalized neoliberal capitalism. His call for ecological justice, what the ecumenical movement used to call a theology of justice, peace, and the integrity of creation, resonates strongly with me. Also, while writing this, the pope was in the United States, and it was fascinating to watch and observe as this visit unfolded.

---

22. Moltmann, *God for a Secular Society*, 16, emphasis mine.
23. The following two paragraphs draw on my *Tenderness of Conscience*, 221.
24. Moltmann, *God for a Secular Society*, 20.

In a somewhat irreverent article, journalist Matt Taibbi raises the question, "Why do we care which side the pope is on?"[25] Taibbi's concern is not theological or ecclesial of course. His concern is with journalism, on the "left" and the "right," whatever the meaning of these terms in contemporary America. Conservatives feel "betrayed" by this pope, Taibbi writes. When George Will chastises the pope for failing to understand that "in America people and their desires are not problems but precious resources" he is in fact saying that what the pope refuses to accept about "us Americans" is "that our greed and selfishness are actually our best qualities."

Taibbi is equally offended by the journalists of the left as they drag the pope to their side on the questions of the environment, income inequality, and of course immigration. "The American Left is always at its most unlikeable when it is being pious." He means the sudden piousness that opportunistically flares up with the unparalleled media event of a popular pope on whose back they can showcase their rightness. "Watching progressives fawn over a pope is depressing."

Taibbi's criticism of the church is harsh indeed: "I was raised Catholic. To me the Church is just a giant evil transnational corporation operating on a dreary business model, one that nurtures debilitating guilt feelings in its followers and then offers to make them go away temporarily in exchange for donations."

One does not have to share this negative view of the church to recognize that there is some validity in the argument and the question. Besides, Rabbi Michael Lerner's warning against the US media's "trivialization of the pope's message" (not to mention their trivialization of the message of Jesus)—"the pope is above politics and only a humble servant of Jesus"— is to be taken seriously.[26] Certainly, while it does not matter whether the "right" or the "left" in media or political circles can claim the pope, it does matter *where the pope stands* in matters of justice and peace.

That this pope has taken up the cudgels with the powerful forces of the rich and privileged across the world, has spoken up for the global poor and the destitute, the global landless and the homeless, the global oppressed and exploited, and dares to name the globalization of indifference with this state of affairs as the evil it is, is a cause for rejoicing and deep gratitude to

---

25. Matt Taibbi, "Why Do We Care Whose Side the Pope Is On?" http://reader-supportednews.org/opinion2/277-75/32575-focus-why-do-we-care-whose-side-the-pope-is-on, 9/25/2015.

26. Michael Lerner, "Save the Pope's Radical Prophetic Message from Media Trivialization," September 23, 2015, http://www.huffingtonpost.com/rabbi-michael-lerner/save-the-popes-radical-pr_b_8182502.html.

God. On these matters the pope almost speaks with the cadences of a black Baptist preacher:

> Do we realize that something is wrong in a world where there are so many farmworkers without land, so many families without a home, so many labourers without rights, so many persons whose dignity is not respected? Do we realize that something is wrong where so many senseless wars are being fought and acts of fratricidal violence are taking place on our very doorstep? Do we realize something is wrong when the soil, water, air and living creatures of our world are under constant threat? So let us not be afraid to say it.[27]

It is words such as these, especially the last sentence, and taking Pope Francis at his word that embolden me to raise some critical questions. The *Belhar Confession* was conceived in 1982 and adopted in 1986 by my denomination during the darkest years of the State of Emergency, the apartheid regime's response to the oppressed people's determined struggle for freedom and justice.[28] *Belhar* endures as a major challenge to the integrity of prophetic witness to my own church as well as to the church ecumenical. *Belhar's* Article 4, and standing as a central truth of the confession, reads in part as follows:

> We believe that God has revealed Godself as the One who wishes to bring about justice and true peace on earth; that in a world full of injustice and enmity God is in a special way the God of the destitute, the poor and the wronged, and that God calls the church to follow God in this . . . that the church must therefore stand by people in any form of suffering and need, which implies, among other things, that the church must witness against any form of injustice, so that justice may roll down like waters and righteousness like a mighty stream; that the church as the possession of God, should stand where God stands, namely against injustice and with the wronged; that in following Christ the church must witness against all the powerful and privileged who selfishly seek their own interests and thus control and harm others. Therefore, we reject any ideology which would legitimate

---

27. Pope Francis, Speech at the World Meeting of Popular Movements, address at Expo Fair, Santa Cruz de la Sierra, 9 July, 2015, http://en.radiovaticana.va/news/2015/07/10/pope_francis_speech_at_world_meeting_of_popular_movements/1157291.

28. For the complete text of the Belhar confession, see https://www.pcusa.org/site_media/media/uploads/theologyandworship/pdfs/belhar.pdf.

forms of injustice and any doctrine which is unwilling to resist such an ideology in the name of the gospel.

For *Belhar*, and for the Reformed tradition as a whole, it is clear: God is on the side of the poor, the destitute and the wronged. Those of us who call upon the name of Jesus must stand with those, because God stands with them in *any form of suffering and need,* and against *any form of injustice.* The genius of the *Belhar Confession* is not just its insistence that justice is the desire of the God of Jesus Christ. Its genius is in the insistence on the *indivisibility* of God's justice. That is not only its genius; it is its judgment, its power and its blessing. *Every* form of injustice is a form of exclusion. Because of the choices God makes, because of where Christ stands, we are, *Belhar* says, *obligated* "to give ourselves willingly and joyfully to be of benefit and blessing to one another." What *Belhar* is pleading for is the courage, compassion, and commitment to interrupt the globalization of indifference by undoing injustice, and by doing the deeds of justice, peace and love required by Yahweh.

So if the pope rightly calls for a resounding "No!" against an "economy of exclusion," the pope must also denounce a theology and an ecclesiology of exclusion. Women, especially poor, rural women, especially women of color, and persons from the LGBTQI+ community, especially lesbians, to say nothing of trans persons, are as much targets and victims of abuse, exploitation and exclusion as are the poor. They are as vulnerable, and in the global South often the most vulnerable; as destitute, and in the global South often the most destitute; as wronged, and in the global South often the most wronged, and we must not be afraid to say it.[29]

Despite the vilification and vitriolic attacks from the rich and privileged, all respected studies, from Thomas Piketty's masterful work[30] to the most recent Oxfam report on inequality and income distribution, prove the pope has read the global situation correctly. The combined wealth of the world's richest 1 percent will overtake that of the other 99 percent in 2016. The very top of this 1 percent represent just sixty-two individuals. One in nine people do not have enough to eat and more than one billion people live on less than $1.25 a day. The so-called economic recovery of the last few

---

29. See Pollack, "Whose Gay Community?" 437–56. Pollack argues that [certainly in the rich North, and specifically in a city like San Francisco] "the visible and political gay community has been characterized as increasingly a middle-class, white institution" and that this middle-class nature requires economic and psychological resources that are not available to the working class, and thus, may limit the expression of sexual orientation for the working class . . . Thus it is important to incorporate class differences when addressing the social and the political dynamics of sexual orientation."

30. Piketty, *Capital in the Twenty-First Century.*

years was in essence only a recovery for the rich: the richest 1 percent have seen their share of the global wealth increase from 44 percent in 2009 to 48 percent in 2014, and will climb to more than 50 percent in the course of 2016. In concrete terms members of the global elite had an average wealth of $2.7m per adult in 2014. In comparison 80 percent of the world's population had an average of a mere $3,851 per adult. In a time of economic crisis and calls for more austerity for the working classes, the wealth of the richest 80 percent doubled in cash terms between 2009 and 2014.[31] But this is now old news. The year 2017 has scarcely started and we had to revise our data. In January 2017 Oxfam reported that the situation was much worse. Just eight white males own as much wealth as half the world's population.[32]

In his assessment of the realities of climate change and the human hand in it the pope was right as well. In its most recent report from late 2015, quite appropriately titled *Shock Waves*, the World Bank estimates, confirming what many ecojustice activists have argued for years now concerning the intimate relationship between climate change, ecojustice and poverty, estimates that climate change is poised to push 100 million people into "extreme poverty" by 2030. Climate-related shocks and stresses, already a major obstacle to poverty reduction, will worsen with climate change.

> Poor people and poor countries are exposed and vulnerable to all types of climate-related shocks—natural disasters that destroy assets and livelihoods; waterborne diseases and pests that become more prevalent during heat waves, floods, or droughts; crop failure from reduced rainfall; and spikes in food prices that follow extreme weather events.[33]

But for the *Belhar Confession* the scourge of exclusion is inflicted upon *all* who are oppressed, exploited, and robbed of their dignity. The pope has not made gender-based violence, unlike sexual abuse of children, a cause for grave concern and urgent action. Yet globally one in three women will experience physical and/or sexual violence by a partner or non-partner. For the Americas it is 29.8 percent; for Europe 25.4 percent; for the Eastern Mediterranean 37 percent and for Africa 36.6 percent. "Violence against women is a global health problem of epidemic proportions," says the World

---

31. See Winnie Byanyima, "Richest 1% will own more than all the rest in 2016," January 19, 2015, www.oxfam.org/en/pressroom/pressreleases/2015-01-19/richest-1-will-own-more-all-rest-2016.

32. See Oxfam report, January 17, 2017, http://www.oxfam.org/en/pressroom/pressreleases/2017-01-16

33. See International Bank for Reconstruction and Development, *Shock Waves, Managing the Impacts of Climate Change on Poverty*, 1, 3.

Health Organization,[34] and the UN calls it "a pandemic in various forms."[35] Women and girls, the UN report states, "represent 55 percent of the estimated 20.9 million victims of forced labor world-wide, and 78 percent of the estimated 4.5 million forced into sexual exploitation."[36]

These are shattering statistics and we know they become most devastating when we look for and discover the human face of such abject misery, unnamable pain and indescribable violence. To follow Christ means to stand where God stands, and because God is a God of justice—compassionate, *indivisible* justice—it means that unless justice rolls down like waters and righteousness like a mighty stream for battered, oppressed, exploited, silenced and excluded women, it will not roll down for the economically excluded poor, the landless farmers, the penniless unemployed or the racially oppressed.

Neither has the pope said a single word about the brutal exclusion of LGBTQI+ persons, the assault upon their dignity as children of God made in the image of God, and the daily threats to their very lives. The tragic paradox of the unprecedented growth of Christianity in Africa and the global South today is that it is largely driven by a particularly virulent form of Christian neo-fundamentalism not indigenous to Africa but derived from the United States. It is a neo-colonialist, imperialist, ideologized religiosity, a toxic mix of scriptural selectivity, violent homophobia, unrelieved patriarchal power that opens up new forms of spiritual enslavement for the people of a continent not yet fully recovered from the enslavements of the past. Its impact on African societies and the African church in the matters of justice and equality for women and the dignity of LGBTQI+ persons is no less than disastrous.[37] Uganda and Nigeria are only the most

---

34. See "Violence Against Women," July 1997, http://www.who.int/gender/violence/v4.pdf.

35. See UNWomen, "Ending violence Against Women: Facts and Figures," February 2016, http://www.unwomen.org/en/what-we-do/ending-violence-against-women/facts-and-figures.

36. Ibid.

37. See Elna Boesak's as-yet-unpublished research for her PhD at the University of Kwa-Zulu Natal, *Channeling Justice? A Feminist Exploration of North American Televangelism in a South African Constitutional Democracy.* For the impact of neo-fundamentalist theology on the situation of LGBTQI+ persons, see, e.g., Boesak, *Kairos, Crisis, and Global Apartheid,* ch. 4. On his visit to Africa the pope once again could not be faulted on the issues that are close to his heart: poverty, corruption, peace. He is aware also of the "pillaging of Africa's precious resources." He lifted up Africa's "strong traditional families." Many women however, will have been left wondering whether the pope's understanding of the "traditional family" in Africa includes polygamy and the oppressed state of women in the family and society and why he uttered no critical word about that, or about the struggles of women against indefensible traditions

well-known and most obvious examples of what has become an African scourge, and it is growing.

This, too, is what the pope calls "the globalization of indifference." Furthered and justified not by the market fundamentalists of global corporatism, but by the Church of Jesus Christ, thriving on theologies and ecclesiologies of exclusion, it calls into question the very essence of our theological and pastoral integrity. The pope's prophetic words in Bolivia in regard to the harm done to people and the ecosystem as they are being "punished" by the greed and the callousness of the rich in their "unfettered pursuit of money" are equally applicable to the harm done to women and LGBTQI+ persons. "Behind all this pain, death, and destruction," the pope said in Santa Cruz de la Sierra, "there is the stench of what Basil of Caesarea called 'the dung of the devil.'"[38] The pope is intentional in this strong language and rightly so. That the church is shamefully complicit in these daily tragedies should not make us afraid to say it.

Moreover—and we have seen this from Nazi Germany to apartheid South Africa and xenophobic post-apartheid South Africa; from Rwanda to Israel to a Western world obsessed with Islamophobia—behind the carefully cultivated hatred, the deliberate dehumanization, the calculated demonization and the callous exclusion of the other lies the temptation of the deification of the self; and behind the deification of the self always lurks the necessity of the annihilation of the other. From India, author Arundhati Roy, in returning an award she has received from the Indian government in protest against that government's "fostering" of intolerance and hatred against minorities in India, writes about the plight of those minorities in the last few years. She refuses to call this state of affairs "intolerance." "It is the wrong word to use for the lynching, shooting, burning and mass murder of fellow human beings." She knows what is wrong, and she is not afraid to say it as she warns us not to be fooled

> when they talk of "taking evidence for forensic examination." Today we live in a country in which, when the thugs and apparatchiks of the New Order talk of "illegal slaughter" they mean the imaginary cow that was killed—not the real man from the scene of the crime, they mean the food in the fridge, not the body of a lynched man.[39]

---

such as female genital mutilation. See Don Melvin, "Pope Francis to start first day in Uganda with Mass for Martyrs," November 29, 2015, http://www.cnn.com/2015/11/28/africa/africa-pope-francis-trip/ and Bernard Namunane, "Uganda Gives Pope Francis Rousing Welcome," November 28, 2015, www.nation.co.ke/news/-/1056/2975662/-/13inrxiz/-/index.html.

38. See "Speech at the Meeting of World Popular Movements," 4.

39. See Arundhati Roy, "Politics by Other Means," November 10, 2015, http://

It is not only wrong; it is, without question, "the stench of the dung of the devil." Not only should we realize that something is wrong; we should not be afraid to say it.

In the end it is not the vilification of the powerful conservative voices that by the very denial of that truth proves the pope right. It is the joy of the poor, the destitute, and the excluded—*all of them*—at hearing the good news of Jesus that should prove him right. And it is not the expediency of politicians who select what suits them from his words that proves him wrong; it is the unheard cries of the subjugated women and the lesbian, gay, bi-sexual, transsexual, intersex children of God; humiliated, deprived of rights, targeted, hunted down, and killed on a daily basis by Christians emboldened by baptized bigotry and sanctified patriarchy, that should give him pause.

To Not Be Afraid to Say It

Before the US Congress, the pope, in a single, astonishing sentence, offered absolution to the United States for its history of dispossession and dehumanization, genocide and slavery:[40] "It is difficult to judge the past by the criteria of the present," the pope said to sustained applause,[41] not returning to this matter again. I shudder to think of the effect of such words on white South Africans the vast majority of whom, from former president F. W. De Klerk on down, still cannot acknowledge that apartheid was wrong, let alone sinful, idolatrous and evil, disastrous for black people, and harmful to themselves.

From one point of view it can argued that the pope is right. Wide international ratification of the Human Rights Charter and the Geneva Conventions cause us to frown on the savage and inhumane treatment of persons and whole peoples, on genocide, massacres, and wholescale oppression. Slavery was more easily tolerated a century or more ago, and the genocide of whole peoples by the colonizers of the Western world in the

---

readersupportednews.org/opinion2/277-75/33413-focus-politics-by-other-means? Since then more than 100 Indian writers and artists have returned their awards in protest, and thousands have braved horrific retribution by marching in protest against manifestations of intolerance and the Indian government's perceived support of these: BBC World's "Fifth Floor," November 21, 2015.

40. See Zinn, *A People's History of the United States*.

41. See "Transcript: Pope Francis's Speech to Congress," *Washington Post*, September 24, 2015, https://www.washingtonpost.com/local/social-issues/transcript-pope-franciss-speech-to-congress/2015/09/24/6d7d7ac8-62bf-11e5-8e9e-dce8a2a2a679_story.html?utm_term=.226e99626c6e.

Global South did not even register until the holocaust in Hitler's Germany, and the attempted genocide of LGBTQI+ persons, Roma, and persons debilitated by illness.

On the surface, in light of our supposedly growing enlightenment, our world should have a better sense of moral responsibility. However, as in the case of racist ideologies it seems to be always followed by that eternal "but" . . . Nations have ratified international treaties. Child labor is forbidden in the global North, but the same countries have no moral qualms about the child labor in Africa, Indonesia and elsewhere that produces the tanzanite, gold, tin and rare earth so essential to Western vanity, comforts and "civilized standards." The West, and in particular the US and the UK, is full of human-rights rage at the barbaric beheadings carried out by ISIS, and rightly so, but there is no such outrage at the public lashings and beheadings by their closely-held ally in oil, war, and human rights abuses, Saudi Arabia, where we have seen 47 beheadings in one day.[42] So, are the criteria of our age better? The evidence—from the Democratic Republic of the Congo where rape is a weapon of war, to Afghanistan where war means acid in the faces of girls who seek education and drones targeting peaceful communities from Yemen to Pakistan on a daily basis, to daily Israeli brutalities in occupied Palestine—would suggest: not so much, or not at all.

So the pope's words raise yet another pressing question: *which* criteria would that be? It is not as if one can safely argue that the criteria used to judge the present—the denial of rampant, unrepentant racism; the effortless demonization of those whom the powerful wish to rob of their resources and destroy altogether; the lust for endless war for the sake of endless profits; the fascination with drone warfare no matter how many civilians die; the practice and justification of torture as "enhanced interrogation"; the idolatry of money; the mindless indifference to the suffering of others—are demonstrably better than the criteria of the past. And what shall we say of the criteria applied in the US's disastrous interventions in defenseless countries across the Global South since the second half of the twentieth century, the destruction of democracies and the support of ruthless tyrants—all still ongoing, and with the support of the vast majority of those sitting right in front of him?

Precisely how, African Americans rightly ask, are the lynchings of the very recent past—when things were supposedly less civilized—different from the uniformed killings in the streets of inner cities in the United States today? Or for that matter, how precisely does the astonishing, and

---

42. See Alastair Jamieson and Charlene Gubash, "Arab Spring Cleric Nimr al- Nimr Among 47 Executed by Saudi-Arabia," October 18, 2014, http://www.msnbc.com/msnbc/arab-spring-cleric-nimr-al-nimr-among-47-executed-saudi-arabia.

astonishingly quick, exoneration by the judicial system of white policemen who kill unarmed people of color on an almost daily basis, differ from the mockery of justice in the trials of white racist killers and bombers of churches in the South just a few steps back into recent history? What criteria do former president George W. Bush, his vice president, Dick Cheney, and former British Prime Minister Tony Blair employ as they continue to justify their invasion of Iraq, based upon lies, deceit, and the reckless pursuit of wealth? And by the same token, what criteria does President Obama, the Nobel Peace Prize winner, apply as he boasts about the seven Muslim countries he is engaging in undeclared war and the ritualistic selections for extermination by drone killings every Tuesday, nick-named "terror Tuesdays"?[43]

Since the pope had chosen Martin Luther King Jr. as one of the four courageous and exemplary Americans of his speech before Congress—the other three being Abraham Lincoln, Dorothy Day, and Thomas Merton—it is fitting to remind ourselves of what Martin Luther King himself had to say on the issue the pope has mentioned only once in his short sentence. Speaking of the slavery of Africans in this country, Dr. King took a decidedly different view on the question of remembering the atrocities of the past:

> There are few parallels in history of the period in which Africans were seized and branded like animals, packed into ships' holds like cargo and transported into chattel slavery. Millions suffered agonizing death in the middle passage in a holocaust reminiscent of the Nazi slaughter of Jews, Poles and others. *We have an obligation of atonement that is not cancelled by the passage of time.*[44]

Here unlike with the pope, with King there is no sign of the cheap grace Dietrich Bonhoeffer warned us against:

> Cheap grace is the preaching of forgiveness without requiring repentance, baptism without church discipline, Communion without confession, absolution without personal confession.

---

43. See, e.g., Heather Saul, "'Peace' President? How Obama Came to Bomb Seven Countries in Six Years," September 24, 2014, http://www.independent.co.uk/news/world/middle-east/peace-president-how-obama-came-to-bomb-seven-countries-in-six-years-9753131.html. The same article mentions the fact that Obama approved more than 390 drone strikes across Pakistan, Yemen, and Somalia in five years—eight times as many approved during the entire Bush presidency. See also Pratap Chatterjee, "Inside the Devastation of America's Drone Wars," April 21, 2016, http://www.tomdispatch.com/post/176131/tomgram%3A_pratap_chatterjee,_inside_the_devastation_of_america's_drone_wars.

44. King, "Let My People Go," 109–10; emphasis mine.

Cheap grace is grace without discipleship, grace without the cross, grace without Jesus Christ; living and incarnate.[45]

At the World Meeting of Popular Movements in Bolivia, the pope did much more than just slate "*all* forms of colonialism, old and new." He also repented for the "many grave sins [which] were committed against the native peoples of America in the name of God," and asked the Church "to kneel before God and implore forgiveness for the past and present sins of her sons and daughters." But because the pope knows the Church had not only sinned against God, but also against the people, he went on: "I humbly ask forgiveness, not only for the offenses of the Church herself, but also for crimes committed against the native peoples during the so-called conquest of America."[46]

One cannot help being moved by such humble, uplifting, courageous words and actions. Here the pope is speaking of the crimes of the colonialists against the native peoples, but pointedly also of the complicity of the church in those crimes. He was not afraid to say it, because the pope knows, as well as we all do, and as Joy DeGruy Leary persuasively argues, that the effects of and ongoing generational trauma from the violence of the past continue to cast a deep and dark shadow over the lives of historically oppressed and enslaved communities.[47] The pope knows, and we know it too, that the unrepented sins and unaddressed wrongs of the past are not forgotten, they are *unremembered,* by which I mean deliberately covered up, trivialized, and normalized for ideological purposes by a version of history unredeemed by truth.[48] But if they are unremembered, they cannot be forgiven, and if they cannot be remembered nor forgiven, the wounds they caused cannot be healed. This is the bringing together of prophetic truthfulness and prophetic pathos that I spoke of in the beginning of this chapter.

It is the pathos for the people—acknowledging and seeing their pain, hearing their cries for justice and acting upon it. It is the pathos for the oppressor and for the church, who in the words of Jeremiah, "aided and abetted" the oppressor in their wrongdoing, letting both hear the prophetic judgement of God for their misdeeds and at once showing the way to God's grace and mercy through repentance and forgiveness, as necessary for the people, the church and the global community. And in all of this the pope is

---

45. Bonhoeffer, *The Cost of Discipleship*, 36.

46. See, "Pope Francis: Speech at World Meeting of Popular Movements."

47. For an informative and persuasive treatment of the concept, see DeGruy Leary, *Post Traumatic Slave Syndrome.*

48. See my treatment of the concept "unremembering as ideological tool" in *The Tenderness of Conscience,* ch. 4.

doing no more than reflecting the pathos of God: for justice, for peace, for the wholeness of God's people and God's creation.

In Bolivia the pope was not afraid to say it, and in doing so, he interrupted the globalization of indifference that denies the past, refuses remorse and repentance, fails to ask for forgiveness, and nullifies the possibility of healing, a reality tragically evident in South Africa as well as in the United States. Before Congress, he let that opportunity go by. What a difference such a sentence would have made before that immensely powerful political body, the collective representation of America's volatile denialism and tragic hardheartedness on these matters.

Just as the conquistadors, aided and abetted by the church, sinned against the indigenous peoples of Central and South America, so the colonizers, aided and abetted by the church and armed with a distorted and perverse theology rooted in "manifest destiny," sinned, and grievously so, against the indigenous peoples of North America, compounding that sin with the horrors of slavery. The call for remorse, repentance and restitution, conversion, and the doing of justice is as necessary in the United States as it is in Latin America. How hopeful it would have been to the millions in the United States and in the world who find themselves hopeless, beyond the borders of acceptability and inclusivity, the targets of scorn, and indifference and death at the hands of the powerful of the world.

Perhaps, one might surmise, the difference lies in the fact that in Bolivia the pope spoke, not just *about* the people or *to* the people. In Bolivia, the pope, understanding the hearts of the people, knowing intimately the plight of the people—and I truly believe he *does* know—spoke as one of the people. He spoke not as the diplomatic emissary from Rome but as the priest who lived in Argentina and worked for the people in the *villas miserias*, the slums of Buenos Aires. He was expressing the truths concerning their lives and deaths, their hopes and fears, their longings for justice and peace. The pope spoke as one who has heard and understood the cries of the vanquished, the destitute, the "leftovers" of historical and ongoing colonization, the victims of globalized indifference because he was there and considered himself as one of them. In Washington DC, announced as "The Pope of the Vatican," the pope spoke as power to power, as a politician to politicians, a diplomat more intent on negotiating the limits of truth-telling than on the persuasive power of prophetic imagination. In doing that, the pope left Matt Taibbi's question unresolved, and the US media, from the "left" and the "right," had another field day. And so did the rulers of the empire sitting in front of him. The pleas of *Belhar*, and the hopes of the faithful *sizwe* for the church to stand where God stands—on this point at least—were left unheard and unfulfilled.

Interrupting the Globalization of Indifference

Still, the issue refuses to let go. How do we, in the fierce urgency of our times, in which we have not a single moment to waste, hold on to prophetic faithfulness, prophetic imagination, and prophetic pathos in a global community threatened by the globalization of a deadly indifference, where the vast majority of God's people are outcasts, leftovers, deprived of the joy of the Gospel? How do we bring the good news that the first good news is to the poor, the captives, the blind, the oppressed? That these are to receive their sight, be liberated and live free with dignity because the year of the Lord's favor had already been proclaimed? (Luke 4:18, 19).

I would like to suggest that we express that commitment against indifference by beginning to do as Jesus asks: repent, believe the good news, and learn to speak a different language. We are in no position to offer comfort, compassion and justice to a suffering, bleeding humanity overwhelmed by a petrifying indifference, if we do not believe that there *is* good news they should hear. And we cannot speak a language of hope and resilience, of resistance and redemption, if we do not unlearn the language of imperial compliance: of domination and subjugation, of carelessness and indifference, of diplomatic evasion.

We are no longer in a position to deny that the pope is right: something is wrong, and it is more wrong today than ten or twenty years ago. The time has come for us not to be afraid to say it. I am not talking about simply mentioning, enumerating, or bemoaning the wrongs we see. To not be afraid to say it has everything to do with *how* we say it. Do we say it with truth, with courage, with compassion, and with faithfulness to those who suffer? The wrongs we see are not just happening; they are caused to happen, and they are happening to the vast majority of God's children who are vulnerable, targeted and excluded from human consideration. They are not happening randomly, they are deeply systemic, deliberately built into systems of oppression, domination, and dehumanization. And we must not be afraid to say it.

"Let us not be afraid to say it" means that the pope knows that because the perpetrators of these wrongs are powerful and rich and privileged we are always tempted to speak in a language guaranteed not to give offense. Then we speak a language couched in such caution, such ambiguity, such fear, that it becomes almost meaningless. The comfortable are not afflicted by it, and the afflicted are not comforted by it.

We must not only break the silence. We must speak a different language. Our language must be a courageous, liberating, transformative, healing, inclusive language, the counter language to the language of distortion and perversion, of hate and violence, discrimination and demonization; of subjugation and domination, of exclusion and extremism. It must be a language counter to and subversive of the language of preemptive legitimation and post-facto justification. In a word, a language so unambiguously prophetic that we interrupt the globalization of indifference with prophetic truthfulness, resistance, and hope.

We should work much harder to develop a theology, ethics, and hermeneutics of liberation and inclusion, that will be able to counter all forms of domination and subjugation, imperial and global, ecclesial, personal and in the public square. We should learn to resist the temptation to see the global realities through the eyes of the powerful and privileged, but rather through the eyes of the suffering, the weak and the vulnerable, the dehumanized and the demonized, the outcasts and the excluded. Our theology should be a theology attuned to the cries of the poor and oppressed because I believe John Calvin was right: the cries of the oppressed are the cries from the very heart of God. Whereas the pope makes a distinction between the voice of God and the cries of the poor, Calvin is much more radical. "It is then the same," Calvin says, "as though God heard Godself when God hears the cries and groaning of those who cannot bear injustice."[49] God presents Godself as the poor and the oppressed.

We must be much more alert in our awareness of the fact that our global reality is an imperial reality, and we must be much more vigorous in our testimony and work against violence in all its forms. Empires not only create realities of dominations and subjugation; they also create myths: of invincibility, endless power, infinite duration, great beneficence, and divine incarnation. Crucial to all these is what Walter Wink called the "myth of redemptive violence." Instead of acknowledging the violence it uses because it is needed for continued domination, subjugation and exploitation, the empire "enshrines the belief that violence saves, that war brings peace, that might makes right." Consequently violence is not only necessary; it is the only thing that "works". "If a god is what one turns to when all else fails," Wink argues, and he is absolutely right, "violence certainly functions as a god. It demands from its devotees an absolute obedience-unto-death . . . It, and not Judaism or Christianity or Islam, is the dominant religion of our society today."[50]

At the heart of the gospel is the living, breathing vibrancy of audacious hope. And it is a hope that does not disappoint (Rom 5:2). We

---

49. See Calvin, *Commentary on the Twelve Minor Prophets*, Habakkuk 1:2; see also Boesak, *Kairos, Crisis and Global Apartheid*, 11–13.

50. Wink, *The Powers That Be*, 42.

interrupt the flow of indifference by the proclamation of this hope. I do not mean hope as some vague theological, philosophical concept or religious construct. I speak of hope as African church father Augustine did when he spoke of hope as a mother who has two daughters: Anger and Courage:[51] anger at the way things are and courage to see that they do not remain the same. The anger of hope means that one refuses to accept something that is wrong, to put up with what is driving one to despair. The courage of hope means to have the firm resolve and commitment to pull oneself to one's feet and to attack injustice, wherever it may be found, even if one has to pay a price for doing so. To proclaim and live hope is to have the anger and the courage that is needed to interrupt the endless flow of indifference that is engulfing the world.

Apart from the refugee crisis, perhaps taken seriously only since the crisis now festers on the doorstep of Europe as the chickens of colonialist overreach and postcolonial lust for world domination come home to roost, the eyes of all the world are on the Middle East. Attention is riveted on the brutal Israeli occupation of Palestine, the folly in Afghanistan of the Taliban, inept government and futile foreign intervention; the US/Saudi war on the people of Yemen; the war in Syria and the scandalous games of global-power brinkmanship at the cost of the lives of the innocent; the entrenchment of a new tyranny in Egypt; the tragic results of regime change in Libya. All rightly so. But almost no one thinks of the Central African Republic with its civil war and an unprecedented humanitarian crisis two years ongoing.

It is a civil war that was started because of altogether non-surprising realities: the consequences of colonialist divide-and-rule policies, ethnic rivalry, social exclusion and economic inequalities, abuse of power and indifference to the consequences of that abuse. Now religion has cast its shadow over it with Christian and Muslim militias fighting each other, leaving more chaos, death, and unbelievable horrors in its wake. The extreme violence is "blighting a generation" with almost two-thirds of school-aged children suffering from post-traumatic stress disorder, having witnessed daily beatings, killings, artillery fire, or machete attacks during months of violence. The elderly and people with disabilities, including children, are simply left behind to die when villagers flee the violence.[52] But this crisis is

51. I consider this matter in more detail in Boesak, *Dare We Speak of Hope?* ch. 2.
52. See Liesl Gerntholtz, "Abuse of Children, latest Horrors From Central African Republic," May 11, 2015, http://hrw.org/news/2015/05/11/dispatches-abuse-children-latest-horrors-central-african-republic; "Central African Republic: People With Disabilities Left Behind," April 28, 2015, www.hrw.org/news/2015/04/28/central-african-republic-people-disabilities-left-behind; Kit O'Connell, "World Ignores Genocide

called "the forgotten conflict" and it is because, one human-rights activist suggests, "there is no oil." One can hardly find a more poignant example of the globalization of indifference.[53] I draw attention to the CAR however, not simply because of the human tragedy unfolding there, but also because I see there a glimmer of the difference the audacity of hopeful interruption of the flow of indifference seeks to make.

Amidst the tragedy and blood and violence, the tears and misery and suffering, one man, Catholic priest Aurelio Gazzera, is standing up in anger and with courage in actions of prophetic, compassionate, and redemptive interruption.[54] He hears gun shots, and he interrupts the mass. He hears screams in the middle of the night, and he interrupts his rest. He hears news of militias with guns and machetes, and he interrupts his hour of meditation. He hears the screams of terrified children and women, and he interrupts the voice of his own fears. He goes out, into situations of conflict, takes Muslims to places of safety, talks Christians into moments of sanity. He risks his own life by providing sanctuary in his church for those fleeing to escape the flames of violent retribution and the vicious cycles of revenge. He hides them under the cross of Jesus from those who want to slaughter them in the name of Jesus. When his car is stopped at a road block he places his body between the guns and the fearful family he is trying to protect. In doing this, Gazzera is the very embodiment of the hopeful *sizwe* who will not let evil go unchallenged.

What is he doing, this foolish, courageous priest? He dares to interrupt the war. He dares to interrupt the flow of violence and blood, the cycles of hatred, fear, and retribution, the deadly logic of revenge, the tyranny of fear, and the worship of a false God, a bloodthirsty, hate-filled, and blasphemous replacement of Jesus and of Allah. He dares to get out of his bed, get down from his pulpit, leave the sacred bread and wine on the table and interrupt the works of evil and the flood of hopelessness by bringing the sacrament

---

In Central African Republic Because It's not ISIS & There's No Oil," April 23, 2015, www.mintpressnews.com/the-forgotten-conflict-the-world-ignores.

53. It is devoutly to be hoped that the that the general elections held in 2016 were indeed "a victory for the entire population" s former interim president Catherine Samba-Panza says. See https://www.usip.org/publications/2016/03/beyond-elections-central-african-republic, accessed 11 May, 2017

54. Father Gazzera is a priest, peace activist and mediator working in Bozoum, CAR. "Humanitarian priest: 'It is easy to divide the world into armed mobs,'" April 18, 2014, http://www.euractiv.com/section/development-policy/interview/humanitarian-priest-it-is-easy-to-divide-the-world-into-armed-mobs; also, Arthur Neslen, "Peace Priest: CAR Aid mission, a victory for money that never arrives," April 18, 2014, http://www.euractiv.com/section/development-policy/news/peace-priest-car-aid-mission-a-victory-for-money-that-never-arrives.

out of the sanctuary into the streets of conflict and death as an act of redemptive love. Celebrating the Eucharist is the resistance of evil.

Has Aurelio Gazzera stopped the war, the violence, the terror? Clearly not. But every time he dares to interrupt, he testifies that chaos and death do not have the last word; that, as Jesus promised, the darkness cannot overcome the light; that amidst the blood and tears and needless suffering hope feeds us with renewed love and resilience and calls us to hitherto unimagined deeds of courage, justice, and freedom. If even only one life is saved, death is defeated, hope is redeemed and for the helpless families, the terrified children, the fearful women and the desperate men, a little piece of heaven has come to earth and the kingdom of God, already near when Jesus came, is a little closer.

CHAPTER 3

The Divine Favor of the Unworthy

When the Fatherless Son Meets the Black Messiah

> What wicked powers and peoples demonize as savage and lowly, the divinity seeks out and privileges, resulting in the revolutionary reversal of the status quo's naming powers.
>
> —Dwight Hopkins, 2005

The Jesus in the Streets

She lives in Ferguson, Missouri. She is an activist and, like so many in the movement that I have met, the total image of Nina Simone's "young, gifted, and black." She is a leader in the LGBTQI+ community and completely dedicated to the struggle for justice. She confesses to be a "non-believer," which in this context does not mean that she has no faith. It means she has not much trust in the church or the church's call upon the Bible or on Jesus. The Jesus she had come to know in the church of her parents, the spiritualized, inoffensive, "gentle Jesus meek and mild" cannot help her, now that she is laying her life on the line for justice. But she has seen "Jesus in the streets," personified by the courageous Clergy of the Streets, and in the masses risking their lives calling for justice and freedom in Ferguson, and that has made all the difference. She tells of her visit to St. John's United Church of Christ, where Reverend Starsky Wilson, a strong, prophetic presence in the struggle, serves as pastor.

> [Starsky] talked about how Jesus himself was a revolutionary. I'm like, here we go . . . It came from when he was talking about how Jesus went into the tabernacle and he turned over the tables

... because of the corruption and the B.S. that was going on, and Jesus was like, "Nah." And he's like, "That's what's happening in Ferguson. It's a bunch of 'Jesuses' standing at the tabernacle, which happens to be the Ferguson Police Department, and they're flipping over the tables." And I'm like, "That's real. That's exactly what's happening right now" ... So when he said that, I'm like, "Yo, that's the realest thing I've heard from a preacher in years because it's the actual truth. That's literally in the Book."[1]

How Starsky Wilson read "the Book," understood and interpreted it in the pulpit and on the streets of struggle and confrontation made all the difference to his ministry and his being. It also made all the difference to the young people who are involved in the struggle for justice and true freedom as they were looking for a grounding of their faith in that struggle, because he was understanding Jesus from below, from the underside of history. He is seeing Jesus through the eyes of those who suffer, belittled and excluded by a system that tells them in every way possible that their lives do not matter, in resistance against systems of oppression and injustice that make that exclusion and denial of their worthiness as human beings and children of God part of their every-day life. Finding Jesus in the streets of protest and in struggles for justice will impact greatly, in fact decisively, one's understanding of the historical Jesus, the Jesus of one's faith, and the Jesus of one's lived experience.

In the anti-apartheid struggle in South Africa, in the middle of the first state of emergency declared by the apartheid regime, I together with the students and youth from the townships made the same discovery: of the difference the story of Jesus of Nazareth makes to the human story; and to the story of human struggles for justice. I recount this story now as I told it elsewhere.[2]

We were in Bellville Uniting Reformed church where I served as pastor, in a prayer service for the release of Nelson Mandela. The service had already begun but students were still streaming in from the surrounding townships. Someone came in and alerted us that the police were arresting young people as they were coming down the street towards the church. As the hundreds of students were leaving church and moving toward the police vehicles, they were singing a song I was hearing for the first time that day.

Akanamandla! Akanamandla! Akanamandla uSatani!

---

1. See Francis, *Ferguson & Faith*, 61, 62. Francis has titled a chapter in her book "Jesus in the Streets."

2. See Boesak, *Comfort and Protest*, 60–62.

> *Sim'swabisile, Alleluia!*
>
> *Sim'swabisile, uSatani!*
>
> *Akanamandla, akanamandla, akanamdla, uSatani!*

Translated, it goes something like this:

> *It is broken, it is broken, the power of Satan is broken!*
>
> *We have disappointed Satan, his power is broken.*
>
> *Alleluia!*

It is a song filled with power and defiant hope. The young people were singing this, dancing and stamping their feet, pointing in the direction of the police as they sang the word "Satan!" It was an astonishing experience. The students were singing that the power of the apartheid regime was clear to see, frighteningly represented by the might of their police and their army. For the young people though, committed to justice and struggling for freedom fueled by their faith in Jesus, that power was already broken. Satan had no power over them. Clear as well is that the power they are singing of is not their own. They are singing of the power of the resurrected Christ. "We have disappointed Satan": we have heard Satan and seen his power, but we have resisted his temptations; we will not give up, we will not be afraid.

The students were singing, dancing all around the police vehicles in which their arrested comrade was held. The police, somewhat confused and somewhat bewildered, it seemed to me, released the arrested young man. Others, having watched all this, join us as we march, singing and dancing back in to the church, resuming the worship service. That day we, as we would again and again, saw Jesus in the streets. With him, we saw Satan fall like lightning from heaven: indeed, *Akanamandla uSatani!*

This chapter is an engagement with an important historical-Jesus study that opens up interesting possibilities for a new understanding of the historical Jesus. This chapter follows the argumentation of Andries van Aarde and his new, and exciting, understanding of Jesus of Nazareth, but seeks to relate the issues raised in a different context: not just, who is the Jesus that emerges from van Aarde's study, but also, what has that Jesus to do with the Jesus of the streets so central to the life, witness and struggle engagement of the Christian youth for whom their faith is so important? In other words, what might happen if the fatherless Jesus, as van Aarde's book title reads, meets the Black Messiah? And how would such a meeting impact the life, witness and engagement of the prophetic church in the world? How would our ministry change after being witness to such a meeting; how would we talk to young Christians engaged in risk-filled, sometimes life-and-death struggles for justice? What would our theology look like?

Fatherless in Galilee

In 2001, Pretoria University's Andries van Aarde published his *Fatherless in Galilee, Jesus as Child of God*, one of the most fascinating books I have read in some time.[3] It is the work of a consummate New Testament scholar. The book is a careful study of the quests for the historical Jesus, the long endeavor since the groundbreaking work of Albert Schweitzer [4] and explains van Aarde's own quest to discover who God is, how Jesus is related to God, how much we can know about Jesus, and besides a series of important questions, to discover above all "what is at stake when one says that study of the life of Jesus is important."[5]

Right at the start van Aarde makes two crucial points that determine his work as well as the wider framework of his understanding and interpretation. First comes the admonition that it would be wise to take Seán Freyne's advice to heart:

> We can reach an approximation to the truth of things, at least I am convinced that the present "third wave" quest for the historical Jesus is no more free of presuppositions than any of the other quests that went before it. Nor could it be otherwise, no matter how refined our methodologies. If we are all prepared to say at the outset what is at stake for us in our search for Jesus—ideologically, academically, personally—then there is some possibility that for now. Even that would be adequate.[6]

So van Aarde is up front in taking this admonition seriously and—bringing us to the second point—he regards his personal experience as crucial to his theological reflections:

> The "situated discourse" of this book is not only a matter of ideological and academic concern, but one of personal engagement. In my own journey I long ago found great pleasure in knowing Jesus. My voyage began with a strenuous relationship with my father, but as a child and adult I experienced the warmth of the believing community.[7]

3. Harrisburg, Pennsylvania: Trinity Press International.
4. Schweitzer, *The Quest for the Historical Jesus*.
5. Van Aarde, *Fatherless*, 1.
6. Ibid., 3.
7. Ibid.

The important point here is two-fold: van Aarde makes clear that he has not succumbed to the allure of neutral, "value-free" research so much of Western scholarship prides itself in. It is as liberation theology has always insisted: all theology is done in context, and all theology reflects the life situation of the theologian. Second, he is open about the impact of his personal journey and engagement on his academic work. With these two crucial points of departure, Van Aarde, unlike the vast majority of Western scholars of whatever ilk, opens up authentic space for meaningful dialogue with liberation theology.

Van Aarde takes us through the whole trajectory of the most recent scholarship research, and it brings him to a unique, for some perhaps controversial point of view. It is important that we follow him closely. For van Aarde the focal point of his research is to demonstrate that Jesus grew up fatherless and that Joseph, the father of Jesus, should probably be seen as a legendary figure. That explains, says van Aarde, why Jesus was a revolutionary figure in his own time.[8] In antiquity, the consequences of this were vast: disconnected from a father figure, Jesus would have been excluded from being called a "child of Abraham," that is, a child of God; access to the court of the Israelites in the temple would have been denied to him; he would have been excluded from the privilege of being given a daughter in marriage.[9] Van Aarde shows how Jesus' fatherlessness is contextualized within a defamatory campaign that focuses on alleged illegitimacy.[10]

He explores the meaning of the "stigma of being fatherless" in social-scientific terms in antiquity, whether in Sepphoris, Galilee, or Pompeii, Italy. He engages in argument surrounding the virgin birth, the life and ministry of Jesus, the development of the dogma of the "two natures" of Jesus as human and divine and underlines the "subversiveness of Jesus' cause."[11]

Putting on "a different thinking cap,"[12] van Aarde wants neither to be bound by the so-called "third quest" in the historical Jesus research nor to the "renewed quest," a distinction so firmly rooted in New Testament scholarship that N. T. Wright believes there is "no third option."[13] Yet for van Aarde there *is* a third option: "It is not a middle of the road stance," van Aarde insists, "but an uncommitted journey where both Jesus' non-apocalyptic response to Jewish eschatology and Mark's apocalyptic

---

8. Ibid., 4.
9. Ibid.
10. Ibid., 5.
11. Ibid.
12. Ibid., 30.
13. Ibid., 32, 33.

interpretation are not anachronistically understood," for the "cause of Jesus" challenges him to "also consider the faith assertions that are found in the Gospel of Mark."[14] As I understand van Aarde, this means that he will learn from whatever results scholarship offers, but is not willing to entertain a forced dichotomy between the historical Jesus and the "Jesus of faith." The Jesus confessed by the believing community is more than yet another historical figure such as Aristotle, Plato, or Alexander the Great. He is confessed *as* the Messiah of Israel, *as* Lord of the world, *as* the Child of God, *as* God. This Jesus is the *Jesus of faith*, in contradistinction to, yet irrevocably bound with, the *Jesus of history*.[15]

Van Aarde's interest in historical Jesus research is born neither from neo-orthodoxy nor from neoliberalism. "For me, it is a matter of urgency to prioritize and contextualize the sources that could lead to Jesus."[16] The "subversive and dangerous memory of Jesus" compels us to take seriously both the context of the historical Jesus and the context of the believing community.

Van Aarde's "third way" is a "Christology from the side."[17] A "Jesus from above" describes the conciliar debates about Jesus as a figure who descended from heaven and was incarnated on earth—a Jesus who has been confessed as "true God" and "true man." A "Jesus from below" refers to modern biblical scholarship where the focus is "squarely on the humanity of Jesus." Both these approaches represent a "vertical classification," a perspective on the person of Jesus, which is "chiefly, if not exclusively, concerned with symbols of power or force." However, "Jesus from above" reflects Christian tradition only after the time of Constantine, when hierarchy became the expressive social structure with power or force as the primary concern. "Jesus from below" expresses twentieth-century concerns with the relationship between the natural and the supernatural, and the possibility of transcendence in a secular world.[18] Yet, van Aarde argues, within Christian groups before Constantine, the chief expressive social dimension for non-Roman and Roman non-elite was not vertical but horizontal—"from side to side."[19]

All this means that Jesus "as a first-century Israelite from Galilee should be studied like other historical persons and should not be regarded as absolutely unique, whatever material is available and by applicable

14. Ibid., 33.
15. Ibid., 8.
16. Ibid., 33.
17. Ibid., 38.
18. Ibid.
19. Ibid.

methods and models."[20] This reading leads van Aarde to the conclusion that "Jesus' fatherlessness is probably a historical fact that should be taken into account when one considers his social identity, his non-patriarchal ethos, his behavior toward women and children, and especially his trust in God as his Father."[21] Nonetheless, this Jesus, who was not just fatherless on earth, but fatherless *in Galilee,* is Child of God.

Putting on this "different thinking cap" indeed allows van Aarde to effectively pursue his central thesis—that of the fatherlessness of Jesus, dealing along the way with the thorny issues of the virgin birth, the meaning of Jesus' baptism by John the Baptist, Jesus as the "Son of God."

His central thesis that Jesus was the son of Mary who grew up fatherless in Galilee of the Gentiles, having to deal with the scandal and societal uncertainty of what that meant—"the peasant boy who probably became a carpenter and then, definitely, a revolutionary teacher and compassionate healer,"[22] the discredited, dishonored one—resonates strongly with black liberation theology's black Jesus. So, too, does his understanding of and emphasis on the consequences of this status of Jesus in his own historical context.

This raises three critical questions. One: does this approach lead to a better—not just different—understanding of the historical Jesus for us today? Two: does van Aarde overcome the shortcomings of Western, Eurocentric, male-dominated scholarship, leading to a different, and better kind of conversation with Christians in oppressed communities in the global South as well as the rich North? Three: where do the conclusions reached through this approach locate the fatherless Jesus, the revolutionary teacher and compassionate healer in the contexts of strife, struggle, and hurt today? As a consequence, perhaps there might be a fourth question: will we, Christians and followers of this Jesus, as a result of this encounter, be found where Jesus is to be found, namely at the heart of the struggles for freedom, dignity, justice, and meaningful life?

These are the persistent questions that emanate from liberation theology as prophetic theology in all its forms. That question can no longer be ignored or denied by Western scholarship.[23]

20. Ibid.
21. Ibid., 15.
22. Ibid., 73.
23. See, e.g., among the growing body of studies, Odoyoye, *Daughters of Anowa*; Wilmore, *Black Religion and Black Radicalism*; Cone, *Black Theology and Black Power*; Cone, *God of the Oppressed*; Cone, *For My People*; Cone, *Speaking the Truth*; Cleage, *The Black Messiah*; Felder, *Troubling Biblical Waters*; Felder (ed.), *Stony the Road we Trod*; Townes, (ed.), *A Troubling in my Soul*; Weems, *Just a Sister Away, A Womanist Vision of*

It is not only the "first generation" black liberation theologians who have placed this issue central. It remains crucial. Obery M. Hendricks Jr., like van Aarde, makes his study of the life of Jesus an intensely personal one. "I was raised," he writes, "on the bland Jesus of Sunday school and of my mother's gentle retellings, the meek, mild Jesus . . . a gentle, serene, non-threatening Jesus whose only concern was getting believers into heaven, and whose only 'transgression' was to claim sonship with God . . . "[24]

Returning to liberation theology's anchor passage (Luke 4:16–18), Obery Hendricks reclaims that pericope as Jesus's "manifesto" to proclaim radical economic, social, and political change. This Jesus, on whom the Spirit of the Lord rests, is a Jesus who sought not only to address the *symptoms* of the people's suffering, but also to alleviate the *causes* of their suffering. For him the historical Jesus was a political revolutionary:

> To say that Jesus was a political revolutionary is to say that the message he proclaimed not only called for change in individual hearts but also demanded sweeping and comprehensive change in political, social, and economic structures in his setting in life: colonized Israel. It means that if Jesus had his way, the Roman Empire and the ruling elites among his own people either would no longer have held their positions of power, or if they did, would have had to conduct themselves very, very differently. It means that his ministry was to radically change the distribution of authority, power, goods and resources, so all people—particularly the little people, or "the least of these," as Jesus called them—might have lives free of political oppression, enforced hunger and poverty, and undue insecurity.[25]

Womanist theologians are equally clear about their views on Jesus. Jesus is the One that they refer to as "healer and provider" writes Kelley Brown.[26] Raquel St. Clair explains that womanist explorations look beyond the "static absolutism of classical Christology to discern and celebrate the presence of Jesus in the lives of the abused and the oppressed." The meaning of Jesus for African American, and by the same token for women of

---

Women's Relationships in the Bible; Boesak, *Farewell to Innocence, A Socio-Ethical Study on Black Theology and Black Power*; Boesak, *Black and Reformed*; Boesak, *Comfort and Protest*; Hopkins, *Shoes That Fit Our Feet*. For more recent studies, see Hopkins, *Being Human*; and especially Hendricks, *The Politics of Jesus*; also Williams, *Bonhoeffer's Black Jesus*.

24. Hendricks Jr., *The Politics of Jesus*, 1, 2.

25. Ibid., 5.

26. Brown, "God is as Christ Does," 12, cited in St. Clair, "Womanist Biblical Interpretation," 58.

the global South, cannot be merely theoretical postulations, "but concrete affirmations grounded in the everyday experiences of their lives," which involves the discovering of the "presence of Jesus in their own particular existential reality."[27]

In this dialogue with Andries van Aarde I shall explore the extent to which van Aarde has engaged the thinking of prophetic theology in general, and black liberation theology in particular, in his ground-breaking work on the historical Jesus.

Already Dietrich Bonhoeffer has thoroughly questioned the concepts "from above" and "from below," which van Aarde also queries, but Bonhoeffer gives "from below" a totally different meaning than modern Western scholarship could, or would, allow:

> We have for once learnt to see the great events of history from below, from the perspective of the outcasts, the suspects, the maltreated, the powerless, the oppressed, the reviled—in short from the perspective of those who suffer.[28]

The point Bonhoeffer makes is that personal suffering (which one takes upon oneself for the sake of justice and in solidarity with, and in identification with the weak and oppressed in their struggles for justice) is "a more effective key, a more rewarding principle for exploring the world in thought and action than personal good fortune." But Bonhoeffer is not speaking of personal suffering as the suffering of individuals when personal disaster strikes: illness, personal trauma, or the death of a loved one. It is the experiences of suffering *for the sake of justice* when one learns to stand where Christ always stands that will allow one to see "from below," through the eyes of and "from the perspective of those who suffer." This is "beyond any talk of 'from below' or 'from above.'"[29]

It is axiomatic, at least read through the lens of Euro-American interpretations, to assume that Bonhoeffer gained this insight from his struggles against anti-Semitism in Germany. But Bonhoeffer could see this crucial truth because at a pivotal time in his life he was exposed, and opened himself, to black perspective: the people's liberation theology of Adam Clayton Powell Sr., the pastor of Abyssinian Baptist Church in Harlem, New York, and in his engagement with "the black Christ of the Harlem Renaissance," where his encounter with Jesus of Nazareth was taken "beyond any talk" in the academic debates in Berlin or at Union Theological Seminary just up the road.[30]

27. St. Clair, "Womanist Biblical Interpretation," 58.
28. Bonhoeffer, *Letters and Papers from Prison*, 17.
29. Ibid., 17.
30. See Clingan, *Against Cheap Grace*; see also de la Torre, *Liberating Jonah*, 95.

That encounter was in the black experience from slavery, oppression, and lynchings to the struggles against Jim Crow in the American South and the racial injustices of the North, expressed in black preaching, the black spirituals, black intellectual engagement with a Jesus altogether different from the Jesus of European, white, male captivity, all embedded in black resistance to injustice and oppression.

Reggie L. Williams is especially instructive in his persuasive analysis of the ways in which Bonhoeffer was influenced through his experience with the writers of the Harlem Renaissance.

> From their location in modern racial discourse, Harlem Renaissance intellectuals shaped a literary movement that spoke about black culture, black political agency, and a black Jesus... [which was] theologically disruptive to white supremacy, and at times graphic in their explicit rebukes of the oppressive and violent white Christ.[31]

The stark, unvarnished prophetic language of Langston Hughes' "Christ in Alabama" and County Cullen's "The Black Christ," in which the historical Jesus is "the first in a succession of lynched black men in the South,"[32] was like nothing Bonhoeffer would have learned or experienced in imperial Germany. Here, Jesus was indeed not the imperialist, white European Christ. No, in Langston Hughes' scorching words, Jesus was

> Most Holy Bastard
>
> Of the bleeding mouth
>
> > Nigger Christ
> >
> > On the Cross
> >
> > Of the South.[33]

It is hard to imagine the shocking effect of these words on Bonhoeffer's aristocratic, European mind. But Bonhoeffer's experience is what occurs when the fatherless Jesus meets the Black Messiah. In Barcelona back in 1928, Bonhoeffer could still see Jesus Christ as the one who called him to absolute love for the *Volk*, his German people, precluding the love for the neighbor: "It is simply impossible to love, or as the case may be, to protect both my enemy and my people... God gave me my mother, my people. For what I

---

31. See Williams, *Bonhoeffer's Black Jesus*, 54.

32. Ibid., 66.

33. Hughes, *The Collected Poems of Langston Hughes*, 143, Williams, *Bonhoeffer's Black Jesus*, 64.

have, I have through my people; what I am, I am through my people."³⁴ That was the language of German Christian nationalism.

The encounter with the views and realities in Harlem made Bonhoeffer understand, in ways he never could before, that the Christ he knew actually was "the white Christ of the modern colonial construct, [who] was complicit in race terror as an opiate Jesus who sedated black people, convincing them to accept racism and sub-humanity as divinely ordained by God."³⁵

The perspective "from below," of the "outcasts, the suspects, the maltreated, the powerless, the oppressed, the reviled"—the language of the Bonhoeffer after Harlem—the perspective of "those who suffer" is not a perspective one learns from the sedate family discussions in aristocratic German homes or in the academic discourse of post-Enlightenment German universities. *That* perspective was opened up to Bonhoeffer every time he entered the highly charged atmosphere of that black church, and every time he was confronted with the Jesus not shaped by "white civilization." It would be immensely rewarding to ask deeper questions about the origins of Bonhoeffer's "perspective from below," and the origins of his deeply courageous decision to shun the "cheap grace" of honored exile in the United States, and to choose for the costly grace of struggle with the oppressed in Germany.³⁶

The gift of Bonhoeffer in this regard, both through his theology and his personal example of costly discipleship embedded in his intensely personal relationship with Jesus Christ, was to raise fundamental questions about the validity of "conciliar debates" about Constantinian concepts of, and

---

34. Dietrich Bonhoeffer Works English, (DBWE) 10:371; see Williams, *Bonhoeffer's Black Jesus*, 14.

35. Williams, *Bonhoeffer's Black Jesus*, 54.

36. It was enlightening and affirming to learn that it was from Adam Clayton Powell Sr., that great black preacher, politician, and justice activist, that Dietrich Bonhoeffer had learned the phrase "cheap grace," which he embraced and applied with such immortal effect in his work and life's testimony.: "Reverend Adam Clayton Powell Sr., the renowned and dynamic pastor of Abyssinian Baptist Church of Harlem, coined the term 'cheap grace' to refer to white Christian America's tolerance of Jim Crow, lynching, and racism. Dietrich Bonhoeffer, who is usually associated with the term 'cheap grace', learned this ethical principle from Powell while attending his church during his student days at Union Seminary . . . Bonhoeffer was able to transport the lessons learnt from the black church to deal with the rising anti-Semitism of his native Germany." See De la Torre, *Liberating Jonah*, 95. De la Torre in turn learned this from Ralph Garlin Clingan, *Against Cheap Grace in a World Come of Age*. Most scholarship on Bonhoeffer's time at Abyssinian Baptist concentrates only on the influence on Bonhoeffer of the church's passionate worship style, the music and the emotional manifestations, De la Torre remarks. "It is interesting to note that few Euroamerican scholars are willing to explore the intellectual contributions the black church, and Adam Clayton Powell in particular, made to Bonhoeffer's scholarly development. We are left asking, why?" Indeed.

twentieth-century concerns with Jesus, the natural and supernatural, and the possibility of transcendence in a secular world. It is telling commentary, though, that despite Bonhoeffer this has remained the dominant trend in a European-centered theological discourse that liberation theologians experience as a colonial, oppressive, exclusivist epistemology and practice.

Does van Aarde, seeing his point of departure in the main thesis of his study, overcome this? Does van Aarde's "side to side" approach (which rejects the "from below" of liberal theology), take us closer to Bonhoeffer's "from below," and via Bonhoeffer closer to black liberation theology's "from below," the "underside of history" and the Black Messiah?

Van Aarde refuses to be defined by either neo-orthodoxy or neoliberalism, and he is absolutely right. Such a depiction would do him grave injustice. Yet, even with van Aarde's self-acknowledged self-understanding, his honesty about the impact of intensely personal experience on his Jesus study, the question arises: is the distance qualitatively strong enough if nonetheless the only sources and dialogue partners for this "different cap" remain those of Western, Eurocentric Enlightenment, of, as Kelly Brown depicts it, the "static absolutism of classical Christology"?[37]

Would van Aarde's historical Jesus have looked and acted more different still if van Aarde had taken more seriously the results of scholarship emanating from black liberation theology, womanist theology, and African women's theologies, the Jesus of suffering and liberation as seen through the eyes and encountered in the lives of the outcasts, the suspects, the maltreated, the powerless, the oppressed and the reviled—the eyes of those who suffer? And even more pertinently, took into account the Jesus the young activists revealed and discovered in the streets? And what kind of conversation would emerge, with what kind of results for doing theology, and making righteous choices in the struggles raging in South Africa and the world today? Simply put, and as we asked in the beginning of this chapter, what would happen if van Aarde's fatherless Jesus met black liberation theology's Black Messiah? This is what intrigues me in van Aarde's captivating study, and these are some of the questions I will try to explore in this ongoing conversation with Andries van Aarde.

Recognizing the Depoliticized Jesus

One of the main problems with New Testament scholarship as it emanated from and was driven by the European Enlightenment, argues Richard A.

---

37. Quoted in Rachel St. Clair, "Womanist Biblical Interpretation," *True to Our Native Land*, 58.

Horsley, forerunner of a new wave of New Testament research, is its failure to understand that the historical context Jesus lived in, and responded to, was the reality of the Roman Empire. Acknowledging that reality, Horsley argues, opens an entirely new way of doing New Testament studies and simultaneously allows us new insights into the historical Jesus.

Not only does the "Enlightenment reduction of reality to what fit the canons of Reason and Nature" leave theologians embarrassed about the Christian Gospels as sources for the historical Jesus, Horsley states,[38] but "recent interpreters of Jesus still focus primarily on the sayings of Jesus isolated from literary context, and thus also from historical social-political context."[39]

This has produced a less clear, if not distorted picture of the world of the New Testament, the contexts of the first Christian communities, and of the historical Jesus. "A domesticated Jesus," Horsley writes, "reduced to merely a religious figure," and "since by definition empire is political, a Jesus who is merely religious has no relevance to or implications for empire."[40]

But learning from other disciplines and especially non-Western scholars "who press for a hearing of different perspectives, Biblical Studies more generally is also discovering the importance of imperial relations, particularly its own connection with modern empire."[41] This discovery has forced some scholars to rethink several assumptions about the context of the New Testament writings and the historical Jesus that have led to fundamental misunderstandings: a depoliticized Jesus, a depoliticized Judea and Galilee, and a depoliticized Roman Empire.[42]

While the major problem with the standard interpretation of the historical Jesus is the depoliticization practiced in Western Christian theology and established New Testament studies in general, there are other seriously limiting factors, writes Horsley, and he identifies those as "failures":

---

38. Horsley, ed., *Jesus and Empire*, 55. See also Carter, *Matthew and Empire*, 1: "The approach to Matthew's Gospel is not the standard one, and challenges the dominant paradigm or way of reading Matthew's Gospel. The conventional scholarly way of reading this Gospel over the last century has been in relation to a synagogue with which Matthew's community is having or has had a bitter dispute . . . . I do think (this approach) is too limited. It turns the Gospel into an exclusively religious work, concerned only with the religious questions and personal matters."

39. *Jesus and Empire*, 56.

40. Ibid., 6.

41. Cf. Horsley, ed., *Paul and Empire*, 2.

42. Horsley makes a very strong and in my view entirely convincing case identifying key, interrelated factors in this process of "depoliticization" through which interpreters "tend to ignore, obscure, or trivialize the broader political situation in which (Jesus) was operating." Horsley, *Jesus and Empire*, 6–12.

Most important among these are the failure to investigate, in as precise terms as possible, the particular historical conditions in which Jesus acted, the failure to consider the social form of the relationship between Jesus and those who responded to him, and the failure to investigate in as precise terms as possible the cultural tradition out of which he and his followers operated.[43]

Small wonder then, that this process of depoliticization has reduced Jesus "to a relatively innocuous religious teacher"[44] "most recently in the guise of a wisdom teacher."[45]

Van Aarde's Jesus is clearly not an "innocuous wisdom teacher" or mere religious figure. No, his Jesus was born to a single mother, lived and worked in Galilee, "multilingual, inhabited by pagans and Israelites, many of mixed marriage heritages upon whom the Judeans looked down." Visiting Judean priests came to teach and enforce the purity laws of the sacred writings, and Jerusalem authorities came to collect the temple taxes from impoverished people who tried to live according to ancestral traditions. These were peasants who survived on small pieces of land, landless tenant farmers who worked for absentee landlords in the cities, incurring huge debts, while some were forced off their land and turned to carpentry. Bandits, outcasts, and rebels escaped to the mountains and found shelter in caves. "This is the 'Galilee of the Gentiles' where people lived in darkness. Somewhere there, Jesus is to be found . . . He was a revolutionary and healer, teacher and helper."[46]

Thus situating Jesus as "fatherless *in Galilee*" is crucial, and van Aarde is correct in doing so. But this "revolutionary" comes to us almost exclusively by way of Jesus' fatherlessness and the consequences of context-specific patriarchy thereof in early first-century Judean society. The political significance of this is thus somewhat lost. The "darkness" in which the Galileans lived was surely not simply "spiritual," but a darkness caused by occupation, by oppression, exploitation, poverty, powerlessness, and exclusion. There is mention of the social, economic, and political situation of people at the time of Jesus, but hardly any attempt to relate this to the harsh political reality of the Roman Empire or the political context of synagogue leaders and temple authorities in their collaboration with the Romans.

The tensions with temple authorities are focused on the marginalization of and scandal inflicted upon Jesus because of his suspected illegitimacy,

---

43. Ibid., 13.
44. Ibid., 13.
45. Ibid., 6.
46. Van Aarde, *Fatherless*, 75.

rather than because of Jesus' stance regarding the ruling elites and the sociopolitical consequences of his life and teachings. Thus, for instance, van Aarde concludes that Jesus was crucified by the Romans "after an outburst of emotion at the outer temple square,"[47] seemingly completely ignoring the political fact that Jesus was executed by order of the Roman governor, that he was killed by crucifixion, a form of execution that the Romans used to intimidate subject peoples by publicly torturing to death their rebel leaders.[48] It was a deadly effective form of rule by fear through intimidation and terror. The Gospels here tell us more, however. Here that incident is much more than just an "outburst of emotion." The "temple cleansing" was an act of resistance, a rejection of the suppositions of power underlying the political life and power of Israel. Obery Hendricks is nothing if not emphatic:

> This is not a temper tantrum . . . No, this was no spontaneous eruption of emotion . . . The temple was the center of Israel's economy, its central bank and treasury, the depository of immense wealth. Indeed so much of the activity of the Jerusalem Temple hinged upon buying and selling and various modes of exchange that it is no exaggeration to say that in a real sense the Temple was fundamentally an *economic* institution.[49]

That is why what seems to have been simply a burst of outrage against wayward merchants was in reality much, much more Hendricks argues. It was a very public attack aimed at Israel's center of power. In other words, it was an overtly *political* act.

> Mark's Gospel makes this clear. It tells us not only that Jesus attacked the money changers and dove sellers, but that he and his followers also seized the Temple grounds and temporarily halted commercial operations. Why? Because despite its veneer of holiness and religiosity, beneath its proclamations of justice

47. Ibid., 78.

48. "The Romans deliberately used crucifixion as an excruciatingly painful form of execution by torture (basically suffocation) to be used primarily on upstart slaves and rebellious provincials." Horsley, *Jesus and Empire*, 28, 29. Van Aarde, however, takes his line of thinking even further when he declares that it was Jesus' psychological state, what he calls "status-envy" that eventually caused his death: "Calling God father and negating the importance of patriarchy goes hand in hand. This disposition amounts to a redefinition of the whole system of holiness . . . Eventually it led to his killing by the Roman authorities" (127). In contrast, see Horsley, *Jesus and Empire*, 6: "If nothing else, then the fact that he was crucified . . . should lead us to take another look." Obery Hendricks writes, "[T]he charge for which he was executed was seeking to replace Caesar's sovereignty over Israel with the *malkuth shemayim*, the kingdom, or sovereignty, of God." This is an "unassailable fact" (*Politics of Jesus*, 78).

49. Hendricks, *Politics of Jesus*, 113, 114, emphasis original.

and concern, the Temple did not treat the people and their needs as holy.[50]

Is van Aarde continuing the Eurocentric tradition of interpretation that created a depoliticized Jesus? His Jesus is decidedly less political than the Jesus emanating from Horsley's school of thought and the Black Messiah we meet in black liberation theology whose cause *is* the liberation of, and justice for, the poor and oppressed.

In Obery Hendricks' brilliant exposé, Jesus emerges not so much as a "politicized" Jesus, but Jesus as the "political revolutionary," Jesus the "Messiah, Tactician and Strategist," the Jesus "who is as concerned about liberating us from the kingdoms of earth as about getting us into the kingdom of heaven." This is what he was crucified for, and, reminiscent of Alexis' experience in Ferguson, Hendricks says, "this is the Jesus that called me back to the Church—the revolutionary Jesus."[51] This Jesus is the Jesus of the streets where the young revolutionaries of Ferguson, Oakland, New York City and Baltimore are discovering the God of justice and liberation.

Obery Hendricks writes as a black theologian unapologetic in his understanding that "Christianity began as the faith of the oppressed,"[52] an approach that leaves him free to explore the shaping of Jesus' radical politics as well as the historical process of the making of the non-political Jesus from Paul to post-Constantinian Christianity.[53] This also opens the way for Hendricks to explore Jesus' determination to "treat the people's needs as holy," Jesus' determination to "give a voice to the voiceless" and "calling the demon by its name," Jesus' righteous anger at injustice—and that is an anger not for his own sake but because of "the maltreatment of others"— and Jesus' strategy of exposing "the workings of oppression."[54]

Van Aarde's hesitation here is curious, however, and in my view not the logical conclusion of the possibilities van Aarde's line of thinking itself opens up. At the end of his very helpful "picture of Jesus," van Aarde, in reference to the two events that shape the life of Jesus—his birth and his baptism—concludes that "what comes before and after Jesus at thirty seems to be his fatherlessness"[55]—exclusively. He does concede, however, that it cannot be proved that this image is representative of "the real Jesus" even

---

50. Ibid. 114, 115.
51. See ibid., Part Two. The quote here is from Part One, 5.
52. Ibid., 85.
53. Ibid., ch. 3.
54. Ibid., 101–67.
55. *Fatherless*, 78.

though this is, for him, the "Jesus of history and the Jesus of faith,"[56] and it is this we shall have to further explore.

The Jesus of History and the Jesus of Faith

There are several reasons why the insights of the Horsley school of thought and the insights of Obery Hendricks are so important to our discourse. First, they recognize the crucial nature of the historical context of Jesus and his times in terms of the realities of empire. That is a major paradigm shift that allows for a totally new understanding of the New Testament writings. These can no longer be read as mere "religious" writings and the tensions depicted in them are not simply tensions between "the Jews" and the emerging Christian community.

Second, they recognize the failures of Western scholarship in its interpretation of the sacred Scriptures. Jesus can no longer be reduced to a religious teacher who uttered isolated sayings and parables relevant only to individual persons and the Scriptures can no longer be detached from the living, breathing, suffering communities for whom they were written and among whom they emerged. Third, in recognizing the imperial context of Jesus and his followers, they recognize at once the imperial realities of our day, and what that means for both the beneficiaries and the victims of empire. "(After 9/11) we can no longer rest comfortably with such domesticated pictures of Jesus," writes Horsley. "We can no longer ignore the impact of Western imperialism on subordinated peoples and the ways in which peoples whose lives have been invaded sometimes react. The 'coincidental' historical analogy is too disquieting . . ."[57]

Fourth, the acknowledgment of non-Western scholarship in its critique of Western scholarship, the new perspectives that critique offers, and the impact of that critique on their interpretation of Scripture and their understanding of ancient and current political situations, brings a definite shift in our theological discourse. It is not simply a paternalistic "reaching out" to non-Western thinking, it is coming closer to accepting the demand to "reconfigure the very scaffolding of the discourse" itself, as Dwight Hopkins formulates it.[58]

Van Aarde's Jesus of history and of faith, the revolutionary, healer, teacher and helper has long been at the heart of radical black Christianity, recognizing what van Aarde calls the "subversiveness of Jesus' cause." But

---

56. Ibid.
57. Horsley, *Jesus and Empire*, 6.
58. Hopkins, *Being Human*, 20.

this truth did not come automatically to blacks in their encounter with the Christian faith. It is a truth they had to struggle to discover themselves, despite the Christianity whites brought. For, as Vincent Harding writes, and he speaks for all conquered, colonized and enslaved people,

> We first met this Christ on slave ships. We heard his name sung in praise while we died in our thousands, chained in stinking holds beneath the decks, locked in with terror and disease and sad memories of our families and homes. When we leaped from the decks to be seized by sharks we saw his name carved in the ship's solid sides. When our women were raped in the cabins, they must have noted the great and holy books on the shelves. Our introduction to this Christ was not propitious and the horrors continued on America's soil.[59]

Black Christians also came to understand the truth that even the coming of the Reformation would not make any essential difference to the situation of blacks across the world, who would be colonized, enslaved and sacrificed in the wake of what Helmut Gollwitzer called the "Protestant capitalist revolution."[60]

Yet, black Christians needed to make the distinction Frederick Douglass made between

> the religion of our blessed Savior . . . which comes from above, in the wisdom of God which is first pure, then peaceable, gentle . . . without partiality and without hypocrisy . . . which makes it the duty of its disciples to visit the fatherless and the widow in their affliction. I love that religion . . . It is because I love this religion that I hate the slave-holding, the woman-whipping, the mind-darkening, the soul-destroying religion that exists in America . . . loving the one I must hate the other; holding to one I must reject the other."[61]

To learn to love this religion, black people have embraced Christianity not as it was delivered to them by segregated white churches, "but as its truth was authenticated to them in the experience of suffering, to reinforce an ingrained religious temperament and to produce an indigenous religion oriented to freedom and human welfare."[62]

59. Harding, "Black Power and the American Christ," 86; see Boesak, *Farewell to Innocence*, 41.
60. Gollwitzer, "Schwarze Theologie," 45, 46; cf. Boesak, *Farewell*, 31.
61. See Foner, *Selections from the Writings of Frederick Douglass*, 55.
62. Wilmore, *Black Religion and Black Radicalism*, 25.

This understanding came through intense struggle with Scripture and the encounter with God in the black experience of suffering and struggle for freedom. In that experience the God of the Bible, who is a God of slaves, justice and freedom, is revealed as the God of Jesus Christ. And this Jesus is not just a transcendent being—he is the One who in his incarnation has become them, took upon himself their reality of suffering, identified with their humiliation, their hunger, their poverty, their misery, their enslavement, their blackness. But he is also the One who promises liberation from slavery and captivity, healing from sickness, restoration of their humanity and resurrection from death.

It is not that the great debates of the church had simply passed black Christians by. "I respect what happened at Nicea and Chalcedon and the theological input of the Church Fathers on Christology," says James Cone, "but that source alone is inadequate . . . the *homoousia* question is not a black question."[63] So black Christians asked different questions and came to different conclusions:

> The Jesus of Nicea, Chalcedon and the ancient creeds—Light from light, begotten, not made, of one substance with the Father—was beautiful, but so painfully remote, untouched and unmoved by human misery caused by injustice and inhumanity. Indeed, in the rendition of the European Renaissance, this Jesus was *too* beautiful, too aloof, too aristocratic for the pain, filth and ugliness of slavery and degradation, too light for the darkness of our misery as black people. The Jesus of Constantinian Christianity, without the crown of thorns, but with the crown of laurels, with his wounded hands holding the sword and the standard of the empire, in whose holy name we were caught and chained, disrobed and shamed, flayed and slaughtered, disowned, unnamed and unmade and finally baptized—*that* Jesus bore no resemblance at all to the Human Son.[64]

The Human Son is the Jesus of history and of faith encountered in the Scriptures and in the black experience. In the dialectic of Scripture and the black experience black people immediately recognized the "gross inconsistency between the allegation that this all-powerful God of the whites could care so much about their eternal salvation while remaining indifferent to the

---

63. Cone, *God of the Oppressed*, 13. "While not diminishing the importance of [Martin] Luther's theological concern, I am sure that if he had been born a black slave, his first question would not have been whether Jesus was present at the Lord's Table but whether he was really present at the slave's cabin, whether slaves could expect Jesus to be with them as they tried to survive the cotton field, the whip, and the pistol," 13.

64. Boesak, *Running With Horses, Reflections of an Accidental Politician*, 39.

powerlessness and wretchedness of their condition."[65] Their understanding of Scripture taught them that "the God who demanded their devotion, and from whom came the spirit that infused their secret meetings and possessed their souls and bodies in the ecstasy of worship, was not the God of the slave master, with his whip and gun, nor the God of the plantation preacher with his segregated services and injunctions to servility and blind obedience."[66]

The New Testament describes Jesus as the oppressed One who came to liberate and bring justice to the poor, the hungry, the naked, the widows and orphans, the oppressed and the afflicted; those who cannot defend themselves against the powerful. This is how he announces himself (Luke 4:16–18) and this is how he reveals himself in his work on earth and in the experience of black people. So James Cone writes,

> Jesus Christ is not a proposition, not a theological concept which exists merely in our heads. He is an event of liberation, a happening in the lives of oppressed people struggling for political freedom. Therefore, to know him is to encounter him in the history of the weak and the helpless. The convergence of Jesus Christ and the black experience is the meaning of the Incarnation.[67]

Hence, black theology does not separate the reality of the historical Jesus from the reality of his presence in the world today.

> Yahweh, who Israel had learned to know "through what he had done" with and for his people, has now made himself known through his Son, through what Jesus, in his turn, was doing with and for people. Thus we understand John 14:9 to read, "To have seen me (act) is to have seen the Father (act)."[68]

So the answer to the question, how close is van Aarde's "Jesus of history and of faith" to the Jesus of history and faith expounded by black theology and experienced in black Christian life, depends on another question, namely "Whose history? Whose faith?" That in turn might again depend on the question, "Whose Jesus?"

---

65. Wilmore, *Black Religion and Black Nationalism*, 32, 33.
66. Ibid., 33.
67. Cone, *God of the Oppressed*, 32, 33.
68. Boesak, *Farewell*, 41.

Whose Jesus?

When van Aarde says, "My book is about the historical Jesus who filled the emptiness caused by his fatherlessness with his trust in God as his Father," and, "my own sense of fatherlessness propelled me toward my present Jesus studies," and again, "I did, however, become existentially impelled by Jesus' fatherlessness because it addressed my own situation," and yet again, "I have come to learn through my own experience who Jesus was and still is, child of God,"[69] he does a remarkable thing. It is rare in Western scholarship to give so much weight, and with such honesty, to personal experience in intellectual endeavor.

But already in this admission is great resonance with one of black theology's central assertions, namely that the encounter with God in the black experience is a legitimate source for theological reflection and that the theologian is exegete of Scripture *and* of life.[70]

Van Aarde cautions that "an image of Jesus can be either an alienation or and affirmation of the biblical model" and that the portrayal of Jesus "is only a shadowy etching,"[71] yet his captivating picture of Jesus shows how much the theme of fatherlessness shapes this picture, and how close he comes to black theology's Black Messiah.[72] His is certainly not "an alienation."

Among other things, van Aarde's Jesus was born out of wedlock, remained unmarried, had a tense relationship with his mother and siblings because of his commitment to his cause. He carried "sinfulness" that led to his association with John the Baptist, was homeless, leading an itinerant lifestyle. He defended fatherless children, patriarchless women, and other outcasts, offended village elders by his subversive teaching and actions. He outraged Pharisees, Herodians, chief priests and elders in Jerusalem, criticized the manipulative ploys and misuse of hierarchical power of temple authorities. Crucified by the Romans, his body was not laid down in a family tomb. He was believed to have been taken up in the bosom of father Abraham, and was believed to be God's beloved child.

---

69. Van Arde, *Fatherless*, 6.

70. See Cone, *God of the Oppressed* 13. Elsewhere Cone writes: "The theologian is *before all else* an exegete, simultaneously of Scripture and of existence . . . to be an exegete of existence means that Scripture is not an abstract word, not merely a rational idea. It is God's Word to those who are oppressed and humiliated in this world. The task of the theologian is to probe the depths of Scripture exegetically for the purpose of relating that message to human existence," *God of the Oppressed*, 8 emphasis original.

71. Van Arde, *Fatherless*, 3.

72. Ibid., 77, 78.

All this affirms van Aarde's central thesis of Jesus' fatherlessness. Much attention is given to "the stigma of fatherlessness" and the social consequences of that fatherlessness—Jesus would have been excluded from being called a child of Abraham, access to the court of the Israelites in the temple would have been denied him because of his sinfulness.[73] Van Aarde's Jesus was a person whose legitimacy, and therefore in the eyes of his detractors his humanity, was in doubt; a "nobody,"[74] derisively called a "Samaritan," meaning a person of mixed race, looked down upon by the Judeans with a contempt well expressed by historian Josephus: "With two races is my soul vexed; and the third is no nation: with the dwellers of Seir and Philistea, and with the foolish race that sojourns in Shechem."[75] In our time and in our societies, race-obsessed and rife with bigotry, homophobia and Islamophobia, the poor, people of color, Muslims, and oppressed communities such as the Palestinians would, exactly as the Galileans of Jesus' time, understand immediately what Josephus was saying and grasp the disdainful intent behind his words.

The Divine Favor of the Unworthy

What is striking about van Aarde's Jesus is not just what is written but also what is left unsaid. It is doubtless a fascinating picture he paints, but it is startling, for example, that he does not point out the one salient feature about Jesus that characterizes all of his mission and has enormous theological implications, in fact, without which every Jesus study remains flawed: Jesus' identification with the poor and oppressed. Jesus was poor, a child of a poor family who could not bring the prescribed sacrifice at his birth but instead the sacrifice of the poor, two turtledoves instead of the year-old lamb (Lev 12:6–8; Luke 2:21–24). He belonged to an impoverished people in Galilee, downtrodden, oppressed and exploited by the ruling elites in Jerusalem and the Roman occupiers.[76]

He came expressly for this reason: to preach good news to the poor, to liberate them from their captivity and to restore their humanity. He identified himself with the poor, and with their struggle for liberation. In the Gospels, Jesus *becomes* the poor, the hungry, the naked, the imprisoned,

73. See *Fatherless*, chs. 4 and 5.

74. Van Aarde, *Fatherless*, 60–61, 127.

75. Ibid., 91, "Samaritans are associated not with Samaria but with Shechem." Reference is also made in the *Testament of Levi*, Chapter 7: "From this day Shechem will be called the City of Fools."

76. See Hendricks, *Politics of Jesus*; see also Boesak, *Farewell*, 43, 44.

and the sick. In black theology these are not mere spiritual connotations, but the actual conditions of people living with naked brutality and oppression.[77] For us, the historical Jesus is the embodiment of God's preferential option for the poor.

Instead of ignoring them or mythologizing them into meaninglessness, black theology, as James Cone shows, understands Jesus' exorcisms as carrying out the theme of liberation of the poor, because freedom for the oppressed can come about only by overcoming the forces of evil:

> [The scandal of Jesus] is that the exorcisms disclose that God in Jesus has brought liberation to the poor and the wretched of the land, and that liberation is none other than the overthrow of everything that is against the fulfillment of their humanity. The scandal is that liberation comes to the poor, and that the Gospel means liberation, and that it gives them the strength and the courage to break the conditions of servitude. This is what the Incarnation means. God in Christ comes to the weak and the helpless, and becomes one with them, taking their condition of oppression as his own and thus transforming their slave-existence into a liberated existence.[78]

This same theme persistently characterizes Jesus' life and work, e.g. in the temptation story (Matt 4:1ff.; Mark 1:12–13; Luke 4:1ff.). "The heart of the matter," writes James Cone, "is Jesus' rejection of any role that would separate him from the poor."[79] Cone is right, but as I have pointed out earlier, there is more here. All the temptations offered Jesus are the things the Emperor boastfully claims: miracle provider for the masses, the arrogance of power, limitless imperial power itself, and a claim on God based on his own power and divinity. Jesus' identification with the poor is also the resistance of the temptations offered by Satan. It is a deliberate rejection of all imperial pretense and the things identified with imperial power, exposing that power for what it is: the works of evil.

His actions were offensive, indeed subversive to the ruling elites, because he posed such a political threat to the privileged life they led at the cost of the poor. Keeping in mind the realities of Roman occupation—the crippling taxes to prop up the military, the hierarchy in Rome and in the provinces; the vast system of patronage, and the "cultural projects" both by the Caesars and the client kings in Judea undertaken at the expense of the

---

77. See, e.g., Boesak, *Farewell*, 43; Felder, *Troubling Biblical Waters*, 19; see also Hendricks, *Politics of Jesus*, 7–8, 326–28.

78. Cone, *God of the Oppressed*, 71.

79. Ibid., 68, 69.

poor, the decades of revolt against this oppression and the terrorizing vengeance of Roman retaliation—it becomes unimaginable that Jesus was the only person unaffected by all this.[80]

In black liberation theology, Jesus' life and mission are paradigmatic of the inverted order of the kingdom of God Jesus comes to proclaim and indeed represents. By "inverted order" I do not mean that "the last shall be first" in a general sense, nor do I infer an apocalyptic divine retribution. Van Aarde knows about this inversion too, but once again his Jesus is exclusively driven by his fatherlessness. "By making the child, and not the father, the model for entry into the reign of God, the fatherless Jesus reversed the hierarchical assumptions that governed all of life."[81] Jesus is partial to "patriarchless women," that is, women without the status accorded by being claimed by a man, therefore vulnerable, and he acted in ways "that women would": referring to himself as a "servant," serving others, taking the last place at the table, forgiving wrongs, being compassionate and healing wounds.[82] Finally van Aarde states bluntly, "In many ways, Jesus acted like a woman."[83] But instead of exploring the enormous revolutionary possibilities these discoveries open up, it suffices to argue that Jesus did all of this because of his fatherlessness. "As a fatherless figure, Jesus saw himself as the protector of fatherless children in Galilee, as well as of women who did not 'belong' to a man."[84]

In black theology, this inverted order is the *intended* purpose and work of God in the life and work of the revolutionary Jesus. All this makes Jesus precisely who he was: the incarnated, liberating, humanizing God taking sides with the oppressed. It is a persistent attack on the hierarchical structures that belittled, humiliated and exploited those who were afforded no status, did not count as fully human, and were marginalized because of their powerlessness. Teaching that "the gateway to God is not through a father figure on earth but through a child," especially if van Aarde is right in asserting that the image Jesus invokes is not just any child, but a street child, an illegitimate child,[85] is indeed truly revolutionary.

Jesus was persistent in taking people from the periphery and deliberately placing them in the center of attention. He did that in his dealings

---

80. See, e.g., Horsley, *Jesus and Empire*. Van Aarde is not unaware of all this, but somehow does not draw these conclusions, e.g. ibid., 128, 129, 130.

81. Ibid., 154, 197.

82. Ibid., 134.

83. Ibid., 197.

84. Ibid.

85. Ibid.

with children, but equally with all those regarded as without status, and therefore without rights or dignity: the man with the withered hand (Mark 3:1–6) who had no "right" to be in the synagogue is "called forward" (placed in the jealously-guarded center) by Jesus. Likewise, the woman suffering from hemorrhages is put in the center while the privileged and powerful Jairus has to respectfully wait until the healing of the woman is done. The story of the daughter of this powerful man is allowed only to "bookend" Jesus' healing of the woman (Mark 5:21–43). The daughter of the leader of the synagogue is indeed restored to life, but what deliberately draws our attention is that the poor, unclean, and despised woman is called "my daughter" by the man who is fatherless but makes every person a chosen and blessed child of God. The woman crippled for eighteen years Jesus first heals, then defends against the leaders of the synagogue, then calls "a daughter of Abraham" (Luke 13:10–17).

So the one with dubious parentage, who would not be allowed to call himself a "son of Abraham" and who would be excluded from access to the court of the Israelites in the temple, claims the authority to rebuke publicly those whose authority is thus thoroughly put to question, and renames this woman a "daughter of Abraham," just as he humanizes and restores Zacchaeus the "sinner and tax collector" and calls him into being as "son of Abraham" (Luke 19:9). Just as it was with Jesus, these persons were all deemed unworthy by those who claimed worthiness by virtue of their birth, privilege, wealth, status, gender, religious purity and power. The discarded are restored, reclaimed, renamed, and redeemed by God. The unworthy are granted divine favor, and that empowers them to reclaim their humanity.

Jesus was born in a stable, lain in a manger amongst the dust, the animals and the dung, in screaming contrast to the palace. From the moment of his birth his legitimacy was in doubt, and the "stigma of fatherlessness" clung to him as he grew up the child of a single mother.[86] Black theology does not join the debate whether the angel in fact appeared to Joseph and instructed him on the name of Jesus. Rather we focus on a fact van Aarde himself alerts us to, but does not pursue: "Apart from Jesus who is called 'the Christ'" Josephus mentions at least twelve others called Jesus who played a part in the history of Israel during the period of Greco-Roman domination. However, "the vast majority of these people belonged to priestly and

---

86. Van Aarde refers to what are called the "Yeshua ben Pentera" traditions in the Talmud that refer to Jesus' illegitimacy—he could be the child of a Roman soldier called Pantera (Obery Hendricks) or, indeed, of anybody—and in the second century CE Justin responded to accusations of (the) rape (of Mary, the mother of Jesus). Van Aarde, *Fatherless*, 73. See also ibid., 60 n. 50.

governing families."[87] Jesus, son of Mary, a "bastard" and a "nobody who would have no identity"[88] was the exact opposite, not even remotely identified with the privileged oppressor elites. He was the One sent from God, the liberator of the oppressed, the defender of the poor and the helper of the helpless. What distinguished him from the others "who all played a role" was not his name, but his self-understanding and his understanding of his mission on earth, his revolutionary words and actions, his relationship with God, his taking sides with the victims of the very power structures that gave the others also named "Jesus" their status.

Whereas van Aarde seeks explanations for the "Son of God metaphor" in Greek-Roman mythology, black theology asks, with Jane Schaberg, "But why could Jesus not be the Son of God and son of an unknown or even son of a nobody?"[89] This is precisely why it is too scandalous to contemplate, but therein lies the power and the glory of the incarnation.

Black theology understands the "shame" and "embarrassment" of Jesus' fatherlessness, not only in the sense of Steve Biko's description of black people in the face of white, racist supremacy as "unwanted step-children of a God whose presence they cannot feel,"[90] but in the actual life experience of millions of township children and single mothers. Understanding the black experience defined by racism, black liberation theology identifies with the stigma of his racial identity, being called a "bastard" and a "Samaritan," a "child of the Mamzerim," of "uncertain parentage,"[91] excluded from the privileges of the temple, being regarded as "sinful" because he did not conform to the criteria of acceptability laid down by the powerful hierarchical structures of the temple authorities.

After all, we have heard how white Christians spoke of us justifying obliteration and genocide. "What," British scientist Robert Knox asked in a lecture in 1847, "signify these races to us? Who cares for the Negro, or Hottentot, or Kaffir?" In his book published in 1850 Knox reiterates the point:

> The wild savage of South Africa, the Tasmanian, the uncultivated Negro merely feel the instinct . . . But can they be taught? They cannot be taught. Animals of today they cannot look for a tomorrow . . . Destined by the nature of their race to run, like

---

87. Ibid., 6 n. 8.

88. Ibid., 127.

89. See the reference to Jane Schaberg's 1994 paper, "The Cancelled Father: Historicity and the NT Infancy Narratives," in Van Aarde, *Fatherless*, 61.

90. This is how Biko describes black people in apartheid South Africa; see *I Write What I Like*, 56.

91. Van Aarde, *Fatherless*, 92.

animals, a certain limited course of existence, it matters little how their extinction is brought about.[92]

Black lives were not considered worthy then, and they do not matter much now. The language is more subtle, but the acts remain as brutal. And my youngest daughter Andrea tells me how some white children at her school had referred to her as a "pavement special." A street dog, a mongrel, in other words. All this, and much more besides, has been part of the black experience. And Jesus, in becoming human, took upon himself the shame and stigma that were inflicted upon black personhood, identified with them in their struggle for human dignity and restored to them their status as children of God. This is what the incarnation, in contrast to white racism, signified to us, and what black personhood signified to God. And Jesus is the Son of God, not *despite* the stigma, the sinfulness and the servanthood, the "effeminate" acts of compassion and forgiveness, "acting like a woman," but precisely *because* of all of those.

Calling God "father" and thereby deliberately "negating the importance of patriarchy" is not a result of "status-envy" caused by fatherlessness,[93] but rather a radical, deliberate and direct onslaught on the rules, the language, the assumptions and the realities that upheld the unjust, unequal and oppressive hierarchical and patriarchal societal structures that kept the ruling elites in power. Jesus' words and actions are not the incidental byproduct of a psychological condition and neither are they solely the consequence of his fatherlessness. It is a deliberate choice. It is Jesus' understanding of his mission as he interpreted it in light of the words of the prophet Isaiah, (Isa 61:1, 2; Luke 4:16ff.), the result of his analysis of the social conditions of the people amongst whom he lived, and this is who he understood God to be, the One he called "Father": "For I, the LORD, love justice" (Isa 61:8). *This is who Jesus is.*

The scandal of the incarnation is that this is who God chose to become, for God reveals that it is in this Jesus from Galilee of the Gentiles, the One who has "emptied himself" (Phil 2:5–11), taking on the form of a slave, identifying with the humiliation, the pain, the debasement of slaves, the poor, women and children, in this love to the very end, that God has entered into the human story, demonstrating true power and majesty. The servant-slave, the emptied one, is Lord; the slave reigns.[94]

---

92. Knox, in a May 1847 lecture, *The Races of Mankind*, quoted in Bernard Magubane, "African Renaissance in Historical Perspective," 26. For the expansion of and more sustained argument on the same point: see Knox, *The Races of Men*, 301, 302.

93. See Van Aarde, *Fatherless*, 127.

94. See Boesak, *The Tenderness of Conscience*, 97–101.

It is as the runaway slave that Yahweh intervenes with Hagar in the wilderness "on the way to Shur"; it is as the runaway slave that she is expressly spoken to and it is as the runaway slave that she is given the promise (Gen 16:10), so that the people in the household of Abraham would not forget her or deny who her son really is, so that the shame of her abandonment would be unmistakable and undeniable, and the promise all the more significant.[95] Moses was given the task of leading God's people out of Egypt not while he was in a position of power in Pharaoh's household, but when he was "on the run, deprived of his status as the son of the daughter of Pharaoh, and no longer able to exercise any of the power and privilege that came with that status."[96] And it is to the fatherless, despised, and stigmatized Child that God declared, "You are my Son, the Beloved; with you I am well pleased" (Mark 1:11). Such is the divine favor of the unworthy.

As such, too, he is the Black Messiah. For us this statement is not metaphorical or iconological, it is christological, and historical.[97] Thus, Dwight N. Hopkins writes, "wherever divinity empties itself in the human realm, divinity creates new possibilities and embraces the full identity of the poor among us . . . What wicked powers and peoples demonize as savage and lowly, the divinity seeks out and privileges, resulting in a revolutionary reversal of the status quo's naming powers."[98]

Throughout this book the issue of *where Christ stands* as formulated by the *Belhar Confession* has been a fundamental one. So too is the question raised right at the beginning in our reflections on the work of M. M. Thomas: is Christ to be found even in the revolutionary turmoil of our times, in the struggles for justice, equality and dignity? The answer is yes, because, we

---

95. See Boesak, *Die Vlug van Gods Verbeelding*, ch. 1.

96. Amjad-Ali, *Islamophobia or Restorative Justice*, 146.

97. See Cone, *God of the Oppressed*, 122–26; Boesak, *Die Vlug van Gods Verbeelding*, 41–45. But this is becoming a more and more contested concept. Van Aarde's insistence on Galilee of the Gentiles as a place where people of mixed race lived, seems an invitation to far more seriously consider what, e.g., Latino theologians like Virgilio Elizondo and Fernando F. Segovia insist on, namely that Jesus was not only metaphorically black but indeed a person of mixed descent: "As a mestizo people, Mexican Americans represent a Galilee of the contemporary world, a modern example of a marginalized and oppressed people" (see DeYoung, *Coming Together in the 21st Century*, 23). DeYoung himself speaks of Jesus as "Afro-Asiatic": "We can only confirm our earlier contention that Jesus, like other Jews in Palestine who had descended from the Hebrew people, was Afro-Asiatic" (DeYoung, *Coming Together*, chapter 2, especially 34–36). See also Obery Hendricks' chapter, "The Marginalization of the Galileans," in *Politics of Jesus*, 70–71. In South Africa's still race-obsessed color coding, this would indicate the derogatory racial category "colored," and it has enormous implications for politics and theology and a new discourse on racial hybridity.

98. *Being Human*, 10.

heard Thomas say, the revolution is about God's choices, social justice and the creation of a new humanity. That "revolutionary reversal" of the status quo's naming powers is taking place before our very eyes today.

So if one should ask where the fatherless Jesus is to meet the Black Messiah, where Jesus is to be found in the turmoil and upheaval caused by struggles for justice today, I would have to answer: Jesus will be found by the side of the mother in Cape Town's Samora Machel squatter camp, where she told of her dilemma with rats. Journalist and documentary producer Elna Boesak, in preparing for a program and public discussion on Women's Day in 2011, had recorded conversations with women in several squatter camps and townships in Cape Town to ask whether South Africa's progressive Constitution was making any difference in their everyday lives.[99] This mother's dilemma is not that the rats overrun the camp and pose a serious health hazard in general. It is more specific. Her dilemma, she testifies in the interview and later to the crowd at the conference, is this: "I cannot afford blankets large enough and thick enough to cover my children properly. So at night I am torn: if I put the blanket so as to cover their feet, their heads will be bare and the rats might chew on the ears and noses. If I cover their heads, the rats might chew at their toes. What shall I do?" At this point, she produces a picture of herself holding a rat she has killed, an enormous creature that sent shivers up the spines of those watching and listening.

The fatherless Jesus will be the Black Messiah by the side of those young people in the Black Lives Matter Movement and the Injustice Must Fall Movement. Those who fight for justice, who challenge the structures of systematized racism and violence, putting their own lives at risk in the streets of Ferguson and Baltimore, outside the gates of Cape Town's Parliament Buildings and Pretoria's Union Buildings. The Black Messiah will be found amongst those young people, black and white, upholding the demands of indivisible justice, stubbornly clinging to a hope that will not disappoint, believing that since in other struggles they have already seen Satan fall like lightning from heaven, their own struggle will see injustice and oppression fall.

Look for the Black Messiah as Jesus the Palestinian—in every sense of the word—in outraged mourning with the Palestinian families whose homes have been destroyed in yet another shameless act of land theft by Israel, or in yet another act of collective vengefulness for a son or a daughter's resistance against the occupation. Look for him amidst the crowd from the West Bank vainly pleading with the Israeli government to show some

---

99. The recordings resulted in a fascinating video production, *Twelve Days in the Trenches* which was presented at the Forum on the Women's Days discussions under the broad title: "Plus-Minus Equal: Do the Scales Balance?"

compassion and to release the bodies of their dead children for burial, instead of holding those bodies as punishment and collective emotional and political blackmail.

The Black Messiah will be found helplessly struggling in the grip of policemen, groaning, like Eric Garner, "I can't breathe," and he will be found lying in the street like Michael Brown, for four and a half hours, an American Calvary as shocking and poignant as the one the Gospels tell of. The Black Messiah will be found in occupied Bethlehem standing with the young Palestinian resister, facing the cordon of Israeli soldiers with a slingshot in his hands: a slingshot against the tanks; literally shooting marbles at the soldiers armed with assault rifles and rubber-coated armor-piercing bullets. The Black Messiah will be with those incredibly brave young soldiers who refuse to serve in the Israeli Defense Forces as long as these forces serve the ends of oppression and injustice and the scandal of the occupation. The Black Messiah is in the struggle to reverse the powers of the status quo to name God's children "savage," "worthless," "demonic" and "unworthy."

The seemingly endless uniformed killings of persons of color on the streets of America and the shameless hubris of the judicial process that sanctifies this with sickening regularity lays bare the dark, desolate heart of America.[100] This is the deadly expression of a deeply felt, deeply ingrained, generational, racist, judgment: not just that black lives don't matter, but that black lives do not matter because black lives are deemed unworthy. At the deepest level, the Black Lives Matter movement, the Injustice Must Fall movement, and the continuing Palestinian intifada are what Dwight Hopkins calls "the divine revolutionary reversal of the status quo's naming powers."

Andries Van Aarde's fatherless Jesus, the revolutionary who redefined the codes, systems and politics of holiness, broke down the barriers and undermined hierarchical structures to raise up those subjected to and denied by them; the subversive who restored the dignity of the downtrodden and shone God's divine favor upon those considered unworthy, not only throws new light on the historical Jesus, but helps us to discover Jesus in our very midst today. Perhaps it will also help to open up heretofore unexplored possibilities for a different discourse with liberation theologies and with black liberation theology in particular.

Van Aarde is right: "To think that the journey (the quest for the historical Jesus) ended with the Old Quest or the New Quest or the Third Quest

---

100. See the chilling assessment of English writer D. H. Lawrence cited in Hedges, *Wages of Rebellion*, 145: "The essential American soul is hard, isolate, stoic, and a killer. It has never melted." Lawrence, *Studies in Classic American Literature*, 65.

or even the Renewed Quest is to miss the reason for the search for Jesus."[101] The "betrayal to the cause of Jesus"[102] is not so much the thinking that the journey ended in the fourth, sixteenth or twentieth centuries; I think the betrayal is the thinking that that journey can even continue with integrity without the confrontation with the victims of such imperial thinking and the consequences of it in the communities of the victimized.

It is perhaps fitting that the fatherless Jesus and the Black Messiah should meet in the streets of struggle and hope, of reversal and renaming, reclaiming and repossessing in impoverished townships in South Africa, the inner cities of the United States and in occupied Palestine and occupied Jerusalem; everywhere where the cause of the fatherless Jesus has been so shamefully betrayed, and where the divine favor of the Black Messiah needs to be so gloriously embraced and celebrated.

101. Van Aarde, *Fatherless*, 204.
102. Ibid.

CHAPTER 4

When *Ubuntu* Takes Flight

Politics, Justice, Reconciliation, and the Spirit of Ubuntu

Somewhere deep inside us we seem to know that we are destined for something better . . . when for a little while we are bound together by bonds of a caring humanity, a universal sense of *ubuntu* . . . Then we experience fleetingly that we are made for togetherness, for friendship, for community . . .

—Desmond Tutu, 1999

Ubuntu is an evolving spirit, existing between memory and an ability to create something new.

—Charles Villa-Vicencio, 2009

Ubuntu in Need of *Ubuntu?*

Ugandan political scientist Mahmood Mamdani, writing about the Rwandan holocaust, speaks of moments in history when victims become killers. Mamdani writes of his visit to one place of massacre. The simple phrasing betrays the sense of tragedy and palpable frustration with the inadequacy of words to describe the indescribable:

> The church was about twenty by sixty feet. Inside, wooden planks were placed on stones. I suppose they were meant as benches. I

> peered inside and saw a pile of belongings—shoulder sacks, tattered clothing, a towel, a wooden box, a *suferia* (cooking pot), plastic mugs and plates, straw mats and hats—the worldly goods of the poor. Then, amidst it all, I saw bones, and then entire skeletons, each caught in the position in which it had died. Even a year after the genocide, I thought the air smelled of blood, mixed with that of bones, clothing, earth—a human mildew.[1]

Those indescribably tragic situations, as with the incomprehensibly violent xenophobic attacks on other nationals in South Africa in 2008, and again in 2015, are situations where we were confounded by what we heard and experienced, by the way all our humanity just seemed to have been swallowed whole by bloodlust. For African people, steeped in the principles of *ubuntu*, the way of life that affirms that we are human because we affirm the humanity of the other, and the conviction that I *am* only because we all *are*, these are bewildering events. It is as if in the face of such self-inflicted horror the African spirit runs from her children and hides herself. We knew better than to pretend that we are able to explain such horrifying events or such an assault upon our identity; we knew only that in such situations *ubuntu* "takes flight."

This wonderful expression is from South African author Sindiwe Magona's novel *Mother to Mother*. She describes the burning anger of the youth during those fateful days of the State of Emergency, when the "necklace"[2] was a preferred form of punishment and execution, the rage and the brutality of a subjugated people who lost their own humanity in their resistance to evil and in the belief that it would bring us freedom.

> Just as we kept on calling, insisted on calling the people who did the necklacing "students" and "comrades," we called a barbaric act the necklace, protecting our ears from a reality too gruesome to hear; clothing satanic deeds with innocent apparel . . .[3]

That loss of humanity, of ourselves and of others, of all sense of human purpose and meaning, and when we are not able to recognise what we are doing to ourselves in what we are doing to others, is when "*ubuntu* takes flight."

I believe, however, that *ubuntu* is not only threatened by raw, mindless, physical violence. Is it not possible that *ubuntu* also takes flight where it is being overrun by other, more systemic and pernicious forms of violence,

---

1. Mamdani, *When Victims Become Killers*, 3.

2. The practice of killing by placing a motor car tire around a person's neck, filling it with petroleum and setting it alight.

3. Magona, *Mother to Mother*, 77, quoted in Villa-Vicencio, *Walk with Us and Listen*, 113–14. See also Boesak, *Running with Horses*, 172–76.

all the more vile because in the process *ubuntu* itself is wrenched from its deepest moral moorings and used to displace justice? Where Africa's children, not just through physical violence, but through the violence of the perpetuation of systemic injustice become refugees from the inhumanity of our own flesh and blood? In the following pages, I will argue that inasmuch as *ubuntu* was used as replacement of justice in the work of the South African Truth and Reconciliation Commission (TRC), the process of reconciliation in our politics and socio-economic life and the justification of ongoing injustice afterwards, this too constitutes a situation where *ubuntu* has taken flight.

But where shall we begin? It is perhaps fair to say that the Western world in general was not very much aware of the ancient African way of life called *ubuntu* until it was popularized through the work of South Africa's Truth and Reconciliation Commission. The world watched, enraptured, as the TRC process began and unfolded into the amnesty process, where some, but by no means all, perpetrators of apartheid's crimes against humanity came to acknowledge their role in the kidnapping, imprisonment, torture and killing of apartheid activists, the persecution of their families and the terrorizing of whole communities. The world seemed rendered speechless faced with such unspeakable horrors, although the half of it has not been told and probably never will be.

Significantly though, and making all the difference, the word and meaning of *ubuntu* were introduced to the world through these processes by that remarkable spiritual leader, Archbishop Desmond Tutu, whose deeply rooted piety and devotion to Jesus Christ made him shape and embrace a Christianized *ubuntu*[4] that would not only influence the very work of the TRC but impact the discourse and praxis of a whole nation. In the history of Truth Commissions this was not only different, it was unique.

So from the mouth of Desmond Tutu, within the context of this peculiar South African apocalypse—a revelation, a horrific unveiling, and a terrible judgment—this is how most of the world learned of *ubuntu*. To explain the meaning of *ubuntu*, Tutu first framed a question. "What is it," he asked, "that constrained so many to choose to forgive rather than to demand retribution, to be so magnanimous and ready to forgive rather than wreak revenge?"[5]

Notice carefully how Tutu constructs this sentence of only 28 words. Immediately, and crucially, *ubuntu* is equated with forgiveness. Notice also his choice of words: "constraint," "forgiveness," "retribution," "revenge,"

---

4. See Michael Battle, *Reconciliation*.
5. Tutu, *No Future Without Forgiveness*, 31.

"magnanimity." He speaks of "constraint," not in the sense of people being forced or coerced, but rather people feeling compelled, as by some deep, irresistible, spiritual force. They are obligated, but not to themselves, for their own benefit or spiritual aggrandizement. It is, rather, an obligation to the quest of the humanization of the other as well as of themselves, and greater still, the humanization, what one could call the ubuntufication, of humanity.

Twice Tutu uses the word "forgiveness" and twice he juxtaposes it with "revenge" and with "retribution." First he speaks of people who "choose" to forgive, then of those same people "ready" to forgive. That is why I understand his use of "constraint" as "feeling compelled" and being "obligated." They "choose": there is no coercion; it is a voluntary action, a deliberate willingness to do something extraordinary. They not only choose, they are "ready" to forgive, that is to say, to forego their right to demand the satisfaction of retribution. It is not simply a feeling they are setting aside. It is a *right, by law*, they are giving up. They are ready to deny themselves the most basic human instincts, and what has become axiomatic in the administration of justice in a country like the United States for example: justice as punishment and revenge, to strike back when hurt, to turn the tables, to teach history's criminals, and thereby generations to come as well as society as a whole, a lesson through the infliction of the same pain they have been subjected to.

They disclaim their right as victims and the empathetic acclaim that goes with it, for who in the world, except the perpetrators and the beneficiaries of apartheid, would begrudge them? To "wreak revenge" is the most natural human response; it is also the historical precedent. To break with such predetermined human response, to turn one's back on historical precedent that would have justified one's vengeful anger and offer forgiveness instead—that comes with great cost and sacrifice. It calls for a magnanimity that is highly unusual, and at some level even incredible.

The "so many" Tutu speaks of—these are South Africa's black people, the victims of crimes against humanity: over 350 years of colonization, slavery, dehumanization, and dispossession. Of fifty years of apartheid's racist oppression, discrimination, and exploitation; of unnamable horrors and indescribable terror, of perpetual impoverishment and unending, daily humiliations. They are the victims of the most calculated viciousness, the most creative evil, the most inventive callousness. These are the ones "ready to forgive rather than wreak revenge."

And why? Tutu is not so banal as to suggest that they are doing this out of a need or pretense to serve the utilitarian politics of what analysts and politicians are fond to call "the equilibrium of the balance of forces." But neither is the answer, perhaps to our surprise, "because of the love of Jesus Christ." At least not immediately. The answer is *ubuntu*. Desmond Tutu himself may very well have had Jesus in mind: "Bless those who persecute you," or Matthew 18:22, where we are instructed to forgive not seven, but seventy-seven times—one of his favorite texts. Or Romans 12:17, 18: "Do not repay anyone evil for evil . . . [and] if it is possible, so far as it depends on you, live peaceably with all."

But for Tutu it is *ubuntu*, albeit an *ubuntu* that resonates deeply with the call of the gospel as he understands it. It is, he says, to be friendly, hospitable and compassionate. It is to know that "I am a person through other persons: I am because I am human, open and available to others, affirming of others." It is not to feel threatened that others are able and good, "for he or she has a proper assurance that comes from knowing that he or she belongs in a greater whole and is diminished when others are humiliated or diminished, when others are tortured or oppressed, or treated as if they were less than who they are." *Ubuntu* means, "I am human because I belong . . . Anger, resentment, lust for revenge, even success through aggressive competitiveness are corrosive" of what serves the common good of social harmony, what Tutu calls "the greatest good." And even though forgiveness is "the best form of self-interest" it is really much more. It is understanding "that what dehumanizes you inexorably dehumanizes me." So *ubuntu* is lifegiving: "It gives people resilience, enabling them to survive and emerge still human despite all efforts to dehumanize them."[6]

No wonder the world was so stunned at learning this while seeing the evidence as it was happening before our very eyes in those amnesty hearings. Tutu asserts that *ubuntu* is not just African, and Charles Villa-Vicencio affirms this: "Tutu's words receive nods and sighs of understanding from many victims and oppressed people around the world. There also those who have never known the reality of deep suffering who in their better moments long for the kind of society in which there is a deeper sense of community and social care."[7] President Obama seems to agree as he speaks at Nelson Mandela's memorial service: "[Mandela] not only embodied *ubuntu*, he taught millions to find that truth within themselves . . . [*ubuntu*] speaks to what is best inside us."[8] But Ambassador Elizabeth Frawley Bagley, US State Department representative for Global Partnerships, shows how careful one must be when she, going further than her president, describes her work—part of US foreign policy—as "Ubuntu diplomacy."[9]

6. Tutu, *No Future*, 31.

7. Villa-Vicencio, *Walk With Us and Listen*, 127.

8. "Remarks by President Obama at Memorial Service for South African President Nelson Mandela," http://www.whitehouse.gov/the-press-office/2013/12/10/remarks-president-obama.

9. Elizabeth Frawley Bagley's remarks at her swearing-in ceremony, http://www.sate.gov/r/pa/prs/ps/2009/06a/125278.htm.

Africans would be surprised and shocked: from unrepented global neoliberal corporatism and economic exploitation to rendition, the justification of torture, and the destruction of "regime change" all in the name of democracy. From endless terror in the name of a war on terror; from drone attacks on wedding parties to air attacks on hospitals unleashed upon the people of the global South—*ubuntu* cannot possibly be this.

On November 14, 2015, news arrived of terror attacks in Paris that ultimately left 130 persons dead. President Obama spoke of the situation as "heartbreaking" and an "assault on all humanity." Rightly so. Two days before, however, when the same kind of terror attacks in Beirut left 40 dead, the president was silent and the reaction in the global North was markedly indifferent. "Without a doubt," writes journalist Belén Fernandez, "when it comes down to it, 'all of humanity' doesn't necessarily qualify as human." Speaking of the president's "heartbreak" because of the deaths of "innocent civilians," Fernandez goes on to ask, "Why doesn't it break the president's heart to order drone attacks and other life-extinguishing maneuvers?" She concludes: "In a world superior to the one we have, the scenario [of people being killed everywhere in the name of a war on terror or the millions of refugees fleeing that same terror in helpless desperation] might qualify as an assault on all humanity. The fact that it doesn't is truly heartbreaking."[10]

In Fernandez' "superior world," the world in which Mandela's *ubuntu* continues to invoke "what's best in all of us," *all* deaths caused by war would break our hearts, and every time it happens, it would be an assault on *all* humanity, since Obama would know and believe that his humanity would be dependent on and inseparable from the humanity of all those in Paris, and in Beirut, and in Yemen. If this is *ubuntu*, it is *ubuntu* desperately in need of *ubuntu*. But in such situations of course, *ubuntu* does not flee. She does not have the chance. She is simply paralyzed by the sight of multiple beheadings, run into the ground by tanks, blown to smithereens by cluster bombs, or in a fiery flash, droned into oblivion, in every sense left speechless by the lethal arrogance of mendacious verbosity, devoid of even the most tenuous reach for truthful intent.

All this raises an important question. Is it possible therefore that *ubuntu* can inspire to greater justice, more political integrity, a more humane world as Desmond Tutu believes?

---

10. See Belen Fernandez, "Beirut and Paris: A Tale of Two Terror Attacks," http://readersupportednews.org/opinion2/277-75/33500-beirut-and-paris-a-tale-of-two-terror-attacks.

Ubuntu as a "Violation of *Ubuntu*"

In South Africa, *ubuntu* and its use in the TRC quickly became highly contested. In the immediate aftermath of the TRC, observer Richard Wilson, severely critical of the amnesty proceedings, recalls how in the amnesty process *ubuntu*, in his view, was used as a kind of emotional blackmail to stifle righteous anger and to persuade the victims of apartheid to once again make the sacrifices, something that "was never demanded of the perpetrators." That is a view that would gain serious traction in the years that followed. Convinced that *ubuntu* was used to bludgeon victims into offering forgiveness while not demanding real remorse from perpetrators, Wilson rejects the term as "a current invention."[11]

Of course *ubuntu* is not a "current invention." *Ubuntu* is an ancient African notion and is doubtless an enormously powerful philosophy and way of life. It is deeply embedded in African jurisprudence, traditions, and religion. The alienation of African law since colonization is well documented, but it does not nullify *ubuntu*'s historic pre-eminence in African life.

But certainly in the last decade or so since the TRC and the euphoria of that early period in South Africa's democratic endeavor, *ubuntu* has become even more a subject of public and academic discourse, even more contentious, and the critique of *ubuntu* more vocal and more pointed, reaching far wider than the TRC.[12] It is one of the most vigorous, and vital, discussions in South Africa today.

Scholars such as Themba Sono, an early harbinger of the less romantic, more critical stance, have warned that *ubuntu* can represent a conservative and reactionary tradition that undermines progress and open, democratic discourse, resistant to dissent, an "overwhelming, totalistic, even totalitarian group psychology . . . stronger on belief than on reason; on sameness than on difference . . . Tradition is venerated, continually revered, change feared and difference shunned. Heresies are not tolerated."[13] Others have pointed to this as well, speaking of *ubuntu* having cultivated a "cult of silence" that does not tolerate individual critique.[14]

---

11. See Graybill, *Truth and Reconciliation in South Africa*, 35. See also Boesak, *The Tenderness of Conscience*, 186

12. Amongst a whole range of publications, see the two most recent volumes in the Africa Thinking Series, both dealing with Ubuntu: Praeg, *A Report on Ubuntu*, and Praeg and Magadla, eds., *Ubuntu: Curating the Archive*.

13. Sono, *Dilemmas of African Intellectuals in South Africa*, 7, cited in Villa-Vicencio, *Walk With Us and Listen*, 118

14. See Keevy, "Ubuntu Versus the Core Values of the South African Constitution," in Praeg and Magadla, eds., *Ubuntu: Curating the Archive*, 54–95.

The critical discourse on *ubuntu* is now much more intense. The *ubuntu* the African National Congress felt entitled to claim as imbuing its history of struggle and the spirit of its politics is now being rejected with utter disdain. Rhodes University political scientist Leonard Praeg is particularly blunt:

> The African National Congress' claim to have founded the new South Africa on the *nomos,* or spirit of law of an extraordinary humanism has bottomed out. After Marikana, no such claim can plausibly be made or sustained. Just as its so-called human-rights-inspired foreign policy revealed itself as a myth soon after it was named as such, any claim by the ANC government to have founded our democratic politico-juridical idea of a shared humanity will and indeed must in future be met with utter derision.[15]

It is not so much *ubuntu* as such that is attacked here, as what is called "an African *nomos*," one "driven less by our concern for a shared humanity than with the violent politics of identity claims," which nowhere manifested itself more clearly than "in the beloved myth of South Africa's so-called miraculous transition," always a function of something as lasting, because essential, "as Africa's exceptional humanism." This is not *ubuntu*. It is rather, Praeg insists, an "*Ubuntu*-driven nationalism, this nationalist, reductive violation of *ubuntu*."[16]

In total contrast with these "vacuous identitarian claims of a bourgeois politics" that constitute the unjust politics of the establishment, Praeg argues, there is a "radically expansive understanding of justice implicit in Ubuntu as a potent critique of neo-liberal constitutionalism." This understanding of *ubuntu*, the *ubuntu* of the ruling elites, is the "domestication of humanism to do the necessary, but not therefore less dirty, work of the politics of the day."[17]

Ubuntu is not rejected. The problem is not u*buntu* but the appropriated, domesticated *ubuntu* as handmaiden of the "violent logic of cultural and political sovereignty" as espoused and practiced by South Africa's political and economic aristocracy. What is needed is an understanding and practice of *ubuntu* that will release its potential for "radical justice."

Would the embrace of such an *ubuntu* make of South Africa, the United States, the State of Israel, and indeed the world a better place? On the face of it, it might seem that such potential might indeed exist. In fact, South

15. Praeg, "Preface," in Praeg and Magadla, eds., *Ubuntu: Curating the Archive,* x.
16. Ibid., xi.
17. Ibid.

Africans proudly claim that their Constitution, one of the most progressive in the world today, embraces *ubuntu* as fundamental, a "shared value and ideal that runs like a golden thread across cultural lines." *Ubuntu*, Constitutional Court Justice Albie Sachs argues, does not only have a "universalistic ethos," it is "in consonance with the values of the Constitution in general and those of the Bill of Rights in particular."[18] If this is so, it argues for a strong synergy between the South African Constitution and its call for radical justice for every single South African in its Bill of Rights, and ancient *ubuntu* values which in turn are not only central to age-old African customs and traditions, but also to African religion.[19]

It is precisely those African traditions and values exemplified in *ubuntu* and so firmly rooted in African religion, however, that make African philosopher Magobe B. Ramose critical of these assumptions.[20] Ramose seriously doubts whether the demand for justice he *does* recognize in *ubuntu* is a driving force of the Constitution at all. *Ubuntu* legal philosophy, Ramose states, "is by definition antithetical to the principle of constitutional supremacy adopted as the legal foundation of the 'new South Africa.'"[21]

Furthermore, a constitution does not by itself guarantee and deliver justice. In truth, for the vast majority of South Africa's people there is no justice. Ramose quotes South African economist Sampie Terreblanche with approval: the negotiated settlement, of which the Constitution is proudly claimed to be its most celebrated outcome, stands in the shadow of what Terreblanche calls "an elite conspiracy" that not only exonerated the white corporations and the white citizens from the part they played in the exploitation and deprivation of blacks, it also enabled whites to transfer all their accumulated wealth—their social and physical wealth, which was accumulated *undeservedly*—almost intact to the new South Africa.[22]

This is the settlement the Constitution protects. "No wonder then," Ramose continues, "that the property clause is the longest in the South African Constitution." For Ramose, constitutional supremacy was no more than a

---

18. See Ilze Keevy, quoting Y. Makgoro, "Ubuntu and the Law in South Africa," Keevy, "Ubuntu Versus the Core Values of the South African Constitution," in Praeg and Magadla, eds., *Ubuntu: Curating the Archive*, 54. This is also the consistent view of the Constitutional Court itself: "Constitutional Court judges introduced the jurisprudence of ubuntu in an effort 'for courts to develop the entrenched fundamental rights in terms of a cohesive set of values, ideal to an open and democratic society'" (54).

19. Keevy, citing Ramose and M'Baye, in Praeg and Magadla, eds., *Ubuntu: Curating the Archive*, 54.

20. See Ramose, "Ubuntu: Affirming a Right and seeking Remedies in South Africa," in Praeg and Magadla, eds., *Ubuntu: Curating the Archive*, 121–36.

21. Ibid., 128.

22. Ibid., 122, quoting Terreblanche, *Lost in Transformation*, 109.

tactic "to defend wealth gained and accumulated on the basis of unjust acquisition. Considerations of *ubuntu*, even of the word itself, were more than remote in the hatching of this wealth-protection mechanism."[23] So Ramose asks the question, "A miracle by whom and for whose benefit?" Ramose concludes, "In these circumstances, it is an ethical exigency to affirm the right to life of *ubuntu* . . . and to seek remedies to the constitutionalized injustice."[24] In affirming the "right to life" of *ubuntu,* Ramose seems to argue, we are affirming the justice inherent in *ubuntu.*

Ubuntu: A Potential for Radical Justice?

Whether *ubuntu* has such a potential for justice as Ramose claims is, however, the question. In her pointed, strongly argued interrogation of this issue, Constitutional Law professor Ilze Keevy questions the assumption of an organic relationship between the South African constitution and *ubuntu*. In fact, she juxtaposes *ubuntu*'s shared beliefs and values with the core values of the constitution, namely, equality and human dignity, and concludes that *ubuntu* is *not* in consonance with the values of the Constitution in general and the Bill of Rights in particular. For her, there is no such thing as a "potential for radical justice" in *ubuntu*, and *ubuntu*, contrary to popular claims, is *not* in synergy with the human rights law and values so distinctive of the South African constitution.

Keevy argues this point by focusing on several critical areas of which I will emphasize only two: one, the question of women and gender justice; and two, the issue of the LBGTQI+ community and sexual justice. All these have to do with justice, equality and human dignity, and they are all fundamental shortcomings in *ubuntu* even as it purportedly "represents the collective personhood and collective morality of the African people, best described by the Zulu proverb, '*umuntu, ngumuntu ngabantu*': I am a person through other persons."[25] For African feminists and feminist theologians such as Mercy Oduyoye, Dorothy Ramodibe, and Rose Zoe-Obianga, however, these are mere words, more utopian than reality. This "folk philosophy" rooted in African religion and tradition oppresses, marginalizes and stereotypes African women, keeps women in a state of submission, sanctifying

---

23. Ibid., 132. I raised this critical point quite sharply in my 2012 publication, *Radical Reconciliation*.

24. Ibid., 123.

25. Keevy, "Core Values," in Praeg and Magadla, eds., *Ubuntu: Curating the Archive*, 66.

oppressive gender stereotyping.²⁶ Rather than being humanizing and uplifting, for women "*ubuntu* represents an oppressive reality: it fosters a deep-seated patriarchy that entrenches gender inequality and disregard for the dignity of African women."²⁷

Africans in same-sex relationships experience discrimination, gang rape, hate speech, harassment, stigmatization, and even murder because of their sexual orientation. Here too, Keevy is correct. South Africa offers the world the horrific phenomenon of "corrective rape" whereby gangs of men rape lesbians "to teach them a lesson," "correct" their wayward ways, and "restore" them to their proper role as women. LGBTQI+ persons are called "subhuman," and "worse than dogs and pigs," and not just by Zimbabwe's Robert Mugabe. Thirty-eight countries in Africa still criminalize consensual same-sex activity between adults. Uganda is only the most conspicuous of these.²⁸

"It has become popular," Keevy writes, "to put great emphasis only on the positive traditional African values, conveniently ignoring the dark side of *ubuntu*, which erodes the human rights of women and others."²⁹ In truth, she argues, as a collective philosophy, "*ubuntu* sustains not only communities, extended families, values, beliefs, tradition, morals, law and justice in these societies, but also the patriarchal hierarchy, discrimination, inequality and stereotyping of women, children, homosexuals, lesbians, witches, strangers, and others."³⁰ A growing number of male African scholars are in agreement. Among others, Lenard Nyirongo offers a ringing condemnation:

> They have said nothing about the violence that goes on within the tribe because of its faulty view of office, authority, power and irresponsibility. This in my view is an illusion . . . the caring and sharing atmosphere we see is not as innocent as it appears.³¹

Keevy's examination from a (feminist) legal point of view, testing the assumed organic link between the South African constitution and *ubuntu*,

26. Ibid., 66.

27. Ibid., 70.

28. Ibid. See also Boesak, *Kairos, Crisis, and Global Apartheid*, 95, 97, and 241 nn. 39 and 40.

29. Keevy, "Core Values," in Praeg and Magadla, eds., *Ubuntu: Curating the Archive*, 72. The argument, among others, always is that same-sex orientations are "un-African" despite evidence to the contrary; see Keevy, citing Osei-Hwedie, "Ubuntu and the Law," in Jacques and Lesetedi, eds., *The New Partnership for Africa's Development*, 72 and 88 n. 76.

30. Keevy, "Core Values," in Praeg and Magadla, eds., *Ubuntu: Curating the Archive*, 78, citing Osei-Hwedie, "Ubuntu and the Law," 154.

31. Ibid., 73, citing Nyirongo, *The Gods of Africa or the God of the Bible*, 149.

leads her to an unequivocal conclusion completely different from those who discern in *ubuntu* a "potential for radical justice": Not only does *ubuntu* have what she calls "a dark side," unmentioned, unacknowledged but indisputable, "it does not guarantee fundamental human rights for individual members, strangers, or outsiders."[32] For her, women, LGBTQI+ persons, strangers and other outsiders would be better off seeking refuge in the guarantees of the constitution and its bill of rights rather than in *ubuntu*.

Our discussion thus far seems to confirm: not only is *ubuntu* is in need of *ubuntu*; in these circumstances, and under these pressures, *ubuntu* takes flight.

Nuremberg, Kempton Park, and the Question of Justice

But what if, taking this discussion yet a bit deeper, we raised the question of *ubuntu* and justice not from a political science or legal point of view, but through the lens of prophetic theology? Let us for a moment take a step or two back. Mahmood Mamdani, who has a great many wise things to say about South Africa's TRC and our reconciliation process, has made a convincing case for the view that South Africa's reconciliation process did not start with the TRC, but in fact already at Kempton Park, where the negotiations between the whites and the black majority took place.[33]

Taking as point of departure Mamdani's intriguing thoughts on the Nuremberg trials, South Africa's political negotiations held in Kempton Park and the TRC,[34] we will once again raise the matter of justice, the way the TRC understood it, and the consequences of that understanding for the TRC and for Christians in the call for the doing of justice.

At Kempton Park, Mamdani says, a historic "paradigm shift" was effected. Instead of following historic precedent (the Nuremberg trials) and dealing with apartheid as the crime against humanity it in fact was, going the route of criminal justice, Kempton Park chose political justice. In other words, to deal with apartheid's perpetrators and beneficiaries not as the criminals they were, but as political adversaries. This was done in return for political reform. At a deeper level this meant that Kempton Park chose not for victor's justice, nor victim's justice, but what Mamdani calls survivor's justice.

---

32. Keevy, "Core Values," in Praeg and Magadla, eds., *Ubuntu: Curating the Archive*, 75.

33. See Mamdani, "Beyond Kempton Park."

34. Ibid.

In his profound and provocative lecture Mahmood Mamdani reflects on the difference between the Nuremberg trials, the Kempton Park negotiations, and the Truth and Reconciliation Commission. He begins with naming "the two great human wrongs that occurred in the twentieth century—the Holocaust and apartheid."[35] He then contrasts the ways in which we have settled accounts "with these great crimes against humanity": in Europe with criminal trials in Nuremberg, and in South Africa with a political settlement in Kempton Park.

Mamdani makes the point that the world has become fascinated with South Africa's TRC, but has not taken the lessons from Kempton Park as seriously as we should have. To begin with, whereas Nuremberg shaped a notion of justice as criminal justice, few recognise that Kempton Park calls on us to think of justice primarily as political justice. Furthermore, and more importantly, whereas Nuremberg has become the basis of a notion of victim's justice—as a complement of rather than a contrast to victor's justice—few acknowledge that Kempton Park provides the basis for an alternative notion of justice, which Mamdani calls "survivor's justice."[36] South African's failure to understand this distinction contributes to the limitations of the South African transition, which Mamdani traces to "the failure to broaden the discussion of justice beyond political to social justice." [37]

Previously Mamdani has uttered telling critique of the workings of the TRC.[38] The problem, he argued then, was that the TRC made an improper distinction, namely between victims and perpetrators. Properly the distinction should have been between *beneficiaries* and victims of apartheid. While *some* white South Africans perpetrated human-rights crimes (for which the TRC tried to hold them responsible), *all* white people benefited from apartheid. Mamdani then warned, "If reconciliation is to be durable, would it not need to be aimed at society (beneficiaries and victims) and not simply at the fractured elite (perpetrators and victims)? . . . And does not justice then become a demand for systemic reform of society as a whole, so that the 'target' is all who benefited, rather than just the personal conversion of 'the perpetrator'"?[39]

Elsewhere I have pursued this issue and pointed to the fact that the TRC has indeed failed to understand the systemic nature of the wrongs done to an economically oppressed and exploited population. It failed too to

35. Ibid., 1.
36. Ibid.
37. Ibid., 2.
38. Mamdani, "Reconciliation without Justice," 4.
39. Ibid.

grasp the *causative* role played by the systems of white political dominance, racial capitalism, and apartheid over a considerable period of time, in bringing about and sustaining white wealth and privilege on the one hand, and black poverty, black deprivation and black humiliation on the other.[40]

Now, however, Mamdani both broadens and deepens his critique. In the popular imagination, he says, the South African transition is mainly identified with the work of the TRC. However,

> The TRC had more in common with the logic of apartheid than is often realised. First, when the TRC held individual state officials criminally responsible, it was only for actions that would have been defined as crimes *under apartheid law*. It did not hold them accountable for the violence that was authorised by apartheid law, but only for the violence beyond the law, violence of which they were individual authors rather than implementers. When it held them accountable, it was for excess, for violence beyond the law. By ignoring the violence authorised the apartheid state and apartheid law, the TRC ignored political violence. Instead, it set out to identify criminal violence, violence that exceeded political orders, violence that would have been punished as crime even under apartheid law had it been fully implemented. In other words, the TRC upheld rather than question the rule of law identified with apartheid.[41]

In my view this analysis has immense political, theological and ethical consequences. Without doubt it had enormous impact on the outcomes and conclusions of the Commission and as a result on the whole reconciliation process. Not only had the work of the TRC been confined to a rather random period of South Africa's history—it did not include the historical wrongs of colonialism and slavery—but in the period it did touch upon, the apartheid era, it worked only with what was lawful under apartheid law. Not only were historic injustices ignored, whole communities—victims of historic wrongs—were thereby excluded from consideration for justice.

But Mamdani moves yet further. The expectation would have been that since Kempton Park has moved beyond the Nuremberg paradigm—moving from criminal justice to political justice and from victim's justice to survivor's justice—the TRC would, as it were, complete the circle, moving from political justice to social justice.

Kempton Park did not at all ignore the question of justice, Mamdani insists. On the contrary, it provided us "with a radically new way of thinking

---

40. Boesak, *The Tenderness of Conscience*, 192–93.
41. Mamdani, "Beyond Kempton Park," 5.

about justice" and this represents "a double breakthrough."[42] First, it distinguished between criminal, political, and social justice so as to prioritize political justice—the reform of the political system—over the other two. This is important, since the object of criminal justice is punishment; that of political justice political reform. Second, "it decriminalised the other side so as to treat it as a political adversary." But this means—and this is a hugely important issue to which we shall return and which should actually be a third, separate point—that political justice prioritizes the claims of the living over those of the dead.[43]

A Paradigm Shift

Whereas Nuremberg was "backward looking" in its preoccupation with justice as punishment Kempton Park sought a balance between past and future, between "redress for the past and reconciliation for the future."[44] The "real trade off" between truth and amnesty was not at the TRC, but at Kempton Park: "The amnesty offered perpetrators and the stay offered beneficiaries was in return for political reform. It is at Kempton Park where the rules changed."[45] Mamdani is right on two counts. Firstly, Kempton Park, far from being just "negotiations" between equals, offered a "stay" to the beneficiaries of apartheid who, in the language of Nuremberg should have been treated as "criminals against humanity." Second, the rules agreed on were the same for *all* survivors, beneficiaries and victims alike, not just surviving victims. "The shift in paradigm changes the meaning of survivor to include all those who survived yesterday's catastrophe, apartheid."[46]

South Africans, white South Africans especially, as well as the global community in general have mostly missed the extraordinary magnanimity in and the huge theological import of this: that we speak of both the victims and the beneficiaries, even the beneficiary as perpetrator, as survivors. *Whites as well as blacks*. As a consequence, they miss the *political* import and the political consequences of this: the fact that here already political forgiveness is at work, and on a scale that would include both communal and personal forgiveness. It also means, amongst other things, that *ubuntu* was already at work at Kempton Park, and on a stunning scale. It did not first lay its claim upon the TRC process proper. Those who argue that the

42. Ibid., 6.
43. Ibid., 8.
44. Ibid.
45. Ibid., 7.
46. Ibid.

call for justice such as made in this book is "setting the bar too high" for politics, should think again about what really happened at Kempton Park.

In a real sense, of course, and looking at this from yet another point of view, the real victims of apartheid survived not simply because they were left alive, but because they resisted and overcame the systems of oppression despite the determination of the beneficiaries to uphold these. Kempton Park "looking forward," shaped not just a common future, because we had no choice, as conventional wisdom holds: there was no clear victor in the struggle against apartheid. One can say that perhaps only in the military sense. *Umkhonto We Sizwe*, the military wing of the African National Congress, really could never be a match for the best equipped defence force on the African continent. In all other ways, however, apartheid was defeated, made "ungovernable," rendered unsustainable. At its heart, it was a victory of nonviolent struggle.[47]

The reconciliation we ascribe to the TRC actually began at Kempton Park, on behalf of the nation, with the inclusion of yesterday's victims, yesterday's perpetrators and yesterday's beneficiaries. This is what the shift from victim's justice to survivor's justice means.[48] This is the beginning of the "miracle" so many speak of. The creation of a common future hereby is not just the result of cold, calculated *real politik* (there was no clear victor) but of a willingness to take the risk of inclusive solidarity in order to make possible the reconciliation the TRC could and should have vested with further meaning.

We do not critique the TRC because it did not send every single apartheid criminal to prison. The crucial paradigm shift discussed above created space for alternatives to retribution and revenge. We critique the TRC for its failure to think beyond the Nuremberg paradigm, to expand the notion of justice to social, distributive justice, so as to make reconciliation authentic, durable, and sustainable.

Giving Preference to the Living

Giving preference to the living is not an excuse for running away from the past, acting as if nothing has happened, or as if it is best to "move on" as quickly and painlessly as possible. Neither does it mean that the living take upon themselves the grave political and moral responsibility of forgiving on behalf of the dead. We can never know what choices the dead would have made. We can argue with equal strength that the dead whom we knew

---

47. Boesak, *Running with Horses*, 157–95, 338–62.
48. Mamdani, "Beyond Kempton Park," 7.

as family or personal friends or struggle comrades would have chosen forgiveness, rather than burdening us with the demand for revenge for which we, not them, have taken responsibility. We are choosing genuine, systemic, sustainable justice for those still alive, who have survived the horrors of apartheid and are alive to harvest the fruits of the struggle for justice. This choice is a *life-giving, life-sustaining* choice. To recall Jessica Breaky: it is the best we can do. It is also the least we can do.

In this regard, the TRC failed, Mamdani says, in what is "the greatest challenge South Africa faces today."[49] In other words, the TRC, as Kempton Park indicated, had the opportunity to give preference to the demands of the living over those of the dead by insisting on social justice. Instead of moving forward on social justice, the TRC moved backward toward Nuremberg. This great lesson we could have taught conflict-torn Africa will remain unlearned, mostly because we did not learn it ourselves.

Defenders of the TRC would argue that what South Africa chose in the TRC was exactly the opposite of Nuremberg. So does, in any case, Archbishop Desmond Tutu, Chair of the TRC and arguably one of the best to explain the work of the TRC. The Nuremberg option was not really a viable option at all, he writes in his insightful and hugely influential book *No Future without Forgiveness*.[50] Nuremberg imposed victor's justice, a term Mamdani also uses. In South Africa, neither side could impose victor's justice because neither side won the decisive (military) victory that would have enabled it to do so.

Like others, Tutu sees as decisive the fact that "the security forces of the apartheid regime would not have supported the negotiated settlement which made possible the 'miracle' of our relatively peaceful transition from oppression to democracy . . . had they known that at the end of the negotiations they would have faced the full wrath of the law as alleged perpetrators. They still controlled the guns and had the capacity to sabotage the whole process." If we had insisted on trials, "there would have been no democratic South Africa."[51] Tutu recognizes other "cogent and important reasons" as well. "We could very well have had retributive justice, and had a South Africa lying in ashes—a truly Pyrrhic victory if ever there was one."[52]

The archbishop then mentions the uncertainties faced in our courts at the beginning of our transition in the 1990s.[53] Discussing first the difficulties

49. Ibid., 10.
50. Tutu, *No Future*, 24.
51. Ibid., 25.
52. Ibid., 27
53. De Lange, "The Historical Context," 14–31. De Lange mentions two cases that

of presenting evidence in court to be proved "beyond reasonable doubt," Tutu then gets to the heart of the matter. First, there was the admission that much of the evidence in terms of documentation had been destroyed.[54] Second, there was the question of the mendacity of those charged with human-rights abuses: "We discovered in the course of the Commission's investigations that the supporters of apartheid were ready to lie at the drop of a hat. This applied to cabinet ministers and commissioners of police right down to rank-and-file supporters . . . (They perjured themselves) brazenly and with considerable conviction."[55] Besides that, there was the important consideration that the majority of judges were still white, "sharing the apprehensions and prejudices of their white compatriots, secure in enjoying the privileges that the injustices of apartheid provided them with so lavishly and therefore inclined to believe that all opposition to that status quo was Communist-inspired."[56]

However, this does not mean that they were ready to "let bygones be bygones."[57] This option would have amounted to what Tutu calls "national amnesia." "Accepting that notion would have victimised the victims of apartheid a second time around. It would have meant denying their experience, a vital part of their identity."[58] Now however, through the TRC, "they would be empowered to tell their stories, and allowed to remember and in this public recounting their individuality and inalienable humanity would be acknowledged."[59] In these stories truth would be found, different from the forensic, factual truth, verifiable and documentable, nor just the social truth, the truth of experience that is established through interaction, discussion and debate, but the personal truth Tutu describes with the words of the late Chief Justice of the Supreme Court Ishmail Mahomed, "the truth of wounded memories."[60] Tutu uses this expression several times since it is intimately tied up with what, for Tutu, lay at the heart of the work of the TRC, namely *ubuntu*.

---

failed in the courts because of the reasons he and Archbishop Tutu expound upon, that of former Minister of Defense Magnus Malan and apartheid scientist Dr. Wouter Basson. See also Boesak, *Tenderness*, 171–73.

54. Tutu, *No Future*, 27; see also Boesak, *Tenderness*, 171–73.
55. Tutu, *No Future*, 27–28.
56. Ibid., 28.
57. Ibid.
58. Ibid., 32.
59. Ibid., 32–33.
60. Ibid., 33.

Of course the TRC cared about justice. The Archbishop devotes one whole chapter to it, titled "What About Justice?"[61] The argument is a discussion about retributive justice "in which an impersonal state hands down punishment with little consideration for the victims and hardly any for the perpetrator,"[62] versus the justice the TRC preferred, namely "restorative justice" for the reasons already mentioned above. For the TRC these were the only forms of justice they considered. Restorative justice, writes Michael Batley, "is a theory of justice that emphasises repairing the harm caused or revealed by criminal behaviour, transforming the traditional relationship between communities and their governments in responding to crime."[63]

But Michael Batley actually makes my point. Restorative justice, firmly embedded in criminology and victimology, is based on three principles. First, it requires the aim to restore those who have been injured. Second, those most directly involved and affected by crime should have the opportunity to participate fully in the process of response, and third, government's role is to preserve a just public order and the community's to build and maintain a just peace.[64] Essential to its success is apology, changed behavior, sincerity, and restitution—the payment of a sum of money by the offender "to compensate the victim for the financial losses caused by the crime."[65] So even though the elements of apology, changed behavior, and (monetary) restitution are brought in, essentially restorative justice remains within the realm of criminal justice, which is what the TRC sought to avoid. But ultimately for Batley too, it is "the spirit of *ubuntu*" that drives the process.[66]

Archbishop Tutu claims that this understanding of restorative justice is the "traditional understanding of African jurisprudence," in which

> the central concern is not retribution or punishment, but in the spirit of *ubuntu*, the healing of breaches, the redressing of imbalances, the restoration of broken relationships. This kind of justice seeks to rehabilitate both the victim and the perpetrator, who should be given the opportunity to be integrated into the community he or she has injured by his or her offence. This is a far more personal approach .... Thus we would claim that that justice, restorative justice, is being served when efforts

61. Ibid., 47–60.
62. Ibid., 51.
63. Batley, "Restorative Justice in the South African Context," 21.
64. Ibid., 22.
65. Ibid.
66. Ibid.

are being made to work for healing, for forgiveness and for reconciliation.[67]

Tutu returns to *ubuntu* as the foundational element in the TRC's work again and again, and links it to forgiveness and healing, justice and reconciliation, as well as amnesty and reparations: "Thus our recommendation to the President and parliament provided that a sum of money reasonably significant in amount would be paid to those designated as victims" even though it should be acknowledged that it was really meant to be symbolic rather than substantial.[68]

No one can accuse the TRC of not engaging the question of justice. The question that is being asked is whether the TRC's conception of justice was radical enough to respond to the demands rising from our situation of persistent, historical, deliberated, generational injustices. Is restorative justice adequate for what was required of the TRC? Is it really the doing of justice and the undoing of injustice that is required? Restorative justice is a concept enjoined to the criminal-justice system, and paradoxically ties the TRC to the "crime" paradigm it is avowed to reject. It works with individuals, their restoration, and their re-integration rather than with communities and systemic social change. It limits itself to criminal justice and personal responses to a specific crime but explicitly steers away from systemic socio-economic justice, which is the main problem we have identified in the work of the TRC in this chapter and elsewhere.[69]

True reconciliation means not just the healing of broken relationships, however important that may be, or even reparations, assuming the government is willing to pay for it (which this government was not—and the TRC did not demand reparations from the perpetrators). Reconciliation in its deepest sense is transformation—of the individual, the community and the systems of society (economic and political)—in order to affect justice as genuine restoration: of integrity, of human dignity, and of human contentment, which makes reconciliation as the expression of compassionate justice and love not only possible but durable.[70]

My contention is that the TRC's only choice was not just between retributive and restorative justice, revenge and forgiveness. It was, however, incumbent upon the TRC to move from victim's justice to survivor's justice and from the foundation of political justice to social justice. For Christians social justice is also the indispensable, irreducible biblical demand, and

67. Tutu, *No Future*, 51–52.
68. Ibid., 57.
69. Boesak, *Tenderness*, 171–212.
70. Boesak, "And Zacchaeus Remained in the Tree," 636–54.

inasmuch as the TRC vested itself with an explicitly Christian understanding of reconciliation, that demand is unavoidable and irrevocable.[71]

We are speaking of the justice *required* by Yahweh that deals directly with iniquitous decrees and oppressive statutes and practices. As North American theologian/philosopher Nicholas Wolterstorff says, it is primary and rectifying justice, the overturning of injustice and the bringing of justice. This is to be done as the cause of Yahweh and of Jesus especially toward the bottom ones, the lowly and the downtrodden whose daily condition is one of injustice.[72]

The TRC could have called for *distributive* justice, and it would have produced a better result than the mere juxtaposition of vengeful punishment and restorative justice. In this we follow Hebrew Bible scholar Walter Brueggemann, who asserts,

> The intention of Mosaic justice is to redistribute social goods and social power; thus it is distributive justice. This justice recognises that social goods and social power are unequally and destructively distributed in Israel's world (and derivatively in any social context), and that the well-being of the community requires that social goods and power to some extent be given by those who have too much, for the sake of those who do not have enough.[73]

Tutu's direct call upon Jesus at the TRC hearings would also have made it natural for the TRC to heed the New Testament not only in its call for forgiveness, but also in its call for radical justice, restitution and restoration, despite what Wolterstorff calls its "de-justicizing,"[74] and Richard Horsley its "de-politicizing"[75] by many. "If there is forgiveness in the New Testament" says Wolterstorff correctly, "there has to be justice in the New Testament." Jesus is "the One who brings justice," is the conclusion of his utterly convincing exposition.[76] If this call had been as much at the heart of the TRC process as *ubuntu* had been, the TRC would have called for restitution, not simply reparations, as the Gospel of Luke makes clear in the

---

71. See Tutu, *No Future*, 86; Smit, "The Doing of the Little Righteousness," 359–78; Boesak, *Tenderness*, 171–212.

72. Wolterstorff, *Justice, Rights and Wrongs*, 75.

73. Brueggemann, *Theology of the Old Testament*, 733–36.

74. Wolterstorff, *Justice*, 96–108.

75. Horsley, *Jesus and Empire*, 6.

76. Wolterstorff, *Justice*, 109; 115.

story of Zacchaeus the tax collector and his life-changing moment of radical reconciliation.[77]

This is what it means to give preference to the living. And it has *political* consequences. For the people of the United States, among many other things, it would mean understanding what journalist William Boardman described so eloquently, discussing President Obama's emotional announcement of his executive action regarding gun control measures:

> Instead of weeping for American children already beyond his help, President Obama could act immediately to save still-living Yemeni children by withdrawing US support of the Saudi-led war on Yemen (carried out with weapons from the US and others) . . . The US could end its role in the naval blockade that keeps Yemenis from fleeing the war zone, a blockade that keeps food and other humanitarian aid from Yemeni children and adults alike, a blockade that enforces mass hunger and one of the worst humanitarian crises in the world.[78]

Perhaps Charles Villa-Vicencio's remarks about "the most controversial aspect" of the South African restorative justice process frame the criticism of the process best. That process allowed,

> Perpetrators, some of whom had committed heinous crimes, to receive amnesty in return for acknowledging those crimes and for making full disclosure of them. This meant that at least some of the perpetrators and all those who benefited from apartheid would be free to share in the new society. They would not be required to pay reparations, undertake community service, or face ceremonial purification of any kind. There was a realization that whites and other benefactors were here to stay. They needed to be drawn into society, excused for past crimes, and allowed to keep the material benefits they had acquired during the apartheid years. The intent was to create space where all who had the necessary skills and resources could contribute to building a new society.[79]

---

77. See, for a full explication of the story of Zacchaeus and the demands of radical reconciliation, Boesak, "Just Another Jew in the Ditch," in Boesak and DeYoung, *Radical Reconciliation*, 57–74.

78. See William Boardman, "Saudi Arabia a Force for Stability? Dream On!," http://readersupportednews.org/opinion2/277-75/34487-saudi-arabia-a-force-for-stability-dream-on.

79. Villa-Vicencio, *Walk with Us and Listen*, 105.

It is right here, though, that we see the dire political, social, and human consequences of a concept of justice that is fundamentally wrong for the situation in South Africa and the way the TRC has used it. The problem is also with the *intent* of the restorative justice enterprise as described by Villa-Vicencio. The intent is exclusively focused on the perpetrator, not on the victims: it is the perpetrator who had to be drawn into society, with no thought of the perennial exclusion of the millions of oppressed people from South African society, and how *they* could be welcomed into a "new society" professing a new reality yet still governed by the untransformed realities of the old one.

The TRC's intent excluded all possibilities for the oppressed to offer their skills and resources (perhaps because there were so few) but without even the vaguest acknowledgement that it was the very crimes for which the perpetrators were so quickly excused that have sabotaged possibilities for black people to gain those skills and resources. So Villa-Vicencio's "all" hardly means all. Almost ironically Villa-Vicencio vindicates Mamdani's critique here, namely the mistake of working with "fractured political elites," confining itself to a personal, individualistic process, rather than dealing with systemic and structural issues of justice. We have already referred to Sampie Terreblanche's criticism regarding the undeserved wealth of white South Africans, but perhaps the most important issue here is that the whole intent of the TRC's restorative justice process, while framing itself within the category of "restorative justice," never intended to include justice as the restoration and distribution of power and social goods, and the affirmation of dignity, and hope.

Furthermore, the "intent" is exclusively focused on white South Africans, their concerns, the retention of their wealth, the use of their skills and resources. There is no intent on the radical justice that is needed for rectification and precisely the creation of that "shared future with repairing and healing" at its center as Nelson Mandela promised the people of South Africa. This is an intent so skewed, a framework so broken, a fracture so fundamental that there never really was any chance of a genuine process of reconciliation, let alone one of *radical* reconciliation so deeply necessary in South Africa.

The Spirit of *Ubuntu*

As we have seen, *ubuntu* has figured prominently in and since the TRC. Its work was driven by "the spirit of *ubuntu*" as Archbishop Tutu states, and it was the compelling force behind the desire to find forgiveness in extraordinarily painful, almost impossible moments. Tutu speaks glowingly about *ubuntu* and its meaning, and he is not the only one.[80]

As we have also noted, *ubuntu* is an ancient African notion and is doubtless an enormously powerful philosophy and as a "concept of brotherhood [sic] and unity for survival" it does "empower people to love and respect each other."[81] It is about human acts, but also about being. It is a "set of institutionalised ideals which guide and direct the patterns of life of Africans."[82] *Ubuntu* is instilled into people as "an obligation of love and caring."[83]

"The most powerful public manifestation of *ubuntu* as a present vital force for humanity is the continuing dissipation of the spirit of apartheid," says theologian Augustine Shutte, not referring to political events but rather "the spirit that underlies them." He writes,

> The continuing nonviolent revolution in South Africa would not be possible if those who were for so long oppressed by the apartheid system were not educated and practised in the ethic of *ubuntu*. The real miracle we have witnessed is the survival of the spirit *on such a scale*. The extraordinary manifestations of forgiveness during the hearings of the Truth and Reconciliation Commission, which must be something unique in human history, would not have been possible without it.[84]

There are, however, deep concerns here. I have grave reservations about the way Shutte uncritically equates the "real miracle" with the "survival" of the spirit of *ubuntu* in the "political arena." The way, *and the scale*, on which forgiveness had taken place in South Africa should not only elicit our admiration as Shutte urges us to do. Shutte speaks almost with reverence, but I fear it might be a more romanticised, socially and politically disconnected reverence.

It should also profoundly disturb us, knowing how little depth of understanding and responsive appreciation, from whites in general to the ANC government, there has been of that "uniqueness" in our political arena, except, as Praeg argues above, for the sake of the political argument

---

80. Teffo, "Moral Renewal and African Experiences," 146–69. See also Villa-Vicencio, *Walk with Us and Listen*, ch. 5.

81. Teffo, "Moral Renewal," 164.

82. Mokgethi Motlhabi and Mluleki Munyaka, "*Ubuntu* and its Socio-Moral Significance," in Murove, ed., *African Ethics*, 63–67.

83. Ibid., 76

84. Shutte, "*Ubuntu* as the Ethical Vision," Murove, *African Ethics*, 99. Emphasis original.

of African "exceptionalism." Arguably, the legalities of apartheid had been removed, but in too many ways—our resurgent racism for example, or the widening wealth/poverty gap, or the blatant and shameless ostentation of the new wealthy elite—the "spirit of apartheid" remains alive. In my view, that makes its "uniqueness" in "human history" more questionable than Shutte seems to realize.

Besides, it is entirely arguable that the nonviolent revolution begun in 1976 with the Soweto Uprisings, continued and intensified in the political campaigns of the United Democratic Front between 1983 and 1990, has been cynically, and tragically, appropriated by the ANC's elitist and thoroughly reactionary "national democratic revolution" and that now, 22 years later as I write, we are faced with the very real prospect of a postponed revolution. That this revolution now seems to have been reclaimed by the youth in the current movements for political and social transformation in South Africa, and that it has also reclaimed its nonviolent character, is yet another reason to speak of South Africa's abiding miracles. But it is a miracle profoundly critical of, and elusive for, those in power.

Our question now, however, is not whether *ubuntu* is something South Africa can offer the world; that is, I think, not in dispute. Neither do I want to argue here whether *ubuntu* is a totalitarian tribal notion that undermines our democratic ideal. The question, rather, is whether *ubuntu* is an adequate concept for reconciliation as we understand it, and for all its humanizing aspects, whether it *enables* us to bring about the justice Christians are called to as required by the Lord, in order to make reconciliation sustainable? Or put differently, if *ubuntu* is used as it is by the TRC, does it not take flight before the forces of systemic injustice it is not equipped to deal with?

Without question the concept of *ubuntu*, meshed as it was with the example and exhortations of Jesus, has inspired some to great acts of personal forgiveness. But did it enable the doing of systemic justice and the undoing of systemic injustice? The answer, regrettably, is "no." *Ubuntu*, as understood and applied by the TRC, created much room for personal forgiveness (a burden mostly placed on the victims without a demand for remorse and repentance from the perpetrators) but not for systemic or personal restoration and restitution; it could not call forth remorse and conversion, infused by a sense of justice. It did, according to Archbishop Tutu, lead to a recommendation to the government to pay reparations and to a call on the business community to play a voluntary role in compensating black people for the disadvantages of apartheid. But clearly, as economist Sampie Terreblanche correctly argues, the exploitation of blacks did not happen voluntarily. "It was compulsory and systemic," embedded in a network of compulsory legislation and justified by ideologies "that were propagated as self-evident truths." To expect big business to compensate *voluntarily* and *to the necessary degree* for injustices done over a century is both "idealistic and naïve."[85] And even though the ANC claims *ubuntu* as philosophical possession, in this matter it did not feel morally or politically compelled by it to do what is right towards the victims of apartheid injustice.

Ubuntu is based on the recognition of human worth and the interconnectedness of all persons, but it has scarcely offered an institutionalised imperative for the restoration of the worth and human integrity of women, and certainly not for lesbian, gay, bisexual, transsexual, queer, and intersex persons, for example. For that reason African women employ a "feminist cultural hermeneutics that warns against the uncritical belief in and practice of religion and African culture, especially those aspects which are harmful to women."[86] *Ubuntu* assumes an interdependent humanity, but it does not address the systemic inequalities that today prevail in the relationships, systemic, personal and communal, of women and men, rich and poor, threatening or obliterating human dignity in South Africa, rendering that interdependence well-nigh impossible. It appeals to assumptions of solidarity but it does not speak of rights and wrongs, of oppression and liberation. Justice may be implied, but it is not demanded.

Rather, *ubuntu* calls us to "deeds of kindness, compassion, caring, sharing, solidarity and sacrifice," as Mluleki and Mothlabi point out,[87] but this is not a call for sacrificial engagement on the side of the powerful and privileged for the sake of justice for the oppressed and exploited in order for wrongs to be righted and justice to be done. Without reciprocal sacrificial acts on the part of the beneficiaries justice will never be done, restitution will not become a reality, dignity will not be restored and human contentment will not be secured. As it is, the sacrifice in our reconciliation process was, and remains, decidedly one-sided, coming from those who, even while embracing and honoring *ubuntu*, have already sacrificed too much.

In Munyaradzi Felix Murove's voluminous anthology on African ethics we have been referring to, *ubuntu* is described as a "spirituality" that must also serve as inspiration to create a different, gentler kind of capitalism, a correction of the "extractive capitalist model."[88] But *ubuntu* is not found as critique of capitalism despite the evidence of devastation caused by neoliberal capitalism globally of which our political and economic elites have become such ardent supporters and willing collaborators; of the crises

---

85. Terreblanche, "Dealing with Systemic Economic Injustice," 268

86. Isabel Apawo Phiri and Sarojini Nadar, "'The Personal is Political': Faith and Religion in a Public University," unpublished paper, University of KwaZulu-Natal, 2010.

87. "*Ubuntu*," in Murove, *African Ethics*, 74

88. Barbara Nussbaum, "*Ubuntu* and Business: Reflections and Questions," in Murove, *African Ethics*, 238–58.

caused by that system and the attendant dangers of blatant consumerism and material greed already ravaging our society and those very values *ubuntu* espouses.[89]

Nowhere is *ubuntu* employed to critique and challenge the reality that our society is arranged in such a way as to deliberately place some (the wealthy and privileged elite) at the top and others (the impoverished masses) at the bottom. Doing justice means that one not only recognizes that the other is human, but that the other is trampled upon, purposely put, and kept, at the bottom.

Nicholas Wolterstorff again offers an extremely valuable insight in this regard. It is an insight crucial to our understanding of justice, of rights and wrongs, and of the bringing of justice to the wronged. "Metaphors common in present-day discourse," he writes, "are those of *the margin* and *the outside*."[90] Some people are in the center, some on the circumference, and some are on the outside. Biblical writers, however, worked instead with the image of up and down. Some are at the top of the social hierarchy, some at the bottom.

They are at the bottom not because of their own fault; they are there because they are downtrodden. Those at the top "trample the heads of the poor into the dust of the earth" (Amos 2:7). "When *center* and *circumference* are one's basic metaphors, the undoing of justice will be described as *including* the outsiders. When *up* and *down* are one's basic metaphors, the undoing of injustice will be described as *lifting up* those at the bottom. The poor do not have to be included in the social order; they have always been there, usually indispensable to its functioning. They have to be lifted up."[91] Remembering Pope Francis's reasoning from chapter 2, it is important to note that the poor are included with the aim of exploitation: they are indispensable as a source of cheap labor. But they are not included with the aim of sharing equally in the rewards of their labor.

The aim, it seems to me, is not charity or even solidarity, but equality:

> God raises the poor from the dust,
>
> And lifts the needy from the ash heap
>
> To make them sit with princes. (Ps 113:7)

---

89. This is all the more remarkable since that same volume offers extremely valuable insights into the contribution of the philosophy of *ubuntu* as a global ethic on the matter of ecological justice and responsibility. See, e.g., Benezet Bujo, "Ecology and Ethical Responsibility from an African Perspective," 281–97; Mogobe B. Ramose, "Ecology through *Ubuntu*," 308–14; Munyaradzi Felix Murove, "An African Environmental Ethic Based on the Concepts of *Ukama* and *Ubuntu*," 315–32.

90. Wolterstorff, *Justice*, 123–24.

91. Ibid., 123, original emphasis.

This is also true of the New Testament, Wolterstorff argues. A striking feature of the New Testament writings and of Jesus' preaching, he says, is the frequency with which the up-and-down metaphor common in the writings of the Hebrew Bible is employed to say something that the writers of the Hebrew Bible at most hint at. "The rectification of injustice requires not only the *lifting up* of the low ones but *casting down* the high ones. The coming of justice requires social inversion."[92]

Ubuntu knows no such radical call. It is a wonderful concept that calls upon values without which human community is not really possible, but justice is irreplaceable. *Ubuntu* needs the imperative to the doing of justice and the undoing of injustice that is so pervasive in the writings of the Bible, the imperative to the radical overturning of the unjust social order so that justice is done. For the doing of even the small deeds of righteousness we need the full power of the conviction that justice is Yahweh's cause, as it is the cause of Jesus; that the pursuit of justice for the lowly and the downtrodden, the weak and the wronged is our enduring calling: "Justice and only justice you shall pursue" (Deut 16:18–20). Turning the present revolutionary fervor firmly towards this understanding of justice as the foundation of reconciliation in South Africa as well as globally seems to me to be a way of keeping the revolution and its drivers most effectively accountable to their own dreams and aspirations and to the common good.

Ubuntu Renewed?

In Charles Villa-Vicencio's view, South Africans have fallen short of the ideal of *ubuntu*.[93] He is correct. We have not only fallen short, we have worked hard to erase whatever potential for justice there might have been in *ubuntu* from *ubuntu* in our zeal to make it as malleable and harmless a concept as possible.

But, Villa-Vicencio goes on to say, it remains nonetheless an ideal those who are trying to extricate themselves from a terrible past would do well to consider, "allowing it to challenge any sense of complacency in their nation-building endeavours. *Ubuntu*, progressively understood and adapted to meet the challenges of modernity, offers a cultural incentive to promote a level of communal co-existence among individuals, clans, ethnic groups, and nations that lingers in the ethos and memory of a continent devastated by greed, conflict and war."[94]

92. Ibid., original emphasis.
93. Villa-Vicencio, *Walk With Us*, 127.
94. Ibid., 127.

These are wise words, and while the African continent itself is in deep need of an *ubuntu* in need of *ubuntu*, it is perhaps the greatest gift Africans have to offer the world. However, in light of our discussion on these matters, simply "meeting the challenges of modernity" would not seem to be sufficient. "Modernity" in and of itself has not brought justice, equity, and a fulfilled life for the vast majority of God's children. On the contrary, "modernity" in every age has brought renewed forms of imperialism, colonialism and oppression, domination and subjugation for the peoples of the world not considered "modern" enough by the empires of the powerful who define the terms of modernity and civilization.

A renewed understanding of *ubuntu* would have to come to mean meeting the challenges of understanding these issues and responding to the demands of human dignity, human contentment, and the indivisibility of justice. It would also mean that we must dare to reclaim our agency so that we do not get drowned in mournful regret that we have perhaps lost both *ubuntu* and her spirit. That means a relentless determination to claim the ability to create something new.

It is only then that South Africa, "a hopeless case if ever there was one," yet chosen by God "for others to look at and take courage," will become "the beacon of hope" as Desmond Tutu prays. It is only then that "this tired, disillusioned, cynical world, hurting so frequently and so grievously," will come to see "more than just a glimmer of hope in what we have attempted in South Africa."[95]

Shortly before his death, veteran ANC leader Govan Mbeki, in speaking of national reconciliation, underscored the need to balance "having and belonging" in the reconciliation process in South Africa and beyond. "People—all people, both black and white, Hutu and Tutsi, Shona and Ndebele—need to feel they are part of a new nation...."[96] Govan Mbeki would not have been offended if we reclaimed his words not just for the peoples of Africa, but for the people of the world, in searching for and working towards a new humanity and the true ubuntufication of our world.

So, stripped of all philosophical mystification, political manipulation, and romantic obfuscation, this is what *ubuntu* must come to mean: people *having*—dignity, justice, worth, security, cherished humanity; and people *belonging*—to each other, to the human family, to that world which is a "home for all" of which Luthuli spoke. There must come a time when *ubuntu* is neither an unattainable ethical dream, nor a fig leaf for our deceit of those who are most vulnerable, looking at the purity of their most

---

95. Tutu, *No Future*, 282.
96. In Villa-Vicencio, *Walk with Us*, 96.

precious traditions through muddied waters from the bottom of the well. Neither must *ubuntu* be the replacement of justice and equality, the blanket with which we smother the hopes and yearnings of the oppressed and the excluded for having and belonging. There must come a time when *ubuntu* must no longer flee from us, hiding herself in fear of being ravaged by our deceitful politics, our destructive rapaciousness, and our mindless violence. Among us and in our search for justice and peace and a reconciled community she must find refuge and safety, and a sacred space to sing and dance with all her children, celebrating herself in our redeemed humanity.

CHAPTER 5

"The Righteousness of Our Strength"

Reconciliation, Justice, and the Historic Obligation of the Oppressed

> So you just start to pay attention, pay a lot more attention to what's going on, and your heart gets bigger because your fight gets bigger.
>
> —ALEXIS TEMPLETON, 2015

Being Responsible for the Miracle

In the course of my work in South Africa during 2011–12 I engaged university students, community leaders, youth leaders, and representatives of community organizations in a yearlong series of discussions we called "Conversations on Reconciled Diversity." Understandably, South Africa's reconciliation process, especially since the work of the Truth and Reconciliation Commission, was a mainstay in these fascinating, challenging, and truly energizing conversations. What is reconciliation and what does it mean when we apply it not only to personal relationships but to the restoration of justice and dignity in politics and society? We have confronted this same question in the conversations with the young activists in Ferguson every time I had gone there at the invitation of the Black Lives Matter Movement and the churches involved in the struggle there.[1]

---

1. Over the weekend of October 29 to November 2, 2015, the whole event was organized under the title "Radical Reconciliation" with a full morning's plenary devoted to "A Faithful Vision of Reconciliation and Justice."

The subject of our present discussion in this chapter is a direct challenge from a student in one of these conversations in South Africa. "Why," he wanted to know with more than just a bit of agitation, "is it always the responsibility of black people in this country to hold out the hand of friendship, to forgive, to beg white people for reconciliation?" It is a question I have been hearing with greater urgency than before, and not just from young people. It is not a comfortable question. This time the young student added a rider. "Your generation," he told me, "you, the Tutus and the Mandelas have convinced us about reconciliation and we believed you. But you failed to bring whites to the table. Why is it now the responsibility of my generation to seek still reconciliation with people who are not interested? I do not want to hear an apology from them. All I want is to see that they are really with us in building this nation. That would be reconciliation for me."

The question has of course far wider implications than just South Africa and our struggle with reconciliation in our striving toward a just, truly non-racial, diverse, and inclusive democracy. It has to do with something all oppressed people have been struggling with for a long time and which, in the now famous formulation by Paulo Freire, goes as follows:

> This then, is the great humanistic and historical task of the oppressed: to liberate themselves and their oppressors as well. The oppressors, who oppress, exploit, and rape by virtue of their power, cannot find in this power the strength to liberate themselves. Only power that springs from the weakness of the oppressed will be sufficiently strong to free both.[2]

This important assertion is the wider context within which our student's question is embedded with its universal implications for oppressed people everywhere. In the face of the present revolutionary upheavals, with young people taking the lead everywhere, the question becomes all the more relevant and urgent. We shall return to this broader context. But first it is necessary to gain some understanding of the immediate South African context within which the question was posed.

In our conversations we had touched on aspects of Archbishop Desmond Tutu's bestselling book *No Future without Forgiveness* and the archbishop's insistence that oppressed Africans, because of both the Christian faith and the African philosophy of *ubuntu,* have an obligation to forgive and create a life of harmony for all, including the perpetrators of the crimes of apartheid. For Tutu the implications are also wider than his concerns about black and white in South Africa. It is not only God's intention and the example of Jesus, the Archbishop writes, but it is the "better thing for which

2. Freire, *Pedagogy of the Oppressed*, 21.

we are meant," for "God has set in motion a centripetal process, a moving towards the centre, towards unity, harmony, goodness, peace and justice; one that removes barriers."[3]

We were also discussing Chief Albert Luthuli who, at the end of his autobiography, wrestles with South Africa's future, his own desire for a non-racial South Africa that he envisions as "a home for all," built in a "new land," for "black, white and brown, from the ruins of the old, narrow groups, a synthesis of the rich cultural strains we have inherited."[4] He believed that beyond the strife and the struggle for freedom "there beckons a civilization, a culture which will take its place in the parade of God's history . . . " That has always been black South Africans' dream, a dream kept alive throughout the decades of struggle and in the face of incredible odds. But simultaneously Luthuli raises an anxious but honest question as he worries about the response of his white compatriots: "Will the outstretched hand be taken? (. . .) I fear not . . . it is a black hand."[5]

At this point of our history, of increasing racial alienation and open racist animosity and growing, unsustainable socio-economic inequalities, it seems that many white people still do not want "that black hand," and increasingly black people, young people especially, are asking whether it is worth it—waiting for that hand to be taken. Simultaneously, and disturbingly, as one watches what happens on social media, black and white racist talk is ratcheted up as the gap widens. And it is not just social media. The intellectual discourse on race is also shifting rapidly, in great measure because of the many disappointments and the very real disillusionments that have set in since 1994.[6] Not since our democratization has South Africa's dream of a non-racial democracy come under such intense pressure.

3. Tutu, *No Future without Forgiveness*, 213.
4. Luthuli, *Let My People Go!* 229–30.
5. Ibid., 230.
6. See Mangcu, ed., *What Colour is Our Future?* One of the problems South Africans face, writes Mangcu in his Preface, is that "the concept of non-racialism has come to take on a different meaning in post-apartheid South Africa, used more now to defend than to fight racial inequality," xviii. Hence also the title of one of the contributions, by Suren Pillay, "Why I Am No Longer a Non-racialist: Identity and Difference," 133–52. Earlier, Mangcu has expressed his deep concern about "black nativism," the "mysticism" that makes it possible, and the political consequences of such mysticism. Mangcu quotes Ivor Chipkin with approval: "Blacks, because of their very blackness are reversing the legacy of apartheid. Anyone who disputes that is against blacks, and therefore against the reversal of apartheid, whether that is actually happening or not. And thus there is a certain form of knowing through belief that is accessible only to black people; belief (that the government is authentically Black) does not derive from the facts (data collected, sorted and interrogated by reason). Rather the facts are revealed through belief"; see Mangcu, *To The Brink, The State of Democracy in South Africa*, 41, 42.

Inevitably also, forgiveness is part of the conversation. Tirelessly, Desmond Tutu pleads for us to remember that in the act of forgiveness "we are declaring our faith in the future of a relationship and in the capacity of the wrongdoer to make a new beginning on a course that will be different from the one that caused us the wrong."[7] Unwillingness to forgive "keeps us in prison," and we should offer forgiveness even before it is asked; "Jesus did not wait until those who were nailing him to the cross had asked for forgiveness."[8]

But the archbishop is not completely unaware of the difficulties and realities, and he sounds a dire warning and an exhortation to whites:

> In South Africa, the whole process of reconciliation has been placed in very considerable jeopardy by the enormous disparities between the rich, mainly the whites, and the poor, mainly the blacks. The huge gap between the haves and the have-nots, which was largely created and maintained by racism and apartheid, poses the greatest threat to reconciliation and stability in our country. The rich provided the class from which the perpetrators and the beneficiaries of apartheid came and the poor produced the bulk of the victims. That is why I have exhorted whites to be keen to see transformation taking place in the lot of blacks. For unless houses replace the hovels and shacks in which most blacks live; unless blacks gain access to clean water, electricity, affordable health care, decent education, good jobs and a safe environment—all things which the vast majority of whites have taken for granted for so long—we can kiss goodbye to reconciliation.[9]

I have quoted Desmond Tutu at length because it remains remarkable how so many people, but mostly whites, in a conscious and unconscious process of domestication, always remember and cite him on his admonitions to blacks to forgive, but forget his stern words of warning and his call on them to do justice.[10]

Mangcu speaks of the time of Thabo Mbeki's presidency and could not foresee what even more disastrous proportions this nativism would take under the rule of the ANC under President Jacob Zuma. This shows that the malady was not only a question of Mbeki and his style of governing; it is a matter of the ANC and its values, politics, and self-mystifying beliefs, no matter who the president might be.

7. Tutu, *No Future*, 220.

8. Ibid.

9. Ibid., 273–74.

10. It is a not unknown phenomenon, similar to the domestication of Martin Luther King Jr., that authors have increasingly begun to recognize. For an excellent discussion

In addition, former president F. W. de Klerk's insensitive repetitions of his "let bygones be bygones" stance have become the impatient mantra from too many white people that black people must, now that the TRC is over and had done its work, allow South Africa "to move on." The disillusionment is widespread. No less a figure than former University of Cape Town principal Dr. Mamphela Ramphele now speaks of our mostly peaceful transition as "the miracle that never was."[11]

But this is what is behind the student's anger, and his polite but unhidden impatience with people like myself and Archbishop Tutu. More recently, Desmond Tutu has become decidedly critical about certain aspects of the TRC, especially the government's tardiness in following up on the matters of justice he himself had raised to which we alluded earlier. In an interview in 2003, Tutu speaks forthrightly:

> Can you explain how a black person wakes up in a squalid ghetto today, almost ten years after freedom? Then goes to work in town, which is still largely white, in palatial homes. And at the end of the day, he goes home to squalor? I don't know why those people don't just say, "To hell with peace. To hell with Tutu and the Truth Commission."[12]

---

on the matter, see Baldwin and Burrow, eds., *The Domestication of Martin Luther King Jr.*. The editors write (xiii–xiv), "'I Have a Dream' may be the best known and the most widely quoted speech in American history . . . it has come to represent the quintessence of American democratic idealism . . . Conveniently forgotten is the man who berated America for its excessive materialism and militarism, who stated admiration for Karl Marx and who regarded Sweden's social democracy as a model that the United States of America would do well to follow." See also, e.g., Dyson, *I May Not Get There With You*, xv: "We have sanitized his ideas, ignoring his mistrust of white America, his commitment to black solidarity and advancement, and the radical message of his later life. Today right-wing conservatives can quote King's speeches in order to criticize affirmative action, while schoolchildren grow up learning only about the great pacifist, not the hard-nosed critic of economic injustice." For my reflections on a somewhat similar process regarding Desmond Tutu, see Boesak and DeYoung, *Radical Reconciliation*, ch. 8. Chapter 6 below, in a different contextual framework, raises the same questions regarding Nelson Mandela.

11. Ramphele, *Laying Ghosts to Rest*, 28. She describes the notion of a miraculous transition as "convenient" for those who want to forget their past role in apartheid; it permits "amnesia over the betrayal of black people" by the UK as former colonial power; it leaves "unexamined" the past role of those who present themselves as "defenders of democracy today" as well as the dubious role of the international community. It poses the "risk" of "losing the lessons of history" and the very language itself promotes "fatalism" in political affairs as well as a feeling of "entitlement to wield power over others," 31–32.

12. Joseph Nevins, "Truth, Lies and Accountability: In Search of Justice in East Timor," *Boston Review*, January/February, 2007, cited in Ramphele, *Ghosts*, 66. My own critique of the TRC, especially as regards its neglect of social justice, apart from my

Many have argued that the great value of the TRC was in allowing the victims of apartheid crimes to tell their stories, to expose the nation to the wounds caused by apartheid, a matter we have alluded to in the Introduction. This was not just storytelling, Desmond Tutu argues. Through the Truth Commission, "they would be *empowered*, allowed to remember and in this public recounting their individuality and inalienable humanity would be acknowledged."[13] And if indeed they did not hear the full truth from the perpetrators of apartheid crimes,[14] and perhaps were too traumatized or bewildered, or simply had no desire to understand the academic distinctions between "social truth," or "forensic factual truth," they at least had, in Judge Ismail Mahomed's memorable phrase, the "truth of wounded memories"[15] with which they could confront their torturers and the nation.

The meaningfulness of this process cannot be underestimated, but inevitably the question arises, and it is not a cynical "*So what?*," but a concerned "What then?"

"Forgiveness Is Killing Us"

These are the words of a religious leader from Mangaung, the township near Bloemfontein, in one of our community leaders' "Reconciled Diversity" conversations. This is a much older person than our student, not angry or cynical, a pastor for whom the word "forgiveness" is "sacred," he says, "because of Jesus." He does not mean that forgiveness in our situation is impossible, or that it is wrong to forgive apartheid's criminals. His concern is that the forgiveness offered is being rejected out of hand, since "no one has asked for it" because they do not think they need it; or apology was given and then rationalized "out of existence" as Archbishop Tutu said of F. W. de Klerk; or it was "accepted" under false pretences, literally making it a cruel joke.[16] It is

---

remarks in chapter 4 above, can be found in Boesak, *The Tenderness of Conscience*, ch. 6; and in *Running with Horses*, ch. 13, a popularized and somewhat expanded version of the more academic examination of the issue in Boesak, "And Zacchaeus Remained in the Tree," 633–54.

13. *No Future*, 33, my emphasis.

14. See Bell and Ntsebeza, *Unfinished Business*, 7: "In little more than six months in 1993, while the political parties of the apartheid state negotiated with the representatives of liberation movements, some 44 metric tons of records from the head quarters of the National Intelligence Service alone were destroyed." They call it a "veritable paper Auschwitz."

15. Tutu, *No Future*, 33.

16. A certain Jacques Hechter, a captain in the apartheid Security Police and a member of the notorious Vlakplaas unit, offers a shocking example of not only the abuse of the amnesty offer from the TRC but also the abuse of forgiveness and reconciliation,

cheapened. When this happens, righteous anger, which has its rightful place in this process,[17] often turns into bitterness. Instead of living in the freedom of forgiveness we offered in faith, we are then left to fester in the loss of retribution that we had declined in trust.

This process is made much more difficult by the fact that black people in South Africa were not only asked to forgive at a personal level, but also at a communal level. Communal forgiveness, writes liberation theologian and ethicist Miguel de la Torre, "is the decision of the whole not to seek revenge, a decision that leads toward, and is also the product of, reconciliation."[18] The best examples of this kind of forgiveness are perhaps the political forgiveness offered in the decision at the negotiations at Kempton Park to accept the paradigm shift in our thinking on the question of justice, and the embrace of survivor's justice as we discussed in chapter 4 and the forgiveness Nelson Mandela, on the day of his release on February 11, 1990, offered to South Africa's white community in that famous speech from the balcony of Cape Town city hall.

There Mandela spoke not just for or about himself, but for all of South Africa's oppressed people, taking the risk on their behalf, or perhaps more precisely, placing the risk of forgiveness and reconciliation on all our shoulders. I speak of the risk of white people not accepting this incredible magnanimity, not even understanding the gift the victims of their oppression were offering them, as well as the risk of black people not willing to make such a commitment on trust and no guarantees of the reciprocity of justice whatsoever. While personal forgiveness of the kind that the victims of apartheid crimes were asked to offer their tormentors during the amnesty hearings was extraordinarily difficult and challenging, in many ways more than those not in such situations can begin to understand, communal forgiveness is no less challenging.

It involves communal and external dynamics that are unpredictable and uncontrollable. It raises questions of power and powerlessness and authority: who has the right to forgive on behalf of a community and how does one get, or dare ask for, community consensus on something as sensitive, as political, and, in the words of our pastor, as sacred, as forgiveness? Personal

---

as well as of the victims of his crimes. After "confessing" and showing "remorse" and receiving the promise of amnesty, Hechter emerged from the room laughing and telling journalists, "Ach, I'm not f***n sorry for what I did. I fought for my country, I believed in what I did, and I did a good job . . . I'll do it again . . . No, man, I'm not really f***n sorry for what I did . . ." Graybill, *Truth and Reconciliation in South Africa*, 52. See also the discussion in Boesak, *Tenderness*, 190–91.

17. See Boesak, *Tenderness*, 195–98.
18. De La Torre, *Liberating Jonah*, 119.

forgiveness calls for a deeply personal response; communal forgiveness needs a sustained systemic response. It raises the bar of spiritual and political maturity very high indeed.

But communal forgiveness cannot unite a disjointed community until injustices that continue to create the powerful and the powerless are dealt with, de la Torre argues. "Communal forgiveness that is substituted for justice makes a mockery of both," he says, and then makes an even stronger point: "There can be no communal forgiveness without a profound realignment of how power operates in society . . . communal forgiveness can only occur within a relationship based on justice and equality."[19]

But this is exactly the problem South Africans are now facing. Beginning with the Kempton Park negotiations and in the TRC process, blacks, the victims of apartheid, have offered political, personal, and communal forgiveness, on the basis of trustful political judgment, the Christian gospel and *ubuntu*, a philosophy of life at whose center is the search for (and the restoration of) harmonious human relationships. They were asked, again and again, to go "beyond retributive justice to restorative justice, to move on to forgiveness, because without it there (really) was no future."[20] President Nelson Mandela in his State of the Nation address on May 10, 1994, and in his address to both Houses of Parliament just a week or so later, was equally insistent, setting the bar for the victims of apartheid, morally and politically, quite high:

> [South Africans] must be constrained . . . regardless of the accumulated effect of our historical burdens, seizing the time to define for ourselves what we want of our shared destiny . . . The nation must come to terms with its past in a spirit of oneness and forgiveness and proceed to build the future on the basis of repairing and healing.[21]

So, on grounds of pure political necessity, and for the sake of an unguaranteed "shared destiny" with their oppressors, black people were asked to "come to terms with" apartheid's past in a "spirit of oneness and forgiveness," building the future on the basis of repairing and healing, *regardless of the accumulated effect of our historical burdens*. This is truly setting the bar high. But we have come to see just how much the weight of those historical burdens, and their unaddressed, unresolved consequences, rest disproportionately on the shoulders of the victims, historically and now presently,

---

19. Ibid., 120.

20. Tutu, *No Future*, 209.

21. Nelson Mandela, Joint Sitting of Both Houses of Parliament, May 24, 1994, cols. 1–15, cited in Villa-Vicencio, *Walk With Us and Listen*, 98.

while the beneficiaries of apartheid had no such burden to shoulder. Certainly not to the same measure.

As we have seen, the secret deals already made long before Mr. Mandela made his appeal excluded the people, their wounds and their longings, their pain and their aspirations and hence *their* healing, from that future. In truth, there has been, and still is, no reciprocity or equality, which could only take the form of social justice, and which would, aside from any moral argument, but precisely *on grounds of political necessity* should have been imperative. There was no restitution. There were not even the meager monetary reparations the TRC had asked the government to consider.[22] If there is no justice and equality; if there is not an equal sharing of the burdens of the past; and if the ongoing situation is one that continues to privilege the beneficiaries of the past and their elite counterparts in the black communities, one might legitimately ask how the future is to be a "shared" future.

Moreover, in South Africa power has indeed changed hands but there was no "profound" realignment of power, no real redistribution of power, and no use of that power for the sake of justice, equality, and dignity, and *that* is the great deceit, the incomprehensible betrayal of black people, and of their trust in the reconciliation process, perhaps even of their faith.[23] While we are not denying that apartheid impaired the humanity of blacks as well as whites and healing is needed for all, there can be no denying as to who caused those historical burdens, who had to bear the brunt of them, who benefited from them and for whom repairing and healing is most needed. Without this historical honesty, this becomes the forgiveness that kills.

I have alluded to this matter in chapter 4; now we should explore this yet further. In a discussion of journalist and political economist Christi van der Westhuizen's book *White Power and the Rise and Fall of the National Party*,[24] South African economist Sampie Terreblanche, in a paper tellingly titled "From White Power to White Wealth: The Unresolved Moral Crisis of White South Africans," spells out in chilling detail the historic injustices that should have been addressed in order to make reconciliation just, humane,

---

22. Tutu, *No Future*, 57.

23. Cf. Calland, *Anatomy of South Africa*: "Indeed, the principal question for us all is this: Having won the vote in 1994, do the people have power and do they govern? Regrettably, despite the dramatic change of 1994, the great majority of South Africans remain marginalized from real power and excluded from full participation in society due to unemployment and chronic poverty" (xiii). After his thorough analysis Calland concludes, "While much has changed on the surface and within the infrastructure of governance—built around the Constitution—beneath it the same interest groups control real power, even though many of the faces have changed. *Plus ça change*" (279).

24. van der Westhuizen, *White Power and the Rise and Fall of the National Party*, 240–46.

and sustainable.²⁵ Terreblanche, as can be seen from the title of his paper, not only sees the history of inequality and injustice in South Africa as a political or economic problem applicable to all South Africans. For him it is especially a *moral crisis* for white South Africans. We shall follow him closely as he develops this argument, since it is crucial for understanding why the reconciliation process in South Africa has become so important and what it has to do with the key question in our reflection, namely the historical obligation of the oppressed for the liberation of the oppressor.

In her impressive book, van der Westhuizen discusses two "Elite Pacts" that have dominated South Africa's political and economic history. The first lasted from 1909 to 1994; the second started in 1994.²⁶ Justified by different permutations of three ideological positions, namely social Darwinism, civilization, and religion, whites used their monopoly of power to perpetuate the Elite Pact of 1909 until 1994. Terreblanche would later refer to these not simply as "pacts," but as "elite conspiracies." ²⁷

Whites, Terreblanche writes, used this power to "enrich the whites *undeservedly* and to impoverish the blacks *undeservedly*."²⁸ Notice three key concepts here Terreblanche deliberately employs: "enrichment," "impoverishment," and "undeserved." Thus from the start we are disabused of the myths of domination, of romantic notions about "poverty" as if it was the natural, God-given state of black people; "enrichment," as if wealth was a blessing from God especially to whites or the just reward for their industry. It is about *processes* of *impoverishment* and *wealth creation* and the fact that both these conditions were not only deliberate, but "undeserved." Both impoverishment and enrichment are interdependent, active, continuing, deeply systemic processes, based on and bolstered by deliberate policies designed to create victims and beneficiaries.

Terreblanche then proceeds to lay bare the systemic nature of both undeserved wealth and undeserved impoverishment. During the first three quarters of the twentieth century, Terreblanche writes, whites were always less than 22 percent of the total population but consistently received more

25. Terreblanche, "From White Power to White Wealth: The Unresolved Moral Crisis of White South Africans," unpublished paper, November 1, 2007.

26. One should point out that these elite pacts did not emerge *ex nihilo*. They come on top of, and as logical consequence of, already firmly established patterns of genocide, dispossession, oppression, and slavery through colonialism and apartheid over almost three centuries since 1652. All of these were deeply systemic and relentlessly generational, and all of these were built on the same ideological rationalizations: social Darwinism, civilization, and religion. Terreblanche is not unaware of this; see, e.g., his *A History of Inequality in South Africa*.

27. Terreblanche, *Lost in Transformation*, 178-79.

28. Terreblanche, "From White Power to White Wealth," 5.

than 70 percent of total income. The Africans were almost 70 percent of the population and consistently received less than 20 percent of total income. "Let us not try to diminish the extent of the whites' *undeserved* enrichment or the blacks' *undeserved* impoverishment," he cautions. "Both were very great," bringing with them high levels of racial inequality and racial hostility.[29]

The period from 1974 to 1994 was a "transition period," the period of struggle. But during this time, the household income of the top 20 percent of black households increased by 40 percent, while the household income of the poorest 60 percent of blacks—who were already poor in 1974—declined by almost 30 percent. The top 20 percent of blacks were "pampered by the whites"—in both the political and economic spheres—in an attempt to convince them of the virtues of apartheid. In 1994 this top 20 percent was a middle class in-the-making, while the poorest 60 percent was already caught in a vicious circle of poverty. "They were already drawn into a pauperization process that was perpetuating itself."[30]

The second Elite Pact of 1994, after the negotiated settlement, took effect under the tutelage of the United States and the Bretton Woods Institutions, instituting a new power constellation and a new politico-economic system. "It was from the outset a *black elitist* and a *neo-liberal capitalist* construct."[31] The economic side is controlled by what Terreblanche calls "the non-racial South African corporate sector," by global corporatism, and by the Washington ideology of market fundamentalism.[32] The second Elite Pact was an agreement between Johannesburg (local corporatism), New York (global corporatism), and Washington (market fundamentalism, the "trickle-down," myth and the conditionality of "good governance").[33]

> ANC policies over the past 13 years have created a black elite ... of +- 2 million people and a black middle class of +- 6 million. The gap between the +-8 million rich blacks and the 20 million to 25 million poor blacks has become dangerously big. The other 10 to 15 million blacks are neither poor nor rich. The fact that +-20% of blacks have become rich and even very rich, while 60% of blacks remain poor and have to live in deteriorating socio-economic conditions, is a deplorable and dangerous state of affairs.[34]

29. Ibid.
30. Ibid., 5, 6.
31. Ibid., 6. Emphasis original.
32. Ibid.
33. See Klein, *The Shock Doctrine*, ch. 10, "Democracy Born in Chains," 194–217.
34. Terreblanche, "From White Power to White Wealth," 9

The point Terreblanche correctly feels compelled to make is that "the poverty of the poorest half of the population represents a situation of *multiple deprivations.*" It is as if the ANC government "does not understand the strong dynamism of the pauperization process that perpetuates and intensifies itself from one generation to the following—especially in a system of neo-liberal global capitalism."[35] The "vicious circle" has also become a downward spiral.

The contradictions caused by these realities are sobering: "We are faced with the contradictory situation that at least 80% of the whites who were already rich in 1994—thanks to apartheid—are now much richer, while 60% of the blacks who were already poor in 1994—as a direct result of apartheid—are now poorer."[36] Then Terreblanche asks the moral question: "*What are we doing in this country?*"[37] As a white person, Terreblanche then has a "final word" for whites: "We have proceeded from white power to white wealth, but we should realize that our moral crisis is far from being resolved. On the contrary, it is as grave as ever."[38]

The unique gift of the TRC, write theologians Emanuel Katongole of Notre Dame and Chris Rice, both formerly from Duke University, "is not that it revealed the truth about historic injustices, but that it did it within an atmosphere of mercy and forgiveness . . . In other words, a new South Africa is not possible without the unique gifts of the TRC . . . without the politics of repentance."[39] But the issues clearly are not this simple. Indeed mercy and forgiveness were abundant, offered almost exclusively by the victims of apartheid, certainly more than any white perpetrator or beneficiary of apartheid deserved. But there certainly was no "politics" of repentance, not from whites in general and not from apartheid politicians in particular. Not even personal repentance by the perpetrators was required before the TRC, only "the truth" such as it was presented, and no political, much less personal repentance was offered by the beneficiaries of apartheid in general. A few cases such as that of Ginn Fourie do more to give credit to the

---

35. Ibid., 8–9, original emphasis. See also Calland, *Anatomy of South Africa*, 279: "Apartheid capitalism has given way to post-apartheid capitalism. Ownership and control of the commanding heights of the economy, the repressive apparatus of the state . . . the army, police and judiciary, the civil service . . . tertiary education and strategic research and development have remained substantially in the same hands as during the heyday of apartheid" (quoting Neville Alexander, *An Ordinary Country*, 64). See also Bond, *Elite Transition*.

36. Terreblanche, "From White Power to White Wealth," 12.

37. Ibid.

38. Ibid.

39. Katongole and Rice, *Reconciling All Things*, 103.

"miraculous" element in South Africa's reconciliation process than the romantic interpretations of Rice and Katongole, in my view.[40] In light of these realities and the daily experiences and ongoing struggles of black, poor, and deprived South Africans, such starry-eyed appraisals are not very useful, and in fact totally misleading.

If one understands the realities spelled out above, one also understands what I have earlier called the permanentization of division, separation, and inequality as perhaps the deepest and most overwhelming legacy of apartheid. It is not just the physical, spatial separation—the townships will forever remain kilometers away from the towns and cities, causing permanent strains on the meager economic resources of township dwellers, as well as making psychological transformation of racialized mind sets through social contact and the building of human relationships extraordinarily difficult. Social cohesion is crippled almost before it can begin. All this is embedded in this history of deliberate, systemic inequality Terreblanche describes, which not only did not end with official apartheid in 1994, but was enshrined in the new Elite Pact of 1994. This has secured a "perpetuation of pauperization" as Terreblanche correctly says, but it should not be reason to allow any permanentization of injustice.

Reconciliation: Hope for a Shared Destiny?

There are some important reasons why the Truth and Reconciliation Commission and consequently the reconciliation process are so decisive for South Africa. It is not only that we chose to reject the Nuremberg model of retributive justice in favor of a model of political justice.[41] In itself that is significant enough. The victims of apartheid gave up (some might argue "were deprived of") the right to punishment for perpetrators and absolved them from "crime," even though apartheid was indeed a Crime Against Humanity. But on top of that, our model of reconciliation has been held up as example for the world, which countries like Rwanda and Liberia were urged to follow. We did not become a Bosnia, Serbia, or a Croatia, drenched in blood. "Our freedom has been bought at a very great price," Desmond Tutu concedes, but to compute the price properly,

> we should compare the high level of stability that we enjoy with the turmoil and upheaval that have so sadly characterized similar radical change in the former Soviet Union, not to mention the awful carnage and instability in the former Yugoslavia . . .[42]

40. See De Gruchy, *Reconciliation*, 165–66, 170.
41. See the discussion in chapter 4.
42. Tutu, *No Future*, 52.

That is doubtless true, but also I think our process is so important for South Africans because we have invested so much in it: our struggle with its hopes, ideals and aspirations; the sacrifices made in the hope for the future, for justice and equality and dignity; our trust in the revered and iconic political leadership for whom we fought when they themselves could not; our belief in the rightness of our cause; the very spirituality of our politics upon which we staked our lives. Fundamental to this is the belief that through reconciliation we would become, in the words of Nelson Mandela, "a nation at peace with itself and the world."[43] At stake is also our faith, the very faith which carried black people through more than three centuries of struggle and suffering, determination and hope.[44]

Politicians have known this from the very beginning; in fact have made it both a point of national pride and an effective political tactic. Johnny de Lange, Deputy Minister for Justice in the first democratic Cabinet, stated unabashedly that "our call for a truth commission did not come from the Constitution or any law, *but from our morality as a people who want to heal our nation, and restore the faith of those in our country and the international community in our common future.*"[45]

This made our South African process "unique"—a uniqueness that arises from "our morality as a people," from our desire to achieve both justice and reconciliation, "not just one or the other"; to rise above party-political interests to a "higher, nobler goal for our divided country as a whole to emerge from a shameful past as the winner."[46] With this process South Africa defied the "despair and cynicism" that history teaches, becoming "a safe place for idealism, the sort of place and time when hope and history rhyme."[47]

Former president Thabo Mbeki, too, pressed South Africans to understand that they "cannot escape a shared destiny."[48] Reconciliation "had to be based on the removal of injustice," and had to do with "fundamental transformation."[49] And it was president Mandela who crowned it all by hold-

43. See Boesak, *Tenderness*, chapter 6.

44. "The only thing that stands between us and despair," the great Sol Plaatje confessed in 1916, "is the thought that Heaven has not yet failed us." See Boesak, *Tenderness*, 127. This centrality of faith has always been typical for the struggle; see ch. 4, "My Power and the Strength of My Hands."

45. De Lange, "The Historical Context"; Villa-Vicencio and Verwoerd, eds., *Looking Back, Reaching Forward*, 14–31. The citation is on 18, my emphasis.

46. Ibid., 23.

47. Kader Asmal, Louise Asmal, and Ronald Suresh Roberts, no doubt inspired by Irish poet Seamus Heany, *Reconciliation Through Truth*, 216.

48. Mbeki, *Africa*, 41.

49. Ibid., 55.

ing before us Albert Luthuli's vision of a truly non-racial, just South Africa, his dream of our "ascending unities," a "home for all"; and Mandela's and the country's public commitment to build "a nation at peace with itself."[50]

One can understand why ordinary South Africans put so much faith in the TRC and the reconciliation process, and why the expectations of justice were so high. It was not just our hopes, dreams, and political aspirations that were at stake. At stake was our very soul.

So, in light of the question that informs this discussion one must not only ask what reconciliation truly means, but also: how do we restore faith in the reconciliation process and in the promises, not of politicians, but of the gospel? And as a consequence: how do we reclaim the wholeness of our soul? Has South Africa, through reconciliation and justice, in fact become the sort of place where the hopes of the people and the making of history rhyme?

In too many ways, as we have seen earlier, South Africa has not become the place where "hope and history rhyme." In too many ways, South Africa is beginning to feel the consequences of reconciliation sought too cheaply because justice was deemed too costly. There seems to not only be a disconnect, but an asymmetry between the hopes of the people and the making of our history. A history that betrays the hopes of the people cannot at the same time be a history that nourishes and responds to the hopes of the people. This is what the students and the youth who are flooding the streets in anger, scaling the walls of Parliament and storming the Union Buildings, bringing the nation to a standstill in hopes of bringing Jacob Zuma and the ANC to their senses, are shouting from the rooftops.

The Historic Obligation of the Oppressed

We have taken this longer, more painful route to this point so that there is no misunderstanding: there is no such thing as cheap reconciliation. Knowing and understanding all this, however, what then of the "historic and humanistic" obligation and task of the oppressed to free the oppressor, as we have heard Paulo Freire say? It seems that oppressed people do not have a choice: it is not an option we may ignore or leave to someone else. It is no less than an "obligation." This obligation is not merely "historic"; it is "humanistic." Freire does not mean humanistic in the sense that it is not driven by any particular religious feelings or inspiration, but that it is a task the oppressed assume for the sake of humanity, for the humanization of the

---

50. In his speech in Parliament, accepting the TRC Report, February 25, 1999; see Boesak, *Tenderness*, 176–77.

world. Without it, our own liberation would be incomplete. The fate of the oppressed is linked to the oppressor, but even more so to the salvation of humankind.

The oppressed can do, and must do, argues Freire, what the oppressor cannot. It is not just that the oppressed, passively, must avoid becoming "oppressors of the oppressors." They must actively, Freire says, evoking our discussion on *ubuntu*, become "restorers of the humanity of both."[51] Only the oppressed understand what Freire calls humanity's "vocation," that is, the quest for becoming more fully human.[52] This vocation is constantly negated by the works of the oppressor. "It is thwarted by injustice, exploitation, oppression and the violence of the oppressors"; yet at the same time it is affirmed by the yearning of the oppressed for freedom and justice, and by their struggle to recover their lost humanity."[53]

In the oppression of others, the oppressors not only oppress those directly under their subjugation. They nullify the essence of all humanity. Only the oppressed can recapture this humanity, and they do it by acting on their yearning for freedom. This yearning is not a romantic feeling or an empty dream, leaving historical realities intact. It is a yearning expressed in struggle against the dehumanization caused by the oppressor. This dehumanization marks those whose humanity has been stolen, just as it marks those who have stolen it. Dehumanization is not our destiny, Freire insists, it is the "result of an unjust order which engenders violence in the oppressors, which in turn dehumanizes the oppressed."[54]

Paulo Freire makes a further point. The oppressors, "who oppress, exploit, and rape by virtue of their power cannot find in this power the strength to liberate either the oppressed or themselves," says Freire. "Only power that springs from the weakness of the oppressed will be sufficiently strong to free both." The power of the oppressor is only the power to destroy, bringing death, despair and poverty. This is true of even their acts of "false generosity" which seek to keep unjust orders secure, and therefore fail to transform the world.[55]

By fighting for the restoration of their humanity, the oppressed will be attempting the restoration of true generosity, because only they "understand the necessity of liberation." And this liberation will not be "defined by

---

51. Freire, *Pedagogy*, 21.
52. Ibid., 20–21.
53. Ibid., 20.
54. Ibid., 21.
55. Ibid., 22.

chance, but through the praxis of their quest for it, through recognising the necessity to fight for it."[56]

The struggle, therefore, is for freedom, "true liberation" and the defeat of false generosity, false consciousness, and false humanity. It is a struggle against the violence of the oppressor, against exploitation and dehumanization. But it is a struggle in order to make the oppressor see the necessity of their own liberation, because ultimately the quest is not just our own "national" liberation, but the humanization of the world. Only the oppressed possess the power to "create a new situation to make possible the pursuit of a fuller humanity."[57]

> Although the situation of oppression is a dehumanized and dehumanizing totality affecting both the oppressors and those whom they oppress, it is the latter who must, from their stifled humanity, wage for both the struggle for a fuller humanity; the oppressor, who is himself dehumanized because he dehumanises others, is unable to lead this struggle.[58]

The oppressed can and must do this, because only they have the "strength," which comes from their desire for freedom and humanity for all.

South Africa's Steve Biko understood this perfectly and speaks of "the righteousness of our strength."[59] He speaks of this while giving evidence in court as a banned person himself. He explains his belief in nonviolence, and in the "righteousness of our strength." This strength is not the power of violence or ideology, not even the power of numbers, but the power of belief. He spoke not of the weakness of others that is to be exploited, but of the strength of the oppressed that is there to inspire and to be shared. It is a strength anchored in the power of the powerless, in the power of the resilience and inviolability of their own humanity. In saying this, Biko affected a fundamental and critical reversal: it is not those with the power of being in government, of undeserved social and economic position and privilege or unbridled military strength who are strong, but those who are powerless and exploited, oppressed and victimized. They are strong because their strength is righteous, rooted not in the desire for power for power's sake but in the longing for freedom and justice. They are strong because this longing is not just for themselves, but for others as well—even their oppressors.

Biko spoke not of the "strength of our righteousness" for that would have been too arrogant, self-righteous, and hypocritical. That is the speech

56. Ibid.
57. Ibid., 24.
58. Ibid.
59. Biko, *I Write What I Like*, 120–37. See also Boesak, *Running with Horses*, 187.

of the powerful and hubristic. He spoke, rather, of "the righteousness of our strength." He knew black people were not strong because they were politically and economically powerful, but because they were right. They were right to believe in themselves, in the inevitability of their own freedom, in the justness of their cause, and that in their freedom lay also the freedom of their oppressor.

It is the strength that comes from knowing your ability and willingness to persuade even the oppressor of that rightness, because you will not give way to the brute power of oppression and you will refuse to turn away from your vision of justice and humanity. It is the strength of having embraced a vision and running with it. It is the strength of those daring to dream a different world, even if you are standing in the midst of death, not knowing whether you will yourself taste the fruits of final victory. It is the strength that comes from the willingness to sacrifice and struggle, not just for one's own sake, but for the sake of generations to come, and, ultimately, for the sake of all humanity.

> We have set out on a quest for true humanity, and somewhere on the distant horizon we can see the glittering prize ... In time we shall be in a position to bestow on South Africa the greatest gift possible—a more human face.[60]

It is the strength that comes from knowing with Hannah that "not by might shall one prevail" (1 Sam 2:9), and with Mary that the strength of God's arm has already "scattered the proud in the thoughts of their hearts, brought down the powerful from their thrones and lifted up the lowly" (Luke 1:51–52).

Throughout the struggles of oppressed peoples, understanding this crucial difference between oppressive power and liberating strength has been a guiding and salvific conviction. From the slave-holding United States, Reverend Nathaniel Paul speaks in moving and vivid terms of the horrors of slavery, through which "the laws of God and the tears of the oppressed are alike disregarded," of the "savage barbarity" of slave masters and those who benefit from slavery, until he cries out to God:

> O Thou immaculate God ... why [was it] that thou didst look on with the calm indifference of an unconcerned spectator, when thy holy law was violated, thy divine authority despised and a portion of thine own creatures reduced to a state of mere vassalage and misery?[61]

---

60. Biko, *I Write What I Like*, 98.
61. Paul, "An Address On the Occasion of the Abolition of Slavery in New York," 184, 187.

Yet Nathaniel Paul knows this too:

> But [slavery's, cruelty's] pernicious tendency may be traced still farther: not only are its effects of the most disastrous character, in relation to the slave, but it extends its influence to the slaveholder; and in many instances it is hard to say which is most wretched, the slave or the slave master.[62]

The hopeful *sizwe* hold onto their humanbeingness in the concern for the humanbeingness of the oppressor, not because of some investment in self-interest, but because of a selfless, sacrificial investment in the future of generations to come, and therefore in the future of humanity. In this tradition stands Howard Thurman with his longing for a "community based on reconciliation, which recognizes and celebrates the underlying unity of life . . . for in the eyes of God every human is His beloved child"[63]; Martin Luther King Jr. and his striving for a "beloved community"; and Albert Luthuli's dream of a non-racial South Africa created from "our ascending unities" to a "home for all."[64] Such is also the testimony of Nelson Mandela, whose "hunger for freedom" for his own people became a hunger "for the freedom of all people, white and black":

> I knew as well as anything that the oppressor must be liberated just as surely as the oppressed . . . I am not truly free if I am taking someone else's freedom just as surely as my freedom is taken away from me. The oppressed and the oppressor are alike robbed of their humanity . . . When I walked out of prison that was my mission—to liberate the oppressed and the oppressor both.[65]

Black people, writes James Cone, are God's suffering servant, not because they are called to a life of endless, senseless suffering, but because suffering "in the context of the struggle for freedom is liberating . . . Black people, therefore, as God's Suffering Servant, are called to suffer with and for God *in the liberation of humanity* . . . Humanity's meaning is found in the oppressed people's fight for freedom . . . "[66]

---

62. Ibid., 184.
63. See Smith, Jr., *Howard Thurman*, 176.
64. Luthuli, *Let My People Go!*, 229.
65. Mandela, *Long Walk to Freedom*, 544.
66. Cone, *God of the Oppressed*, 178. Emphasis added. "For the oppressed, justice is the rescue from hurt; and for the oppressors it is the removal of the power to hurt others—even against their will—so that justice can be realized for all" (159).

It is in joining the oppressed in that struggle for all humanity that oppressors will find their freedom and recover their own humanity. Their freedom shall be validated by the freedom of the oppressed. What Cone writes about black people is true, but we shall keep in mind that in post-1994 South Africa whiteness no longer has sole claim on the category of "oppressor." South Africa's oppressor classes have shifted depressingly quickly to include the new black political and economic aristocracy, and the yoke of neoliberal capitalist classism they put upon the people is as hard and unyielding as the burdens of white-sponsored apartheid once were.

In South Africa in the 1980s the United Democratic Front understood this when we made those three crucial decisions: (*a*) that our struggle should be above-ground struggle, an open defiance of apartheid and its regime, and an open challenge to the international community; (*b*) that it should be a nonviolent struggle in open defiance of the violence of apartheid and the belief in the salvific power of violence; and (*c*) it should be a non-racial struggle, an open defiance of the very foundations of racist apartheid and a continued belief that our very struggle should embody the noble ideals of the future society we were fighting for.

And today the youth of the "Injustice Must Fall" movement in South Africa and the youth of the Black Lives Matter movement in the United States understand it superbly. Despite the ongoing racism and systemic oppression still felt by their generation after the anti-apartheid struggle and the civil rights struggle, it has not made them cynical. Those marches in Cape Town and Ferguson, in Johannesburg and New York, in Baltimore and Pretoria are stubbornly, liberatingly inclusive: they are marches for social, racial, gender, and sexual justice. They are recognizing, and joyously affirming, their strength in the righteousness of their rebellion.

Despite the violence and brutality of police in the grip of an imperialistic siege mentality, they remain stubbornly, and liberatingly, nonviolent. Despite the betrayal of the struggle by the ANC in South Africa and despite the blatant carelessness of cynical politics in the United States, they retain the buoyancy of hope, the freshness of righteous anger, the incomprehensible courage of those who have seen Satan fall like lightning from heaven. Despite the cynicism and mendaciousness of the white-controlled mass media, they remain the defiant remnant of the hopeful *sizwe*.

So do oppressed people have an "historic and humanistic obligation" to free the oppressor? I would say yes, and that "yes" does not relieve the oppressor from understanding their own responsibility for their own freedom. Oppressors ignore the "outstretched hand" of the oppressed only at their own peril. They free themselves of their fear of freedom and true humanity only if they join the oppressed in the ongoing struggle for genuine freedom for all, if they exchange the power to oppress for the strength to set free, thereby claiming freedom for themselves.

In South Africa that means that white people understand that freedom cannot be secured by clever yet ill-conceived elite pacts with a new political aristocracy, and that the new black elite understand that the new humanity is not to be gained by new moneyed alliances against the impoverished masses. At this point in our history, Luthuli's "outstretched hand" is not rejected because it is "a black hand." It is rejected because it is the hand reaching for justice and equality. That hand is open, not to receive the charity of false generosity, but to grasp and own the gift of fulfilled humanity. In the final analysis that gift is not the oppressor's to give or deny. It is a God-given heritage.

The oppressed do have an obligation, not because of a particular desire to coddle the oppressor (which, in the cruel twist of our historic irony, now includes South Africa's black political and economic aristocracy), but because our struggle never had been for ourselves alone. It is embedded in the struggles of oppressed peoples of all places and all times. And it is historic, not because it is historically predetermined, but because it is of historic proportions every time it happens. How seriously we take this does matter—not just to us, but to the world. Not simply for the sake of particular oppressors in particular situations but for the sake of a reconciled humanity. Not so that the oppressor can be indulged, but because there truly is much at stake: the building of a non-racial, inclusive, reconciled community, the humanizing of the world, the creation of a new humanity. And in doing this we are doing for ourselves as well, so that we do not become alienated from our own ubuntufication.

In South Africa, the United States, and Israel/Palestine it is more than just the fact that we are forced by historical circumstance to live together, and the desperate and politically vile efforts of the Israeli government to create an apartheid more efficient and ruthless than the white minority regime in South Africa could dream of or achieve cannot change this fact. It is because we truly have to share the same destiny. We have, after all, each in our own way, chosen justice for the living above revenge for the dead. But it is a destiny not forged of secret elite pacts, nor built on deceit of the poor and vulnerable, nor on the betrayal of their trust and their faith, by running away from historic culpability and responsibility, by trying to keep in place an occupation that cannot last. It rests upon the struggle for justice, a struggle that sees beyond our own situations into the world where a new humanity waits to be born.

This is what we mean when we say that the struggle continues, because it never was a struggle of black against white, or Palestinian against Jew; it was a struggle for a fuller humanity through the establishment and flourishing of justice and dignity. For in South Africa, United States, Palestine and the larger Arab world, the struggle for full humanity continues. And in this, too, Freire is right:

> Although the situation of oppression is a dehumanized and dehumanizing totality affecting both the oppressors and those whom they oppressed, it is the latter who must, from their stifled humanity wage for both the struggle for a fuller humanity; the oppressor, who is himself dehumanized because he dehumanizes others, is unable to lead this struggle.[67]

In this ongoing struggle, in these historic moments of renewed opportunity and relentless temptation, we should let ourselves be guided by the wisdom taught us by our ancestors and elders in words left to us by Robert Sobukwe, in our situation today still ringing clear as a bell: "We still have a mission, a nation to build, we have a God to glorify; a contribution to make towards the blessing of humankind."[68] Or to return to the wise insights of Paulo Freire: "The man or woman who emerges is a new person, viable only as the oppressor-oppressed contradiction is superseded by the humanization of all people."[69] And that of Alexis Templeton, speaking of the struggle against sexism and homophobia within the struggle against racism in the United States: "So you just start to pay attention, pay a lot more attention to what's going on, and your heart gets bigger because your fight gets bigger."[70] That is our historic obligation, and without it the world will be a desolate and terrifying place.

---

67. Freire, *Pedagogy*, 24

68. Robert Sobukwe in a speech at his graduation ceremony from Fort Hare in 1949, see Karis and Carter, eds., *From Protest to Challenge*, 332.

69. Freire, *Pedagogy*, 49.

70. L. Francis, *Ferguson and Faith*, 73.

CHAPTER 6

Deification, Demonization, and Dispossession

Mandela, Prime Evil, and the Hope That Will Not Go Away

> Basic to the revolution is the new sense of dignity and historical mission embraced by the people and the demand of the people for power as the bearer of dignity and for significant and responsible participation in society and social history.
>
> —M. M. Thomas

An Unreconciled Society?

Since the coming of democracy, as a nation South Africans have without a doubt achieved much. Our decision, in dealing with the crime against humanity called apartheid, to make a fundamental choice for reconciliation rather than retribution and revenge, for what social scientist Mahmood Mamdani called "survivor's justice" rather than either victor's or victim's justice, thereby creating a foundation for political justice, remains an enormous gift to South Africa and the world, spiritually and politically.[1] I remain convinced this fundamental choice is foundational for the building of open, democratic, inclusive, humane, and peaceful societies, and not just for those emerging from situations of protracted, serious, and deadly conflict. South Africa, in making this choice, has done itself, and the world, a great service.[2]

1. See Mamdani, "Reconciliation without Justice"; "Beyond Kempton Park."
2. It is in this fundamental choice that South Africa, in my firmly held view, is a

At this moment in history, as we have discussed throughout this book, South Africa is convulsed in upheaval and not just in the streets. South Africa's people are rising up in revolt against their government in defense of South Africa's constitution, against systemic injustices the African National Congress, in its tenure of over twenty years in government, has dismally failed to address. In this chapter we endeavor to probe deeper into what I consider to be important reasons behind the uprisings.

At the same time our reconciliation process is under intense scrutiny and even more intense pressure. It is vital that we hold on to the fundamental decision for a truly reconciled community, with justice, dignity and inclusion all the more tenaciously. Yet, as we have seen, this very same reconciliation process is wracked with contradictions with immense political and social implications for issues regarding the restoration of human rights, human dignity, and justice.[3]

Our civil society organizations, despite great difficulties, not least created by the present ANC government, have remained vigilant and vibrant, and judging by the negligible effect of public opinion on the United States Congress in crucial matters such as gun control, gender justice, women's rights and voting rights, or regarding the influence of money on the democratic process for example, seem to have been more effective than we sometimes give them credit for.

Simultaneously, though, and at the levels where it matters most, we have been grappling with seemingly unsolvable problems and invincible challenges. Foremost on the agenda is the struggle for the sanctity of the constitution, and the question how to continue to build South Africa as a genuinely just, equal, and inclusive constitutional democracy. Every day brings new stories of an unconquered, unrepentant racism, corruption in government, revelations of shocking criminal activities at the highest levels of our law enforcement agencies, chaos in education, service delivery protests and violent crime. And running through it all like poison through the nation's blood stream is our ongoing, relentless and unaddressed poverty, and the distressing, growing, and utterly dangerous gap between the rich and the poor, symbolizing the chasm between the nation's stated goals of reconciliation and social cohesion and the bitter realities of raging

---

model to the world, not so much in the process we followed and that we called reconciliation. That process needs to be seriously reconsidered and subjected to some vigorous (self-) critique as South Africans seek to pursue genuine, sustainable reconciliation before its example is uncritically followed by nations and societies other than ours. That, in part, is the point this book is trying to argue.

3. See Mamdani, "Beyond Kempton Park." See also Boesak, *The Tenderness of Conscience*, ch.; "And Zacchaeus Remained in the Tree," 635–64; and Boesak and DeYoung, *Radical Reconciliation*.

inequalities exacerbated since apartheid by the economic policies of our ruling political aristocracy.[4]

As a nation we have framed one of the most progressive constitutions of any modern democracy based on what we claim to be the principles and values of *ubuntu*. We have deleted political and social apartheid from our statute books, yet not from the political, economic and social life of the nation. In fact we have vigorously defended, and continue to defend and justify our enthusiastic embrace of neoliberal capitalism despite the quite disastrous consequences of this policy choice for the vast majority of the people of South Africa, especially women. Especially poor, rural, black women. Today South Africa is one of the most unequal societies in the world.

At another level, as I write this, South Africans are still reeling from the spate of revelations of vile incidents of gender-based violence that continue to ravage both the young women involved and the soul of our nation: the seventeen-year-old mentally impaired girl from Soweto, gang-raped over days by young boys who then let the video they made of the crime go viral; or the twelve-year-old girl from KwaZulu-Natal raped by a fifteen-year-old boy who gouged her eyes out for good measure. I make this point to underline the shocking realities of gender-based violence in South Africa, the broadness of it as a phenomenon, and the dangers of regarding it as more and more a "normal" feature of life in South Africa.

On top of this came the shock of the death of the forty-four Marikana miners at the hands of the police and the scandalous use by the National Prosecuting Authority of oppressive apartheid-era laws to charge the workers with murder.[5] In a previous publication I have ventured the considered opinion that the Marikana massacre will come to be an iconic turning point in South Africa's history: just as the Sharpeville massacre in March 1960 finally defined the apartheid regime and simultaneously redefined the struggle against apartheid, so Marikana will come to redefine both the ANC and the ongoing struggles for justice in South Africa.[6] We are a shell-shocked nation, writes Archbishop Tutu. "We suffer from a profound sense of anxiety, and—increasingly, disillusionment—over the moral and spiritual well-being of the nation."[7] More than secular analysis might care

---

4. See, e.g., Terreblanche, "Dealing with Systematic Economic Injustice," 268; Mosoetsa, *Eating from One Pot*, and Terreblanche, *Lost in Transformation*, and Terreblanche, *Verdeelde Land*.

5. For details of the killing of forty-four miners at the Marikana platinum mine near Rustenburg, North West Province, South Africa, see DLF News: www.democraticleft.za.net, and Boesak, *Dare We Speak of Hope*, 6 n. 7; 6–8.

6. See Boesak, *Dare We Speak of Hope*, 6.

7. From an e-mail from Archbishop Tutu, May 3, 2012.

to admit, this concern is at the core of what is driving the present revolution sweeping the nation.

"We are," the archbishop continues, "a deeply wounded people. We carry the recent scars of apartheid and the ingrained hurt of centuries of colonialism before that. Some of us feel superior to others, and some feel inferior. For generations, instead of following the universal golden rule of reciprocity, to love one another as ourselves, we have been trained to be mistrustful, to dislike, even to hate."

Desmond Tutu is right. We are indeed a traumatized people. Among perhaps many reasons, I should like to advance only four. First, we have, despite vehement and angry denials, not dealt as honestly and thoroughly with our past—centuries of colonialist oppression, slavery, and apartheid—as we should have. In a self-inflicted process of what I have called unremembering,[8] we have sought refuge under a thinly veiled, selective, national political and social amnesia as we entered our reconciliation process, and ever since we have been struggling with the moral amnesia that has produced. We have indeed not allowed ourselves to come face to face with our wounded selves. Desmond Tutu rightly sees our unbelievably violent past as a source for our violence today still, even though it should be said we are at a point where the violent past can no longer be the exclusive cause of the violence of the present.

Second, we have taken our reconciliation process, its blessings and gifts, for granted—as if we were entitled. Third, and for our purposes here perhaps the most important, we have not had the courage to accept the burden of culpability for our past, nor the responsibility for genuine, all-encompassing transformation necessary for a secure, humane, and dignified future. A fourth reason needs a separate discussion and reflection for which we have neither space nor time but should still be noted: we have not dealt with the legacies and continuing ideologies of perverse conceptions of masculinity that come with centuries of oppression, violence, and dehumanization as well as unredeemed cultural, political, and religious notions of patriarchy.

We have perhaps understood the art of negotiation and political compromise, but we have not shown that we have fully understood the nature of power. Nor have we wholly embraced the challenges of moral responsibility and personal and political accountability that are essential to truth and reconciliation processes, and we have not completely come to terms with the impact of this truth on our political and communal life. We have closed

---

8. For the way I use this term as "a deliberate political act for reasons of domestication and control, in which a nation's history is falsified, rewritten or denied," see Boesak, *The Tenderness of Conscience*, ch. 4, esp. 103–4.

our eyes to the consequences of our reveling in a kind of political pietism, boasting of our quite wonderful policies on paper and the values of our Constitution while remaining, at heart, an un-reconciled society, not able to implement those policies with the same vigour with which we expounded them and not able to embrace the values of our Constitution as habits of the heart.[9] We have become fearful of challenging our glossy, official narrative, of being accused of "pathologizing the nation" with a "spiritualized" notion of reconciliation based upon biblical demands for the restoration of justice, rights, and human dignity in order to find the restoration of proper human and communal relationships.[10]

We have, to put it differently, sat back and waited for miracles to happen, even as we professed no belief in miracles and depended only on the hard realities of politics, our negotiation skills, and our ability to manipulate the "balance of forces." We have consistently confused the political accommodation in our secret agreements among the political aristocracies (*before* the agreements at our famed Kempton Park negotiations) and our concentration on our "fractured elites"[11] in the Amnesty Committee hearings with authentic, durable, and sustainable reconciliation. Not just in economic terms but much more in terms of what Nicholas Wolterstorff calls primary justice[12]—that is, the justice persons are not granted out the generosity of the powerful, which can be withheld as it pleases the powerful, but the justice to which one has a *right*. Not heeding Bonhoeffer's wisdom regarding cheap grace, and not honoring justice as essential to our understanding of reconciliation, we have worked far too hard at avoiding a costly reconciliation.

In the process, we have, and this is the thrust of my argument in our reflection here, discarded our responsibility to work for real change and genuine reconciliation while we created new mythologies we could hide behind. For our guilt, we hid behind a demon of our own creation. For our responsibility, we hid behind an angel as gift from God. In our reconciliation process we have fallen prey to the temptation of deification, demonization, and renewed dispossession, and the question is: how has this impacted the workings of reconciliation in South Africa and what will reconciliation become in those places where the South African model is being or

9. The concept of "habits of the heart" is used to great effect in Bellah et al., *Habits of the Heart*. For my understanding of the concept of "political pietism," see Boesak and DeYoung, *Radical Reconciliation*, 1.

10. See Jakes Gerwel's argument of "excessive spiritualization" of our reconciliation process as a danger to its essential nature, a "secular political pact" and what he sees as "pathologizing an essentially healthy nation," in "National Reconciliation," 277–86.

11. Mamdani, "Reconciliation without Justice," 4.

12. See Wolterstorff, *Justice in Love*, 85–92.

planned to be followed? Will the hopeful *sizwe* once again be turned away empty-handed?

Prime Evil, the Ultimate Good, Culpability and Responsibility

Two names have become symbolic, indeed, paradigmatic for what I regard as a tragic error, and the dilemmas it now causes for South Africans: Eugene de Kock and Nelson Mandela. This is how I see our mistake and our dilemma: South Africans, I argue, have hidden all our culpability for the injustices of the past behind Eugene de Kock, and we simultaneously have hidden all our responsibility for justice in the present behind Nelson Mandela. Both men have grown to larger-than-life proportions in our minds, have become our over-powering symbols of absolute good and absolute evil, and have been made to vicariously carry the burdens and responsibilities of reconciliation for the rest of us. Now that President Nelson Mandela has died, and his iconization around the world has stunned even South Africans, this has become more of a reality than we might be ready to admit.

Eugene de Kock is the former colonel of the South African Police Force (SAP) during apartheid, a commander of the infamous C-1 Unit in charge of one of the most notorious police quarters in South African history, *Vlakplaas*—a name associated with the most terrifying images and evil possibilities the human mind is capable of. *Vlakplaas* was the headquarters of the SAP's most efficient counter-insurgency group, who made their name by the kidnapping, torture, and murder of hundreds of anti-apartheid activists. De Kock himself became known through his testimony before the TRC. His frank testimony and the revelations of the workings of that unit earned him the nick-name "Prime Evil," first given to him by investigative journalist Jacques Pauw, after the title of Pauw's very popular television program.[13] What Pauw had discovered through his own investigations, and what de Kock confessed before the Commission, was indeed so horrendous that it numbed the senses.[14]

De Kock was found guilty, not offered amnesty, and sentenced to 212 years in prison for his past crimes against humanity. Psychologist Pumla

---

13. See Pauw, *Dances with Devils*, 125–53.

14. Ibid., 145–46. "Without ever being debriefed or receiving psychiatric care, de Kock was transferred from one fighting unit to the other . . . After that, Eugene de Kock was not just a highly skilled and professional assassin, but a savage and perverted killer who took great pride and satisfaction in what he did . . . If de Kock was Atilla, his men were his Huns . . ." (145).

Gobodo-Madikizela, who served on the TRC's Human Rights Violations Committee, was gripped by the story of de Kock, obtained permission to visit him in prison, and despite thinking of him as "the incarnation of evil," found him, and his situation, more complex than the simplified public image allowed and the public mind demanded. He was, she thought, symbolic of "the compartmentalization of South African thinking, a private world and a public world," the split realities of "the polite church-goers, the cultured suburbanites, the voters and the 'grim' but 'good' business of terrorising blacks."[15]

It is safe to say that in the mind of ordinary South Africans there is no single person as horrifying as de Kock. Jacques Pauw's *Prime Evil* television series presented de Kock and the events at *Vlakplaas* without adornment and in shocking detail, not to sensationalize the matter or just to demonize de Kock, Pauw says, but because he wanted to "horrify and stagger white television viewers in particular with compelling and frightening accounts of a bitter war and a searingly demented past. Never again did I want my countrymen to be able to say: 'I am as shocked as you are about these many revelations. I didn't know...'"[16]

De Kock testified that as any good soldier, he followed the orders given by his superiors, who in turn followed the orders coming from the apartheid politicians. This, the fact that he was a soldier, specifically trained for what he did,[17] and his upbringing, were perhaps some of the reasons why Pumla Gobodo-Madikizela found it in her heart to forgive him. His remorse was another.

But white South Africa could not live with a de Kock that reminded them that he dedicated his life to a cause they had persistently chosen, to protect the white supremacist, privileged life-style they cherished too much; that he tortured and killed because he believed that was expected of him in order to keep them "safe." He was not just a soldier; he was an *apartheid* soldier. It became absolutely necessary, as a matter of life and death, to turn him into a person so evil, so much Satan personified, an evil so great that it cannot only not be forgiven, but it cannot be imagined in any other person, let alone be recognized as an evil that *represented* the white community in their perverse lust for the maintenance of apartheid, white power and white privilege, and the benefits these brought them.

15. Gobodo-Madikizela, *A Human Being Died That Night*, 13.

16. Pauw, *Dances with Devils*, 146.

17. Ibid., 144–45. See Gordin, "De Kock 'followed orders in murder'": "De Kock was not an out-of-control madman—he was an officer acting under orders."

However, the sheer enormity of de Kock's evil also made it impossible for him to be called merely insane, following the "mad, lone-wolf" theory so beloved of culpable communities refusing responsibility for someone from their own ranks who commits great crimes they associate only with an "enemy Other." Madness on such a scale might be excusable and hence certainly not permissible for de Kock. It had to be pure, unadulterated evil, making any complicity unthinkable, even though it was clear, as Jacques Pauw shows, that he was not a "lone wolf" or just a "bad apple," as F. W. de Klerk called him while he, before the TRC, blithely trivialized the deeds of apartheid's killing machines by comparing them to mere "theft."[18] Having built their wealth and privilege through the system of apartheid, that system being defended by men like de Kock, white society was now content to let de Kock vicariously bear the full weight of the guilt they should have felt. Pauw argues that "Eugene de Kock became the incarnation and human face of evil, the inalienable combatant who rose in defence of an indefensible system. In that sense, he stood accused on behalf of every white man and woman who grew fat and prosperous under National Party rule—all four and a half million of us."[19]

And Jacques Pauw's brutal honesty is the heart of the matter. In a perverse inversion of the truth, de Kock was turned into white peoples' "suffering servant," bearing all the guilt and the sickness, the destructive lust and the evil of apartheid. He was not a man in prison, nor an apartheid soldier, he was pure, prime evil, and he truly belonged on the cross. White South Africa could wash their hands of him. Suddenly it was not the depravity of the apartheid system and its benefits for whites that were "unimaginable." What became unimaginable was the horror embodied in a single man, disconnected from collective culpability, collective moral responsibility and collective accountability.

After his testimony, and even more after his remorse, he was shunned by white society, by those who were his military and political superiors, and by the justice system. "Then," Pauw writes, "without preamble, apartheid's ultimate weapon was not just defeated, but shunned."[20] The community who had used him was the community who now despised, stigmatized, and isolated him. While de Kock was found guilty, Magnus Malan, the apartheid

---

18. Pauw, *Dances with Devils*, 148–49. Pauw quotes from the transcript of de Klerk's appearance before the TRC. "Is it possible," he was asked, "that the commander of Vlakplaas would have been able to sustain, taken all the resources he needed, finances and so on, that situation on his own and keep it secret from everybody higher up?" De Klerk responded, "Yes, it is possible. It happens all the time with theft."

19. Ibid., 147.

20. Ibid.

defense minister while white South Africa waged wars against neighboring countries and in the townships against black activists and communities, and Dr. Wouter Basson, the apartheid scientist and head of apartheid's chemical and biological warfare program, and who the popular press had come to call "Dr. Death," were found not guilty by our courts. Consequently, in the eyes of large sections of the white community white blamelessness was established because in the acquittals of these two apartheid operatives white innocence was reaffirmed.

Jacques Pauw is vivid in his anger as he tells of de Kock's "pariahdom":

> He awakened from his long nightmare alone and forlorn. The politicians who had spawned the hate and funded the killers, the generals who spurred them on, the *dominees* [white DRC pastors] who prayed for their deliverance from enemies, the judges and magistrates who excused their deeds as self-defence, the civil servants in grey shoes who did the paperwork that let the system classify, remove, disinherit and control, clucked their tongues and shook their heads, then gave silent thanks for their personal escape from retribution. De Kock's pariahdom was one of the most despicable acts of betrayal in the history of South Africa.[21]

"In the name of reconciliation," Pauw asserts, "they cast him on the heap of yesterday's putrid offal" in order to get on with the business of "cultivating a new land."[22]

Mr. F. W. de Klerk's testimony before the Commission, his failure to recognize the evil of apartheid (not to mention apologize for it) is matched only by his failure to accept governmental responsibility for men like de Kock who merely did as they were led to believe was their sacred duty for God and country.[23] To be sure, this is not at all an argument to absolve de Kock of his personal responsibility. Indeed, Mr. de Kock's crimes against his victims, their families and the communities, as crimes against humanity, may well be described as crimes that, in the words of journalist Elna Boesak to which we shall return below, may be forgivable but not excusable. He himself accepted that responsibility; "went on a remarkable, what might be described as a crusade to expose the generals and politicians for whom he killed on the one hand, and on the other to seek forgiveness from the families of his victims," even though he knew that it was something he "could

---

21. Ibid., 147–48.
22. Ibid., 148.
23. Ibid., 148–49.

never rectify."²⁴ But still, it was from his victims that he found forgiveness, even though Pauw finds that "ironic" since he himself had for such a long time "resented no one more than de Kock." But his victims forgave him, "restoring some dignity to his tattered remains."²⁵

So in a strange and compelling sense, it is de Kock who has come to most resemble the image Archbishop Tutu has yearned for in his search for the restoration of human relationships and human communities through reconciliation and the embrace of ubuntu.²⁶

What is strange and compelling, though, is that de Kock has not been restored to the white communities on whose behalf he has tortured and killed to preserve their power and privilege. He has instead been offered restored humanity by, and restored community with, those whom he had made the victims of his zeal for apartheid. These are the miracles South Africa, despite everything, still produces, these acts of forgiveness that are possible when the powerless gird on strength and show that what is essentially inexcusable can indeed be forgivable. For both his victims as for Eugene de Kock himself, and for the country, these are acts of true redemption.

But the other side of this coin is Nelson Mandela, *uTata we sizwe*, "the father of the nation," the paragon of virtue, forgiveness, and reconciliation. We do not have to introduce Mr. Mandela to any audience in the world—he remains by far the greatest political icon of the twentieth century, and of the twenty-first, so far. But Mr. Mandela's greatness is not in dispute here. What I want to highlight is the fact that Mr. Mandela is not merely iconized, he is *deified*. The late Reverend Leon Sullivan of the United States was the first who famously called Mr. Mandela "Jesus," but any number of articles on any number of websites reflect that view, as is clear from a post by a Methodist pastor in New Jersey.²⁷ Johannesburg businessman Mxolisi Mbetse formally

24. Ibid., 149.

25. Ibid.

26. "In the spirit of *ubuntu*, the central concern is the healing of breaches, the redressing of imbalances, the restoration of broken relationships, a seeking to rehabilitate both the victim and the perpetrator, who should be given the opportunity to be reintegrated into the community he has injured by his offense." See Tutu, *No Future without Forgiveness*, 54–55.

27. See, e.g., Reverend David LeDuc of Vincent United Methodist Church, on Mandela and Jesus, "Opinion: Reflecting on the Ideas of Nelson Mandela and Jesus," February 17, 2011. http://www.northjersey.com/community-news/religion/reflecting-on-the-ideas-of-nelson-mandela-and-jesus-1.276634. After the death of Mandela the debate on this issue fairly exploded. A BBC journalist called Mandela "Jesus" and the responses were immediate. British journalist Dominic Lawson abhorred the idea because "Mandela had shortcomings," while others defended it. The idea itself appears nonetheless endlessly appealing, see Danie. "Jesus and Mandela: Two of the Good Guys":

offered artist Dean Simon 2.5 million US dollars for a painting of the "Last Supper" depicting Mr. Mandela as Jesus.[28]

Nelson Mandela is in every way the opposite of Eugene de Kock, and if there are those who might refrain from calling him "Jesus," they certainly would refer to him in the words Mephiboseth addressed to David: "My lord the king is like an angel of God" (2 Sam 18:27). In that sense Mandela has come to embody all that is good in South Africa, canceling out all that is bad, the virtuous glue that holds the nation together. Sharing in his unifying greatness, we allow ourselves to ignore the growing fractures, fissions, and chasms. What we also ignore in the process is the contradiction with Nelson Mandela's own magnanimity towards white people, a magnanimity that seems impossible, if not unseemly, to extend to de Kock. The more we embrace Mandela, the greater our need to despise de Kock. But such contradictions are not sustainable, and sooner rather than later South Africa will have to face up to this reality.

In February 2011 Nelson Mandela became quite ill, foreshadowing the illness that would finally take his life two years later. The panic that news engendered in South Africa was astonishing to watch. It was also unusually instructive. Rumors about his health and even his death rotated endlessly on radio, television, and the social media. Assurances from government that he was doing better were greeted with wide public skepticism. Pundits were already speculating on the "after Mandela" scenarios. But it was worse than that. For me all this collective hyperventilation raised a question: why are South Africans so panic-stricken at the thought that Madiba—at the age of ninety-two!—might die? It has much to do, I think, with Nelson Mandela as savior of the nation, as the personification of our collective goodness, over against Eugene de Kock, the symbol of prime evil.

In South African minds, then, Nelson Mandela was already firmly lodged as our vicarious fulfilment of reconciliation, hope, and future. We have made him the incarnation of everything we have been mercifully granted in the miracle of our peaceful transition and which we, like the prodigal son, have wasted with unthinking recklessness in our neglect of justice. He is all the justice South Africans did not seek or work for; all the hope of the poor we refused to be; all the warm human inclusion of the uncomfortable Other we have continued to treat with such heartless carelessness. We have made him the dream of reconciliation and unity we, in hot pursuit of our own interests, otherwise regard with such scorn. He

---

http://www.chicagonow.com/bronzeville-urban-green/2013/12/jesus-and-mandela-two-of-the-good-guys. My intention is not to enter into these journalistic debates. My point is an entirely different one.

28. http//www.timeslive.co.za/local/article612624.

remains the moral refuge for our denied racism and our secretly nurtured ethnic selfishness, for all the compassion that we so easily discard except on special occasions like "Mandela Day"; for all the wasted energy we should have spent on love and sharing and instead lavished on self-enrichment and ostentatious self-aggrandizement.

Mandela has become the hiding place of our unfulfilled promises to the poor and now of our unnameable fears; he is the fig leaf behind which we seek to hide the shamelessness of our pursuit of self-indulgence, fiercely protecting our Elite Pacts and interests. Mandela is the ever-rising wall behind which we take refuge against the growing anger of the destitute and the wronged; he is the excuse for our failure to be disturbed by the injustice we inflict upon the victims of our violence and greed. Because we re-created him in our own self-protecting, self-justifying image, we have made him God's visible pardon for our frigidity towards the weak, the wounded and the downtrodden in our society. We have not done what we should have done because we held him up in our stead. If de Kock is our reflected but unthinkable shame, Mandela is our reflected, but embraced salvation.

So in competitive sycophantic frenzy we heap mindless praise upon him, hoping that that would substitute for the systemic justice we withhold from the masses he had sacrificed so much for. He was the one who suffered twenty-seven years in prison, yet could emerge a symbol of forgiveness and reconciliation. Instead of embracing this as the astonishing symbol of political forgiveness it was, and in return responding to the magnanimity of black victims of apartheid crimes with remorse, repentance, and the reciprocity of justice, the vast majority of the beneficiaries of apartheid grasped Mandela's forgiveness as political entitlement.[29] If he could forgive so unconditionally, is the argument, why could not *all* blacks forget their anger, likewise forgive and "move on"?

He was, and remains, in complete reversal of the de Kock image, the "suffering servant" who forgives, loves, and heals in our stead. He lifts us up and offers us vicarious salvation. Is that not why we call him "Jesus"? But it is a completely contradictory image, I would suggest. Privileged South Africans love Mandela because he does not make on them the radical demands that Jesus does. When Mandela talked about reconciliation, he talked about political accommodation and nation-building, calling us a "nation at peace

---

29. Tutu laments this: "I have sadly to note that a very large section of the white community have forgotten far too easily and far too soon, that our country was indeed on the verge of catastrophe which could have seen us overwhelmed by the kind of carnage and unrest that have characterized places such as Bosnia, Kosovo, the Middle East and Northern Ireland. We should all be overflowing with immense gratitude that things turned out differently" (*No Future*, 164).

with itself." When Jesus talked about reconciliation, he was not nearly that diplomatic. He would remind us of the story of Zacchaeus; of repentance, restitution, and justice (Luke 19:1-10).[30] If Mandela had called Zacchaeus out of that tree to testify and set the example for remorse, restitution, and restoration, white South Africans would not admire him nearly so much.

Even so, by 2011 South Africans knew that they would be faced with one remaining, inescapable truth: when Mandela goes, we shall be forced to acknowledge that all along we were the ones we (and the poor) have all been waiting for; that *we* shall have to do what is right; that the struggle for justice, for human dignity, shall have to be *our* life, as the struggle for freedom had been his. *We* shall have to be the glue that keeps the nation together; *we,* not him, shall have to be the best that is in all of us. Now that he is indeed gone this is the serious question the nation continues to face.

A Dispossession of a Different Kind

But in creating our own images of ultimate good and ultimate evil, South Africans have deflected and denied our culpability for injustice over generations, and our responsibility for justice in our lifetime. Our greatest error, I suggest, is not that we have made reconciliation an arbitrary instrument of negotiation, as we did, nor a calculated tool for political accommodation serving an elite pact, which we also did. One of our gravest errors is that we, after delinking reconciliation and social justice, have carefully, in our official national narrative and in the narrative of our private lives, created images of absolute good and absolute evil, of demons and angels to which we cling, and behind which we hide our culpability and our responsibility. If the moral justification of apartheid was apartheid's theological heresy, this abuse of reconciliation is our political heresy.

In this process, however, a further grave injustice is being perpetrated, one that has totally re-disempowered, indeed re-victimized, the people. The people who struggled with, for, and on behalf of Mandela during his forced absence cannot deny the existence of prime evil, since they have been its undeniable victims. And they dare not disavow a beloved Madiba, since he is the symbol of their pride and hope, the man for whom they sacrificed so much, even though his generosity of soul has been so shamelessly exploited by the privileged from the old order and the new alike. We have demonised

---

30. For the use of the Zacchaeus story as an example of what I have called "real, radical and revolutionary reconciliation," see Boesak and DeYoung, *Radical Reconciliation*, 63-74.

one person and deified the other, while we have de-sanctified the needs of the poor, which we should have held holy before God.

The same process, too, has robbed the masses of their rightful place in history, has dispossessed them of their pride in their heroic role in the struggle for liberation, and has disowned the sacrifices they have made. Before the TRC, F. W. de Klerk has casually reduced centuries of pain and suffering to simple, petty "theft," as we have seen. After the dispossession of colonization, the dehumanization of slavery, and the thingification of apartheid, the victims of oppression are now subjected to the trivialization of their suffering.

But in other ways as well, the oppressed masses have been disenfranchised. The process of deification has not only impinged on the issues of justice—it goes much deeper. Reconciliation in South Africa, write Emmanuel Katongole and Chris Rice, would not have been possible "without the forgiveness of Tutu," or "the presidency of Nelson Mandela," for while it is important to note "the politics of power" behind these processes, "it is just as crucial to see the politics of repentance."[31] The politics of power is clear for all to see, but of the "politics of repentance" there was no sign—not from Mr. F. W. de Klerk, or the white political leadership; not from the military and police commanders who gave Eugene de Kock his orders, and not from the white South African public in general. South African theologian Charles Villa-Vicencio, who had worked with the TRC, would later describe how Douglas Gibson, senior politician of the Democratic Alliance, reflective of the views of the white community in South Africa, would severely criticize a civil-society initiative by some white South Africans calling on whites to simply acknowledge that they had benefited from apartheid.[32]

The repentance of whites for apartheid, inasmuch as it was seen, was seen in extraordinary, and utterly moving, but individual, and regrettably rare, acts of remorse. It is the spiritual power of forgiveness from the black victims of apartheid abuse and from ordinary white citizens, victims of black political violence, that turned our politics, whenever that happened, into a politics of repentance and forgiveness. But Rice and Katongole, fixated on white South Africa's imagined "politics of remorse," hardly recognize this, and it is such politically pietistic and romanticized notions of reconciliation that create room for ongoing injustice and in fact makes the realization of

---

31. Katangole and Rice, *Reconciling All Things*, 102–3. I have referred to their views in the previous chapter but am here making a different point.

32. See Villa-Vicencio, *Walk with Us and Listen*, 102: "The Democratic Alliance [the official opposition in South Africa's parliament] made no attempt to persuade or enable whites to acknowledge culpability for accepting the benefits of apartheid or to take responsibility for any form of reparation."

genuine reconciliation more difficult because these deny the people their rightful role in history, their agency in their own liberation, and the power of their extraordinary gift of love, reconciliation, and forgiveness.

Fairly typical, too, is what celebrated American historian and biographer Taylor Branch writes:

> In 1990, Nelson Mandela emerged from twenty-seven years in a prison to a Cape Town balcony, where he destroyed the iron rule of apartheid not with Armageddon's revenge but a plea for hopeful consent: "Universal suffrage on a common voters' roll in a united, democratic, and non-racial South Africa is the only way to peace and racial harmony."[33]

No black South African in their right mind would even think of diminishing Nelson Mandela, trivialize or deny his sacrifices, resilience, or exceptional leadership. We speak from the depth of our African soul when we call him "Tata." Neither would any one of us deny Archbishop's Tutu's life of struggle, his inspirational faith, his spiritual leadership at the TRC, or indeed the prophetic leadership he still provides. After all, long before white South Africans and the rest of the world knew, recognized, or claimed them and their leadership, they were ours. While the world despised Mandela as a Communist and a terrorist (he was not taken off the "terrorist list" of the United States until 2008!) and classified his organization, the African National Congress, as a terrorist organization—and while the world took no notice of Desmond Tutu and white South Africa derided him as an irritatingly meddlesome priest—black South Africans acclaimed their courage and embraced them as our rightful leaders.

While Western governments supported and benefited from apartheid, backed its white minority regime's despotism, and never protested Mandela's imprisonment that robbed us of his leadership for twenty-seven years, his people marched and worked for his release, making amazing sacrifices in the process, and with their very blood assured the world that without Mandela's freedom we would not consider ourselves free and that we would not rest until that day would come to pass.

Now it is claimed that Mandela—all on his own—"destroyed the iron rule of apartheid from a Cape Town balcony," as if the mere act of standing on a balcony and making a speech could ever do such a thing. It is the same as stating that Martin Luther King Jr. destroyed segregation in America on his own by merely making the "I Have a Dream" speech in 1963. It is an astounding claim, recklessly sweeping aside, and completely disconnecting Mandela from, South Africa's long history of struggle, from the first slave

---

33. Branch, *At Canaan's Edge*, 771.

revolts to the Defiance Campaign to the resistance of the youth, de-voicing the masses and nullifying their sacrifices.

By the same token we are told that it was Desmond Tutu's capacity for forgiveness that *made* our reconciliation, not the forgiveness, magnanimity, and grace of the millions who suffered, were imprisoned, tortured, and whose loved ones were murdered, and who were so magnanimous in their forgiveness of white people, as Desmond Tutu himself testifies.[34] And the ironic truth is that neither Mandela nor Tutu would ever make this claim for themselves. They would recoil at such a crime against their people. But such purposeful unremembering serves the hegemonic narrative, alienates Mandela and Tutu from their people and their ongoing struggles, and it eliminates the historic claim of the poor upon the rich, white world whose prosperity and power were built on their blood.

This is not just a political miscalculation. This is a moral crisis, for whites in the first place certainly, who still benefit from past injustices and the present pain of the poor as well as for those blacks who have become the new imperial heirs to the sinful pacts that secure their enrichment at the cost of justice for the destitute. But at heart, it is a crisis facing the nation as a whole. The dispossession of the poor over the course of our history runs deep, and it is more than land, dignity, worthiness, and true deliverance. And the truth is that long before Mandela's death the rich and powerful have cynically claimed Madiba, the symbol of hope for the masses, for themselves and their own ends.

The Mandela the people of South Africa mourned and celebrated was the Mandela they remembered, *all* of him: the youth leader, the angry activist, the volunteer in the Defiance Campaign, the soldier who "stopped talking peace and nonviolence" and initiated *Mkhonto we Sizwe*, the African National Congress' military wing in 1961. Mandela, the passionate defender of the struggle who faced the apartheid courts at the Rivonia Trial and told the truth about violence and nonviolence; the man who sat in prison and refused terms for release unworthy of the leader of such a heroic struggle; the man who came out of that prison and called for peace, reconciliation, and forgiveness instead of violence, retribution, and revenge. In the eyes of his people there was no contradiction between the Mandela of 1961 and the Mandela of 1990.

The Mandela the Western media celebrated in the weeks after his death was not the complete Mandela. He certainly was not the people's leader as

---

34. See Tutu, *No Future,* 164: "One has longed so eagerly and so desperately for a like generosity of spirit to have been evoked in the white community by the magnanimity of those in the black community who, despite the untold suffering inflicted so unnecessarily on them, have been ready to forgive their tormentors."

they remembered him. The Western mass media praised the incarcerated, courageous Mandela, but were not truthful about the real reasons of his imprisonment and their complicity in it. They celebrated his magnanimity towards whites but did not speak of its source: the sacrificial willingness of his people to forgive rooted in their faith in the God of justice, reconciliation, and forgiveness.

The Mandela of the Western media was a domesticated Mandela, a man refashioned to meet the shallow criteria of their celebrity expectations. In their hands he became a truncated celebrity. He was the palatable, affable African, completely divorced from the disdainful pessimism with which they regard his continent; the continent they had dispassionately spurned while it was bleeding to death as in Rwanda, in the Democratic Republic of the Congo, and now most recently in Mali, Somalia, the Central African Republic, and Yemen. This even as they were making sure that the lucrative business of extracting Africa's minerals while financing her warlords and killing her children remained uninterrupted.

He was a Mandela completely isolated from the messiness of struggle, washed clean of the blood of his people that stained the soil while they fought for his release, against the apartheid regime and the sustained support for it by the governments of the West and their corporations who mercilessly exploited black South African labour for endless profits.

Theirs was the Mandela they could do business with: the "reasonable" Mandela who understood the demands of *Realpolitik* and therefore the limits of the dreams of freedom. They took possession of the freedom fighter and moulded him until he became the politician who was great mainly because, in their view, he understood that whites in South Africa did not have to be called to account for the crimes of apartheid and the rich North for their complicity in those crimes. As such he was perfect for their purposes, and therefore good for South Africa. Even before he died, and now much more so after his death, the oppressed have not only been estranged from Mandela's life and excised from his story; they have been tragically orphaned, alienated from their own struggle, reduced to mere worshippers under that balcony, the unwanted children of a stolen dream.

Beyond Demonization and Deification

The daunting challenges we are facing will not disappear by themselves, nor can they be evaded by political escapism or moral neutrality. The demonization of one person and the deification of another can no longer be the hiding places of our own lack of political and social responsibility and dearth of moral concern. Since the beginning of South Africa's reconciliation process we have made great efforts to try and escape the legacy of our past by forgetfulness, political compromise, or selective indignation. We shall have to learn that only deep and abiding justice to what Jesus called "the least of these"—the poor, the weak, the destitute, the wronged—can help us face the past, confront it, overcome it.

Deification and demonization are the graves wherein we have buried all hope for genuine reconciliation, justice, and meaningful transformation. The songs we sing at that graveside are not songs of mourning and loss; only the sorrowful wailings of self-justification and self-destruction.

In part, this chapter was earlier presented as a public lecture in Johannesburg that elicited quite a reaction from the media. From his prison cell, as his own response, Eugene de Kock has written me a letter, based on what he has read, brutally honest and utterly moving, in which he bares his soul in a way that has left me, a total stranger to him, deeply touched. He speaks of his crimes, his remorse and his pain, not for himself, but for our country, a pain he has carried for eighteen years. "I wish I could have this remorse long ago," he writes, "but I have lacked the insight . . ." He mourns not only his life, but the lives of those he has taken in a cause he now knows never had any justification. He mourns for South Africa and its people, its young white people who should never become victims of the Great Myth[35] as he had been. So he ends his letter with this sentence: "I hope that the South Africa for which you have fought will become a reality in your lifetime; a country where every citizen receives their place in the sun, where every parent knows their children are safe, and where no one ever again would think of another as a lesser human being."

I then thought that South Africans should ask themselves whether keeping this man in prison will continue to be the substitute for the recognition of guilt and genuine remorse, personally, and politically, our undoing of injustice and our doing of justice in our social life as well as in our politics. Our reconciliation is not being realized, promoted, or protected by the demonization of one man while the demons that are ravaging our society and our inner selves have not been confronted nor exorcised. The issue here

---

35. Journalist Elna Boesak writes incisively about "the Great Myth," a powerful ideological driving force in the making of the Afrikaners' image of themselves: "Over three hundred years," she writes, "the fiction, the fable, the narrative, rhetoric and lie has been used to conquer, confuse, poison, and paralyze the hearts and minds of men, women, and children, and to carve, with deliberate intent, from the off-spring of the Creoles of colonization—children of Africa—[a new nation of] white racists." See Elna Boesak, "Tussen Reitz en 'n Rots: Wat het Verkeerd geloop?," unpublished paper, Volksblad Arts Festival, Free State University, Bloemfontein, July 10, 2008, 1, 2. See also Boesak and DeYoung, *Radical Reconciliation*, 98–101.

is not whether Mr. de Kock should have remained in jail. De Kock himself says that he believes that he belongs there. "I represent the worst of our past," he writes. The point, rather, is that that past he is suffering punishment for has not been recognized, or repented for as the evil it was. Neither has it been recognized that he is there having done what he has done on behalf of all white South Africa. He is, in fact, one of the very few white South Africans who have genuinely repented, and publicly asked for forgiveness *without any justification, qualification or reservation whatsoever.*

This is in stark contrast to the man who was one of his political bosses in the apartheid regime, at the top of the table of that infamous Security Council, and who has turned his back on him, former president F. W. de Klerk. In his testimony before the Truth and Reconciliation Commission already, Mr. de Klerk has, as we have heard from Desmond Tutu, "rationalized his apology out of existence." But very recently, in May 2012, de Klerk once again publicly defended apartheid, proving Desmond Tutu absolutely correct in his critical assessment. In an interview with CNN's Christiana Amanpour, de Klerk defended the Bantustans, the apartheid legal system and the courts that found Mandela guilty of treason.[36]

On Amanpour's insistent questioning, de Klerk refused to acknowledge that apartheid was morally wrong and that he has anything to apologize for. Recalling what he did present as an apology, de Klerk went on to say, "What I haven't apologised for is the original concept of seeking to bring justice to all South Africans through the concept of nation states." This, he admits, "failed." He advances three reasons:

1. whites wanted to keep too much land for themselves;
2. whites and blacks became economically integrated; and
3. the majority of blacks said that "this is not how we want our rights."

Asked twice whether he thought apartheid was morally repugnant, de Klerk responded, "I can only say in a qualified way. Inasmuch as it trampled human rights it was, and remains, morally reprehensible." But originally, in its pure form, de Klerk insists, apartheid was not wrong; it was simply "seeking to bring justice to all South Africans."

There is, as Desmond Tutu has remarked and South Africa and the world now once again discovered, no admission that the very thought of a white racist system of domination, held in place by brutal systemic and physical violence and justified by a distortion of the Gospel of Jesus Christ,

---

36. Interview with F.W de Klerk: http://www.globalpost.com/dispatch/news/regions/africa/120511/fw-de-klerk-cnn-interview-amanpour-video.

was intrinsically evil. Of the "politics of repentance," which Rice and Katongole claim to have discerned, there still is no sign.

De Klerk speaks as if the problem was "white people wanting too much land," not at all giving a thought to what was the heart of colonialism and apartheid: dispossession, land theft, disenfranchisement, genocide, and brutal oppression. In de Klerk's view, the fact that apartheid was well-meant but did not "work" makes its failure a matter of mere practicalities, at most perhaps a political miscalculation; not because it was morally repugnant, socially perverted, and politically unsustainable, let alone sinful and evil. Once again de Klerk has set a bad example for whites in South Africa, holding up apartheid as morally acceptable, but practically hampered. "It would have worked, if..." This is why so many have lost hope in our reconciliation process. His is not the language of hope. It is the language of deception, justification, and mortification.

Fundamentally different though, is the language of the man officially designated for contempt and revilement. "Apartheid," de Kock writes in his letter, "could only be maintained through murder, crime, deceit and the abuse of human rights. The crimes of which I was found guilty, are what it took for a few million whites to rob the rest of South Africa of their political rights. Apartheid was not a political system that in the end did not work; it was a distortion of the realities and of the truth with the purpose to undermine and destroy. If I am the one representing the pain of the past, let me be the one to speak on behalf of that past... if we as whites saw our fellow black South Africans as equal to ourselves, no one would have had to shed a drop of blood for this country."

And then Eugene de Kock speaks words his former president and member of the apartheid regime's Security Council cannot bring himself to speak: "I am deeply saddened by what the past has done to my own people; young boys who believed they were fighting bravely, (and God knows they did!) for a righteous cause, men in the army who gave their lives for 'South Africa,' all in vain, and for a leadership that would never accept responsibility."

Of the two, the one praised for his political wisdom in conceding to negotiations with the black majority, and the other, despised for being a foot soldier for apartheid, who speaks with the most integrity? Of the two, the one still defending apartheid, not taking responsibility for the atrocities under his regime, and the other, accepting his guilt, crying out in remorse and seeking forgiveness from the victims of apartheid, who is speaking hope into the lives of South Africans, white and black? Of the two, the one imprisoned in unrepentant self-justification, the other still hanging on a cross but embraced by the forgiveness of his victims, who speaks the language of the future? Now that Eugene de Kock has been released from prison, he will find ways to demonstrate even more clearly his remorse and his commitment to build a truly new South Africa through genuine reconciliation and justice.

Respected civil society leader Dr. Mamphela Ramphele speaks of "the miracle that never was,"[37] expressing perhaps the growing cynicism and despair now palpable in our communities. Seen from one point of view, the ongoing injustices, our unredeemed racism, our fractured life as a nation, she may be right. But perhaps we have been overlooking some miracles that actually did happen. If someone like Eugene de Kock can find such words of honesty, remorse, forgiveness and healing, it is perhaps not too late for the country as a whole to find that language of humility and hope as well.

Mamphela Ramphele also speaks of the vast difference between F. W. de Klerk and Eugene de Kock, and she is touched by de Kock's honesty and willingness to admit his guilt. However, "his demonization was an attempt by the apartheid state to distance itself from the killing machine it had spawned and sustained over the years."[38] As with Pumla Gobodo-Madikizela, the deepest touchstone for her judgment is de Kock's remorse and the amazing generosity of his victims to forgive him, because they sense his sincerity. Like Gobodo-Madikizela, she comes away uneasy with the "Prime Evil" label and asks the ultimate question concerning the violence in our liberation struggle: "Who is not evil?"[39]

I would suggest, though, that we look not for where we can discern the evil that makes us all equal in guilt, but that we instead look for the miracle that can lift us all up toward justice and redemption. And in truth the miracle has already happened. We struggled against all odds for over three centuries and we won. We were locked in battle with truly demonic forces and we never gave up. We stood alone in the world for so long but we believed. We were traumatized by indescribable violence and dehumanization but when the time came for fundamental choices we chose the open hand reaching for a shared future, not the closed fist grimly gripping the past. We chose solidarity with and justice for the living rather than revenge for the dead. We chose reconciliation over retribution, the risk of forgiveness over the triumph of justified condemnation. And even Eugene de Kock can find the cleansing power of remorse and the humanizing power of forgiveness. Such restoration is a miracle waiting to be recognized, embraced, and emulated.

---

37. Ramphele, *Laying Ghosts to Rest*, ch. 2.
38. Ibid., 60.
39. Ibid., 61.

Deification, Demonization, and the Politics of Broken-Heartedness

Parker J. Palmer suggests a way of thinking that might be helpful to South Africans and to us all as we struggle with our past, our guilt, our responsibilities and our longings for justice and wholeness. I am persuaded by the way he speaks of "the politics of the broken-hearted." [40]

We think of heartbreak, Palmer says, as a personal, not a political, condition. "But I believe that heartbreak offers a powerful lens through which to examine the well-being of the body politic." He speaks of the "gaps" between Americans and their global neighbors that continue to grow, the conflicts and contradictions of twenty-first century life "that are breaking the American heart and threatening to compromise our democratic values." He points to the "threats" to our common, global community. What Palmer says of Americans can easily be said of South Africans with our violent, fractured past that has made of us such a traumatized nation. But broken-heartedness is also the heart "broken open into the largeness of life, into greater capacity to hold one's own and the world's pain and joy," helping us not to "shut our hearts down," either withdrawing into fearful isolation or angrily lashing out at the "alien other."

Recognizing our own broken-heartedness as a political-social condition is not to be filled with self-pity and hopeless longings that things might somehow be different for myself, but rather looking at myself in the clearest possible mirror, "trying to penetrate the illusions about myself and the world that have taken me into this pain until I touch the painful truth behind my illusions, so that conflict and confusion can settle and deeper wisdom emerge."

South Africans, black and white, may want to ponder how such honest recognition of our common broken-heartedness, not a political weakness to be exploited but as human openness to be embraced, might help us in understanding the pain of the other in the situations we are facing.

Perhaps, too, in so remembering our own broken-heartedness as a result of our wretched past, we would then better understand the broken-heartedness of the threatened children, the exploited poor, the oppressed and silenced women and the marginalized lesbian, gay, bisexual, transsexual and intersex persons in our post-apartheid but unreconciled society today. We may even come to understand the un-reconciled, unhealed apartheid soldiers, who maimed, tortured, and killed to prove their Christian

---

40. See Palmer, *The Politics of the Brokenhearted*, Essay No. 8. All citations in this section are from that essay. See also Palmer, *Healing the Heart of Democracy*.

patriotism, as well as the too-quickly forgotten and unredeemed black youth who embraced the "necklace" at the behest of their MK commissars as a sign of revolutionary faithfulness. By God's grace we may be able to come closer to the truth of Jesus of Nazareth, who, anointed by the Spirit of the Lord, came precisely to heal the broken-hearted (Luke 4:18). In so doing we may be able to touch the painful truth behind our illusions, to emerge into the deeper wisdom of hopeful living in the doing of justice and the affirmation of our common humanity.

There is a power in heartbreak, Palmer says, "for better or for worse," but the choice is ours. We can find power for good "in acknowledging our wounds and thus opening them to healing," but it starts, for all of us, Americans, South Africans, Palestinians and Israeli's with honestly facing the question: "What shall we do with our heartbreak so that it yields life, not death?"[41] Perhaps that, finally, might be what lies behind Eugene de Kock's remarkable conversion, repentance and transformation, and perhaps that is how de Kock's spiritual transformation may become an inspiration for all of us.

In this way we might discover that we do not need to demonize one another because we all too keenly aware of our failures to make our countries and the world the places we long for them to be. Likewise, we do not need to deify one another because the greater good that is in all of us and the infinite grace of God enables us to do what is right—with honesty, integrity, and justice.

For reconciliation to be the justice-bringing, restorative power it is meant to be, and for hope to be the transformational, life-affirming power *it* is intended to be, neither angels nor demons are necessary. What our world needs are ordinary human beings. But I speak of a humanized, redeemed and redemptive ordinariness: committed, steadfast, courageous, hopeful, and single-minded toward justice, together in all our rich diversity. Hopefully we will then remember that history may be written by the victor, and the past may be manipulated by the powerful, but the future is moulded by those who dream it, believe in it and live into it.

The Suffering Servant and the Hopeful *Sizwe*

Perhaps, finally, Christians would do well to ponder the truth that no human being can serve as our "suffering servant" absolving us from our guilt and our culpability, our responsibility, and the call to do justice. It is a vainglorious idolatry that we seek to create such "suffering servants" for ourselves as

---

41. Palmer, *Healing the Heart*, 59.

substitute for the One we cannot face, whose demands we find too radical, whose love we find too revolutionary, even while being embarrassed by him because the powers and principalities of this world find him too unimpressive, even as they fear him as subversive and dangerous, a severe threat to their imperial designs.

We will also do well to remember that the world belongs to God; it is the whole world that is the theater of God's glory. Our calling is, in the words of liberation theologian José Miguez Bonino, to "dare to name God, to confess God from within the womb of politics, from within the very heart of commitment."[42] But naming God means to "stake our lives for and with" precisely those who are considered of "unimpressive status" by the rich and powerful. Naming God in our lives and in our politics is "naming the hope that never dies, the future that still exists, that is waiting to be claimed by all of us on behalf of all of us, the love that will not let us go."[43] Naming God means "standing where God stands, fighting for whom God fights—the children, the women, the undefended."[44]

We do justice and reclaim reconciliation in the name of this God because we ourselves have been redeemed, called, and empowered by the One who himself took on our unimpressive proportions, who has become acquainted with the grief inflicted on God's children because of injustice, taken upon himself our woundedness because in the woundedness of God's children God is wounded, and grieved.[45] Elsewhere I have tried to find the words for this and it seems worthwhile to repeat them here:

> He was despised and rejected by those who thought him a danger to their positions of power and privilege within the status quo, *and* by those who found him not pliable enough, as well as not hard enough, to fit into the predetermined mould of their revolutionary zeal. They knew, as we do, that the unimpressiveness of his incarnation was not the absence of his glory, but the heavenly solidarity with the poor and the lowly. Those who found him offensive would not look at him because looking at him means looking at the human face of the poor. They hid their faces from him because they could not bring themselves to look upon the misery their greed had visited upon the helpless. They held him of no account because the powerless do not feature

---

42. Bonino, *Toward a Christian Political Ethics*, 8.

43. See Boesak, *The Tenderness of Conscience*, 239.

44. See Bonino, *Christian Political Ethics*, 8; see also Boesak, *The Tenderness of Conscience*, 238–39.

45. See Wolterstorff on "The Wounds of God," 114–32; see also Boesak, *Dare We Speak of Hope*, ch. 1.

in their reckoning except as sacrifices on the altar of political expedience. They held him cursed because he carried in his body the afflictions they have wrought upon the wounded by keeping them outside the gate, outside the circle of protection. They crucified him because he was the tender conscience [the persistent prophetic resistance to their power] that would not let go of their hardened hearts. But because God awakens in the hearts of the poor the longing for freedom, justice and contentment, they are doomed to hear his voice as long as the poor cry out. They shall see him as long as the poor have a face. They shall have to face him as long as the poor have hope.[46]

The suffering God, like the hopeful *sizwe*, will not go away.

---

46. See Boesak, *The Tenderness of Conscience*, 239.

CHAPTER 7

"A Hope Unprepared to Accept Things as They Are"

Prophetic Theology—Speaking Truth from the Edge

> Finally we assert that true revolutionary and systemic change will ultimately only be brought forth by ordinary working people, students, and youth—organizing, marching and taking power from the corrupt elites.
>
> —Aislinn Pulley, 2016

"This Ends with Us"

The renewed struggles for justice and equality are, as previous struggles did, once again presenting themselves, in the words of the 1985 *Kairos Document,* as "a challenge to the church."[1] In South Africa the young people and the students have been filling the streets in protest for weeks as I am writing this, and the oppressed masses of the black townships, have never really stopped their resistance since the turn of the century. And as we have seen in the previous chapter, the struggles are not confined to protests in the streets.

The inner cities of the United States remain filled with tensions, and in Palestine many are speaking of a third intifada. They are filling the air with their demands for justice, dignity, and equality. They are not only

---

1. See *The Kairos Document: A Challenge to the Church*: http://www.sahistory.org.za/archive/challenge-church-comment-political-crisis-south-africa-*kairos*-document-1985.

confronting the church with fundamental choices, they are challenging our theology, its assumptions and content, its awareness of its prophetic calling. They are pushing theology to the edge, presenting it with the very same life-and-death choices they have to make. They are the people, poor, oppressed, and destitute, relentlessly pushed to the edge of existence by the brutal policies of imperial forces without and their surrogates within. They are, in the words of *Kairos Palestine,* crying "from the heart of suffering." It is the edge of exile from a life of dignity, empowerment and meaning, or, as William Herzog frames it, speaking of the lives of first-century Palestinian peasants, "barely able to survive from one planting season to the next, in perpetual debt and near the razor's edge of destitution."[2] It is there, at that edge, that prophetic theology is called to join them, and it is from that edge that prophetic theology must again find its voice and speak truth to power.

As Aislinn Pulley has made clear, these students and youth from Ferguson to Cape Town, from Johannesburg to Baltimore, from Chicago to Pretoria to Bethlehem, and on the university campuses across these countries, are making it clear that they are tired of the politics of mendacity, deceit, and delusion; they are creating a new politics of struggle and hope. They are tired of being lied to by politicians always ready to sacrifice young lives for the old injustices because these fill the troughs the politics of injustice feed from. They are disillusioned by an older generation who, made complacent by piecemeal power, piecemeal privilege, and piecemeal prosperity, can only fall back on the faded street-creds of a yesterday too far removed from today and not even remotely connected to tomorrow: "I shook Nelson Mandela's hand"; "I marched with Dr. King"; "I was in exile."

These young people have become a compelling, restless, disturbing presence in the midst of an apathetic society far too occupied with the comfort of the privileged and a complacent church far too self-absorbed with survival; far too intimidated by the power of the few to understand the power of the hopes of the people. Their voices are ringing with the anger of authenticity because they speak from where they have willingly and determinedly gone: to the frontline of the struggle for a new humanity. They are calling us to account and to understanding: of our complicity in the status quo, our misreading of the present, our not having learned from the past, and our still-hovering hesitation even while the fires are burning. They are calling our urgent attention to things the prophetic church, in South Africa as well as elsewhere, seems to have forgotten, refuses to remember, or no longer even recognize as the glaring sins of our societies.

---

2. See Herzog II, *Jesus, Justice, and the Reign of God,* 101.

The young people and the students who are challenging the church and her theologians have every right to simply write us off. After all, they are fighting the battles we, for reasons not always noble, have not completed. Along the way we have become outmaneuvered by the system, lulled by the privileges of the system, coopted by the system, and intimidated by the power of the system. Or we have not been able to withstand the lures of privilege and comfort and closed our eyes to the burning and persistent injustices despite the price tag for our children. Or we have simply given up. We have too easily accepted the oppressor's definition of freedom and we have told ourselves that the struggle was over, despite the overwhelming evidence all around us. Now the children are determined to do what we, in the last quarter of a century, have left undone; they are determined to undo what we have done, or have allowed to be done in our name.

Theirs is a commanding voice, inescapable because it is a voice not coming from strangers but from our own children. It is not at all just a voice of anger and reproach; it is an invitation to remember and reclaim the heritage of the prophetic tradition, the legacy we, they are still saying even now despite our years of quietism, have left for them. In that sense, it is an astonishingly hopeful voice. This is what our daughter Sarah, at that point studying law in South Africa, posted on her Facebook page at the height of the battles in October 2015, after the students have stormed the gates of Parliament in Cape Town and the Union Buildings in Pretoria:

> The history of protesting for equality, our rights and justice runs deep within our veins. This is the stock from which we come. Too many thought that 1994 was the end of the struggle in South Africa, whether that was out of ignorant privilege and arrogance or genuine hope for our future, only they know deep within themselves. The only fact that remains unquestionable for me today is that for the first time since 1994, the youth of South Africa are picking up the torch which was passed onto us by those who came before and were willing to fight endlessly to break down a brutal system of oppression. They killed their demon and for that we remain eternally grateful. But now it is our turn to face our devil. And as we have started to do this week, it is clear to me that we are doing so with the fearlessness of those before us, but with our own renewed sense of unity and resilience. Today is a new day in South Africa. To those who still doubt, I say, open your ears and you will hear; open your eyes and you will see . . . the voices of thousands of South Africans calling for justice ringing across the country at a volume that has not been heard since the height of the struggle against Apartheid. You will see

how these echoing voices cause the foundations of the current system of injustice and oppression to shake and crack until the walls which keep some in, but most out, crumble and crash to the ground . . . Today we face our devil, and today, we will kill it.[3]

Sarah Boesak goes on to rejoice in the fact that this struggle—and she might as well be speaking of what we are seeing across the globe—is an inclusive struggle, infused with an understanding of the indivisibility of justice. "South Africans from every university, from every race, from every gender, from every province and from every economic grouping" are uniting to "say in one, collective voice that this oppression (which South Africans have been fighting for far too long) ends with us." These are words I have heard also across the United States, wherever I have had the privilege of meeting and speaking with the young people who are leading the struggle there. We understand that the *kairos* moment has come for us, is what I hear them saying. The struggle for justice will continue, but we are equally determined that it should end with us.

A Theology at the Edge

The invitation is an invitation to join the struggle against injustice that must "end with us." It is an invitation to a new conversation with the future. It is a conversation that pushes theology to the edge. But the conversation itself is double-edged: it invites reflections on "a theology at the edge" and on the fact that the struggle for justice, peace, and the restoration of human dignity in South Africa and the world, as well as the struggle for the integrity of the prophetic witness of the church in South Africa and in the world continue, and in a real sense continue to represent the sharp edge of our engagement with the world. In and of itself this is an extremely important understanding and point of departure. It determines whether our theology, in the words of the Belhar Confession of the Uniting Reformed Church in Southern Africa as it speaks of the church, is ready to "stand where God stands": namely "with the wronged and the destitute," . . . on the side of the poor and the oppressed, and "against every form of injustice"[4]

This calls for prophetic theology to recognize that first, there is a struggle and second, that it is continuing in its multi-faceted realities across the globe. Third, that the struggle we are speaking of is not the struggle within the halls and the politics of academia: for example whether theology,

---

3. Email message to the author, November 6, 2015.
4. For the full text of the Belhar Confession, see *World Alliance of Reformed Churches, Semper Reformanda:* http://wcrc.ch/belhar-confession/.

as a discipline, a science if you will, even the "queen of sciences," actually belongs in a public university, and has come under renewed attack from the so-called New Atheists.[5] "The struggle" is the life-and-death struggles of people, oppressed, destitute and excluded from a life of meaning and dignity. Driven to the edge of despair by fear, intimidation, and the sheer exhaustion of constantly living on the edge of survival against forces too brutal to adequately describe, it is a struggle to cling to the life-giving force of hope and faith.

This is true whether we speak of children pulverized by drones in Pakistan or Yemen or Afghanistan; women subjected to rape as weapon of war as is the case in the Democratic Republic of the Congo; men and women, Muslim and Christian, derided, persecuted, and finally beheaded in Iraq or Libya by the Islamic State (IS) because they are considered "infidels"; young women in India killed by a mob of men because they refuse to submit to arranged marriages with men thrice their age; or young African American men murdered by police while walking down the street in Ferguson, Missouri, or Baltimore, Maryland, or Long Island, New York, simply because they happen to be black.

Finally, we are speaking of a theology deliberately conscious of the fact that it is "a theology at the edge." So we are not speaking of theology in general, the kind the nineteenth-century Dutch theologian Abraham Kuyper referred to as "ethical philosophizing" that does nothing to transform the world.[6] We are speaking of a certain expression of theology, a prophetic theology, the theology that responded to the struggle in South Africa with prophetic truth and faithfulness, standing as the oppressed and with the oppressed in our struggles against oppression in colonial times and during the reign of apartheid, and now in global struggles against the devastating reach of imperial powers and their underlings everywhere.

The expectation is for theology not just to be "relevant," whatever that may mean, although one hopes that at the very least it means reflecting intellectually and with integrity *on* the people's struggles. But it should mean even more, we are informed. It means, in the words of S'bu Zikode —of

---

5. See, e.g., Tara Isabella Burton, "Study Theology, Even If You Don't Believe in God": http://www.theatlantic.com/education/print/2013/10-study-theology-even-if-you-dont-believe-in-god. Burton points out that in the United States thirty-seven states have laws limiting the spending of public funds on religious training. She quotes New Atheist Richard Dawkins who argues that "a positive case now needs to be made that [theology] has any real content at all, or that it has any place whatsoever in today's university culture."

6. See Kuyper, *Six Stone Lectures*, 123; see also Boesak, *The Tenderness of Conscience*, ch. 7.

Abahlali baseMjondolo, the Shack-Dwellers movement in KwaZulu-Natal, South Africa—who has been fighting such brave battles against the powers that be in that province for the last twenty years, the ability and willingness "to be inside the struggles of the people and to be inside the discussions inside the struggles of the people" recognizing the people as equals and the primary agents in their own struggles for justice and dignity.[7] In other words, having the humility and courage to let the cries of the people, emanating from the depths of their struggles, their hopes and their determined courage shape *our* theological reflections and responses to the struggles for justice in the midst of which we profess our faith. It is when this happens that one can begin to speak of a prophetic theology rooted in a people's theology, a concept the 1985 South African *Kairos Document* so powerfully embodies.

In the twenty-fifth anniversary edition of his classic *The Church Struggle in South Africa*, renowned South African theologian John de Gruchy suggests four "significant and interlocking challenges that have emerged for the church in South Africa at the start of the 21st century." The first is the livelihoods of the poor. The second: human sexuality and gender justice. Third is the impact of pluralism; and fourth, the effects of globalization.[8]

De Gruchy knows that although the struggle against formalized, legalized apartheid has come to an end, the struggle for justice is not over, and that that struggle has evolved into global struggles, against new forms of global apartheid, new and renewed struggles for justice, all struggles that challenge prophetic theology at its deepest core. There is nothing romantic or sentimental about it. What has kept the struggle against apartheid alive, de Gruchy asserts,

> was not any romantic optimism that all would eventually work out for the good, but a "hope against hope" that engendered action. Such hope is unprepared to accept things as they are because it is founded on the conviction that this is not how things are meant to be, and that good will triumph over evil. Keeping such hope alive is the heart of Christian political witness, a hope that celebrates every achievement of justice, no matter how small, en route to the kingdom of God.[9]

De Gruchy is absolutely right, of course. The important point he makes here, in my view, is not just that we struggle in hope, but that both the

---

7. See Gerald West, "Peoples' Theology, Prophetic Theology and Public Theology in Post-liberation South Africa," http://www.academia.edu/7263452, 13, 14.

8. De Gruchy, *The Church Struggle in South Africa*, xiv.

9. Ibid., xiv.

struggle and the hope that drives it are rooted in hope against hope. This, at its essence, means that despite the "realities" we are facing, political, economic and otherwise, threatening hopelessness and deadly retaliation from the powers that be and their collaborators even in the church, it is unprepared to accept the world as it is, that it is driven toward justice, grounded in the expectation of the kingdom of a God who is all in all justice. This God is One who, we are promised, shall not rest until justice is established in all the earth (Isa 42:1–4).

During the past two decades, both at the start of our democratic era and as events have unfolded in South Africa, even though to a large measure the prophetic church has lost its voice and its presence, some of us have engaged, and continue to engage those challenges for the church and for theology. The struggle for justice and peace, for dignity and equality, for a genuinely transformed society reflecting, nurturing, and promoting true, reconciled diversity; for a better, ecologically responsible, justice-responsive, more humane, inclusive world continues, and it is waged on many more fronts than we foresaw twenty years ago.

There were those, theologians still standing in the tradition of critical, prophetic theology, who insisted early on amidst the euphoria of, and following, 1994 that in South Africa we are nowhere near a "post-apartheid" society, that political liberation must be followed by socio-economic liberation and that this liberation is not to be found by plunging blindly into the abyss of neoliberal capitalism in unthinking imitation of the rich North. We argued that the mere shift of political power into black hands is not *ipso facto* a shift toward the kind of justice that defines freedom, and that the people having the vote is not the same as the people finding their voice. We argued that the struggle to understand the nature and the power of power and its ways with human beings did not end with the struggle against apartheid.

We pointed out that our reconciliation process would remain incomplete, unfulfilled, unsustainable, and cheap if it is de-linked from the costly demands of the systemic *undoing* of injustice and the equally systemic *doing* of justice, from personal and political repentance, restitution and the restoration of human dignity. We warned that an incomplete revolution is the same as a postponed revolution, and that if we could not find the courage to squarely and honestly face the sins of our past, we would not gain the integrity to face the challenges of our future. We were largely ignored, marginalized, and in some ways attacked and vilified because our expression of a liberation theology within the context of post-1994 South Africa did not fall in line with the demands of the new, national, official narrative of a post-apartheid, de-racialized, rainbow nation desperately wanting to be called "reconciled," but lacking the courage to run the risk of costly reconciliation.[10]

In that sense, prophetic theology is, as all true prophetic theology always is, indeed a theology "at the edge"—always at the edge of challenge and risk, of confrontation with the powers and principalities of our present age. In South Africa, we are called to do our theology within the context of a constant awareness of a post-1994 government who, in perfect, and distressing, imitation of the pre-1994 government is a government, as John Calvin admonishes King Francis I of France, "presently turned away and estranged from us—even inflamed against us."[11] Calvin ends his letter to the king with the prayer—in my view not incidentally but in fact quite consciously—reminding the king of the One who has ultimate authority and to whom *all* authority is subject, "that the Lord, the King of kings, establish your throne in justice and your seat in equity."

This is not wishing-well politics, pious sophistry, or sycophantic babble. It is prophetic admonition. First, the king may be king, but the Lord is "King of kings." The king is subject to a Higher Authority. Second, the "throne" and the "seat" is not to be equated with untouchable elevation and unchecked power. Rather, "throne" and "seat" is Calvin's understanding of the way earthly authorities should rule and the manner in which the power entrusted to them should be used, namely as the pursuit of justice, equity, and dignity. Third, this is the only way in which the king's throne shall be "established," that is, have stability, authority, and legitimacy. These are the criteria God has laid down, by which the king's, and derivatively all governmental rule, will be judged. These are also the legitimate expectations of the people. These are the criteria that will determine whether any rule is legitimate and worthy of loyalty.

Thus it is also a theology *with* an edge: a prophetic, political edge that comes from the edge Jesus himself gave to his ministry in the proclamation of the kingdom of God, and in his embrace of the struggles of the poor and

---

10. For a sermon from early 2001 (on Ps 126), critical of South Africa's socio-economic and political choices in the negotiations and since 1994 and the resultant processes of impoverishment and oppression of the poor, see Boesak, "The Tears of the Sower"; for more sustained critique, see Boesak, *The Tenderness of Conscience*; Boesak, *Running with Horses*, especially chs. 11, 13, and 18; Boesak, *Dare We Speak of Hope*; Boesak and DeYoung, *Radical Reconciliation*; Moluleke, "May the Black God Stand Up, Please!" 115–26; *The Evil of Patriarchy in Church, Society and Politics,* papers from a consultation hosted by Inclusive and Affirming Ministries (Stellenbosch: 2009). For a secular prophetic critique raising the same concerns, see, e.g., Calland, *Anatomy of South Africa*; van der Westhuizen, *White Power*; Alexander, *An Ordinary Country*. See especially Terreblanche, *Verdeelde Land*; also my *Kairos, Crisis and Global Apartheid.*

11. Calvin, *Institutes*, preface to vol. 1.

the powerless, in such stark contrast *with*, and in opposition *to* the reign of Caesar in Rome and the Temple elites in Jerusalem. That struggle, reminding earthly powers and authorities of the limits of their power and the criteria for judging their rule, continues.

It is a theology at the edge in another sense as well, I think. It is one that de Gruchy only fleetingly refers to, but then it is one that none of us discerned adequately in the final years of the eighties and the beginning of the nineties. I am speaking of the waves of Christian neo-fundamentalism washing over Africa and much of the global South with its toxic neo-colonialist package deal of scriptural selectivity, presented as "biblical inerrancy," violent homophobia, patriarchal power, and anti-justice agenda. Its justification of war and violence in the name of Jesus, its religious exclusivism coupled with unbridled political ambition in its so-called dominion theology, and its prosperity gospel grounded in the embrace of and enslavement to capitalist consumerist ideology. In its neo-colonialist alliances with capitalist power and the global media, it represents an edge, perhaps in the sense of a precipice, and prophetic theology should be much more aware and much better prepared to take on the challenges posed here. It certainly is dragging Africa, its churches, and its societies, to the edge of a disaster every bit as devastating as colonialism.[12]

However, John de Gruchy also points out that we have misconstrued that hope itself, and ended up with the "hope for a time after apartheid, articulated by many in the churches as an anticipation of the kingdom of God."[13] While such a hope provided the energy for perseverance in the dark night of despair he says, it also showed us as "somewhat naïve." De Gruchy explains: "The end of apartheid did not mean the end of colonial power relations, or more precisely, the power relationships that had been established in the colonial era along racially discriminative lines."[14]

In our reflections on the meaning of a theology at the edge from where the struggles for justice, freedom, and human dignity are waged, some socio-historical, theological reflections on de Gruchy's thoughts may not be out of place, keeping in mind my suggestion that a "theology *at* the edge" is

---

12. The highly negative impact of this religious force on the questions of justice, equality, and dignity as embraced by the South African Constitution for the life of women, especially with regard to gender-based violencem, for example, is only just beginning to be scrutinized in any systematic, academic fashion. See Elna Boesak's 2016 PhD dissertation at the University of KwaZulu-Natal, "Channeling Justice? A Feminist Exploration of North American Televangelism in a South African Constitutional Democracy." The impact on the rights and dignity on the lives of LGBTQI+ persons is another example of what exactly we are facing here.

13. De Gruchy, *Church Struggle*, 230.

14. Ibid.

as much a theology "*on* the edge" and a theology *with* an edge. There are, I think, one or two valuable lessons to be learned here.

The Church of the Streets

Throughout the history of struggle in South Africa, prophetic Christian leadership had always had a strong presence.[15] For all intents and purposes this leadership came to an end with the exile of the liberation movements in 1960, and probably definitely with the deaths of Chief Albert Luthuli in 1969 (for the ANC) and Robert Sobukwe (1978) for the Pan Africanist Congress. One can, of course, certainly argue that as far as the ANC is concerned it did find some expression in the leadership of Oliver Tambo, albeit in drastically changed circumstances in exile that made its recognizability, let alone its acknowledgement and practical application, much harder. I suspect that Tambo had to have held his Christian convictions as much more personal than political and public, except where it was expected of him as leader of the ANC in their efforts to build relationships with churches in the struggle.[16]

This leadership represented the presence of a prophetic church, never fully reflected in the institutional church, but in the prophetic witness and faithful resistance of the multitude of Christians whose faith led them to political activism and participation in the struggles for justice and dignity within their contexts. We have in mind what we have referenced before: Charles Villa-Vicencio's description of that church as "a restless presence that disturbed the church and the world"[17] who understood the call to costly discipleship, righteous choices, and sacrificial witness; Martin Luther

---

15. Ibid., 47–49. See also Tambo's "The Church and Our Struggle," an address to the World Council of Churches' World Consultation in the Netherlands, June 1980, in Tambo, *Preparing for Power*, 180–93. Tambo himself refers to the "proud history" of the ANC that included among its founders and early leadership "true Christians" who participated in the struggle on the basis of their faith. "These are men and women who read in the Scriptures a clear message that it was impermissible that he who had been made in the image of God should be debased and enslaved" (186). One paragraph later Tambo repeats the sentence almost word for word, which, in my view, indicates not mere repetition but rather the importance Tambo himself attached to such a belief.

16. For example, in 1988 Oliver Tambo and I shared a platform in New York City's Riverside Church in the context of that church's decision to honor the legacy of assassinated Swedish Prime Minister Olof Palme. Tambo's speech was about the struggle and the enormous contribution of Palme to the cause of peace, but clearly written for a Christian audience, and one I felt he was not uncomfortable with at all. See *Preparing for Power*, 235–45.

17. See Villa-Vicencio, *Trapped in Apartheid*, 5.

King Jr.'s "the church within the church, a true ecclesia and the hope of the world."[18] It is a church driven by a radical gospel of compassionate justice, hope and liberation, who understood the call to costly discipleship, righteous choices, and sacrificial witness.

That is why throughout the Defiance Campaign of the 1950s for example, the struggle was so much characterized by a spirituality of politics, so inspired by prophetic faithfulness, so infused with sacrificial commitment. It is a spiritually that would not be so explicitly reclaimed until the final phase of the struggle against apartheid in the 1980s.

But then came the 1960s, the decade of the Sharpeville massacre, the Rivonia trial, exile, and Robben Island, bannings and persecutions on a scale not experienced before, the ruthless, unprecedented suppression of dissent and all political activities. In that period the voice of that prophetic church fell silent. We—I am speaking of those of us in the black churches who followed our prophetic calling in our participation in the campaigns for freedom—allowed our fear of the apartheid regime to overcome our fear of the Lord and our commitment to prophetic faithfulness. The black church as a whole did not seem able to muster the courage of an Albert Luthuli who railed against the silence of the church because the church bent so easily under the threats from government, "virtually cowering," too afraid to speak.

"What is becoming of [prophetic] Christian witness?" Luthuli asked, warning the church that he was "extreme on this point."[19] Speaking of the tendency in the church to succumb to intimidation by the state because of the state's power to issue or revoke permits for church properties, and knowing where that might lead, Luthuli is blunt in his critique:

> Let us lose church sites and keep our integrity. I disagree with those who want to "save something from the wreck" because what I see happening is the wreck of Christian witness, and what I fear is a slow drift into nationalist state religion.[20]

On these matters, the struggle for freedom and the prophetic witness of the church, Luthuli remained consistent and unshakable, even, as we have seen, considering himself an extremist on the question of prophetic faithfulness, challenging both the church and the government on matters of justice. All this changed quite dramatically during the 1960s. It was as if the exile of the liberation movements was also the exile of the prophetic church, and as

---

18. See King, "Letter From a Birmingham Jail," 142.
19. See Luthuli, *Let My People Go!* 132.
20. Ibid.

if the imprisonment of the leaders of those movements was also the captivity of the prophetic church.

There were of course Christian voices that made themselves heard throughout that difficult decade, mainly through documents and declarations, and not for one moment do I underestimate their value and the expressions of protest they represented at the time. But in truth they were by and large the voice of white Christian leadership, moderate voices who could not authentically reclaim the radical, nonviolent, Christian militancy of an Albert Luthuli for example. Nor could they speak with any credibility for the black masses or for the black church.[21] Too strongly tied to their white churches, white privilege, and white solidarity, and not ready to accept and follow radical black (Christian) leadership, in the final analysis they remained, in the words of Charles Villa-Vicencio, "trapped in apartheid."[22]

The militant masses in the United States would be confronted with the same issue during the civil rights struggle, and Martin Luther King Jr. would describe them well: well-intentioned white moderates who could not understand the impatience of the black oppressed people of America, not understanding that they cannot "set the timetable for the Negro's freedom"; representatives of a white church "that appears to be more white than Christian" seeking safety "behind the security of stained-glass windows,"[23] too trapped in their whiteness to realize that "speaking truth to power" meant in the first place speaking to themselves in their privileged positions.

At best, these voices may have represented a theology of cautious protest, while what we actually needed was a theology of militant, nonviolent resistance. Those church leaders, well-intentioned though they may have been, did not completely overcome the white paternalism that assumed it could speak for black people.[24] And the black church, unlike Albert Luthuli, did not yet understand well enough that protest, without the framework of resistance, without the proper understanding of the realities of power and powerlessness, and without the vision of enduring liberation, was doomed to remain a form of begging.[25] Black people, for the most part, and the

21. I refer especially to the *Cottesloe Declaration* (1960) and the *Message to the People of South Africa* (1968). I pursue this argument in more detail in Boesak, *Kairos, Crisis and Global Apartheid*, ch. 3.

22. See Villa-Vicencio, *Trapped in Apartheid*.

23. King, *Where Do We Go from Here*, 36.

24. See Luthuli, *Let My people Go!* 125: "White, paternalist Christianity—as though Whites had invented the Christian faith—estranges my people from Christ. Hypocrisy, double standards, and the identification of white skins with Christianity do the same . . . We know Christianity for what it is, we know it is not a white preserve . . . It is not too late for white Christians to look to the Gospels and redefine their allegiance."

25. It was philosopher and literary scholar Adam Small who in 1973, at the beginning

black church, for the most part, would beg to be listened to; beg to be responded to; beg for crumbs from the oppressor's table because we did not vigorously enough claim our seat *at* the table. More importantly, perhaps, neither did we make clear enough that the table set by the oppressor is not acceptable to a people bent on defining their freedom for themselves. So we protested against the *consequences* of the decisions made for us by others while we should have been the ones making the decisions regarding our own future for ourselves.

As far as the black church is concerned, however, while we may have turned silent on the issues that mattered, we did not stop preaching. We did not understand that in a very real sense, we had come, to use the phrase of American homiletician Richard Lischer, to "the end of words,"[26] or more specifically, to the end of those particular kinds of words. If words were to be spoken, other words were called for. However, as Steve Biko pointed out and we shall see below, we did not preach a liberating Jesus. We preached a colonized, domesticated, de-justicized,[27] depoliticized, spiritualized Jesus, as if the Jesus speaking in Luke 4:16–20 did not exist, could be ignored, or did not speak of *us*. We preached a Jesus that knew nothing of justice or of judgment on injustice. The black church preached a Jesus that would not be offensive to the apartheid regime, not cause discomfort for those whose approval we sought, nor constitute a danger to ourselves. Prophetic faithfulness, for the most part, was alien to the life and testimony of the black church. Unlike Luthuli and Martin Luther King Jr., at that point in our history we were not ready to be "extremists" in the mode of Amos, Micah, or Jesus.

Biko and the Children of Soweto

Then, in the 1970s, two major events occurred: Steve Biko and the coming of Black Consciousness, and Soweto and the revolution of the children. Both would quite decisively expose the alienation of the black church from its prophetic calling. We were at first stunned, then shamed, then converted by Biko's critique of Christianity and more specifically, of the black church.

---

of the waves of protest of that era against apartheid through the Black Consciousness Movement, first raised the question of protest as a form of begging, providing valuable food for thought as we entered the final stages of the onslaught against apartheid through the United Democratic Front; see Small, "Blackness versus Nihilism," 14–15, cited in Boesak, *Black and Reformed*, 7.

26. See Lischer, *The End of Words*.

27. I borrow the term from Wolterstorff, *Justice: Rights and Wrongs*, 96–98.

"If in the past," Biko told us, "Christianity was the perfect instrument for the subjugation of the people, now the interpretation of Christianity and the Bible are the tools for the maintenance of subjugation."[28] In the first instance Biko's critique was historical. He was criticizing the white missionaries and the white church for their use of our faith and the Scriptures to justify oppression. But in the second instance Biko's critique was contemporary, self-critical. He was critical of a black church not being able to break the chains of a colonizing, dehumanizing white Christianity, continuing to believe in and practicing a theology that kept the Bible captive to an enslaving hermeneutic and ourselves subservient to a Christianized, colonialized mind set. We were the ones whose interpretation of the Bible became what he called a "poisoned well" from which our people were forced to drink. His critique was not so much directed at the Bible as to the *interpretation* of the Bible by black preachers. There was, he seemed to say, nothing redemptive, liberating, or hopeful we had to say to the people who listened for the Word of God in the biblical message from the pulpit.

The children of Soweto did not so much critique the black church with their words as with their courage, their sacrifices and their blood. They showed us not only the emptiness of our words, but called for the end of those—to be replaced by deeds of courage and commitment. That was the beginning of what African American theologian Gayraud Wilmore, in regard to the situation of black America, called the "radicalization of Black Christianity."[29] It was then that we were able to move from a theology of acquiescence to a theology of refusal, from a theology of resignation to a theology of hope,[30] from a theology of protest to a theology of resistance. We sought to understand not only the question of suffering but the question of *unearned* suffering; and as a consequence not just the relationship between unearned suffering and redemption, but crucially the theological question of resistance *against* unearned suffering *as* redemptive suffering.

Then we began to ask the fundamental questions about power and powerlessness, about power and the use of power and the effects of the use of power. Then we began to understand that the issue was not simply one of equality in society but really the question: what *kind* of equality in what *kind* of society? We then began to inquire not just about justice and injustice, but about the nature of structural, systemic injustice. We talked not just about poverty. We began to debate the systemic nature of poverty, and more

---

28. See Biko, *I Write What I Like*, 58–59.
29. See Wilmore, *Black Religion and Black Radicalism*.
30. See for my thoughts on hope Boesak, *Dare We Speak of Hope*.

precisely the socio-historical processes of generational wealth and generational *impoverishment.*

In the process we began to understand the struggle better and in different terms. It became clear to us not only that there *was* a struggle, but that the struggle was *ours*, not somebody else's, not even another generation's but *ours*; that in that struggle one had to take sides and that neutrality was no longer possible. We understood that the struggle, in a very real sense, was not simply black and white, that in other words, there were black people and white people, for different political, ideological, and personal reasons, on either side of that struggle. Searching for the enemies or allies of liberation and justice based on skin color and racialized sentiment, therefore, was delusional, misleading, and futile.

In 1983, at the launch of the United Democratic Front, we understood this and tried to articulate it as foundational for the new phase of struggle about to commence, as well as for what may lie ahead:

> There is something else that must be said. South Africa belongs to all its people. This is a basic truth to which we must cling tenaciously now and in the future. This country is our country. Its future is not safe in the hands of persons, white or black, who despise democracy and trample on the rights of the people. Its future is not safe in the hands of people, black or white, who, to build their empires, depend upon economic exploitation and human degradation. Its future is not safe in the hands of persons, black or white, who need the flimsy and deceitful cloak of ethnic superiority to cover the nakedness of their racism. Its future is not safe in the hands of persons, white or black, who seek to secure their unjustly acquired positions of privilege by repressing violently the weak, the exploited, and the needy. Its future is not safe in the hands of persons, white or black, who put their faith simply in the madness of growing militarism. For the sake of our country and our children, therefore, whether *you* be white or black, resist those persons, whether *they* be white or black.[31]

In South Africa and the United States we seem to have reached that point, and it is brilliantly illustrated by Aislinn Pulley. We understood as well that it was not just about the prophetic *voice* of the church that needed to be heard but about the prophetic *participation* of the church that needed to be seen in the resistance to evil. It became clearer to us that the church was fundamentally divided: there was the church that benefited from our

---

31. See Boesak, *Black and Reformed*, 161.

oppression and therefore acquiesced in it, and there was the church that suffered under oppression and felt called to rise up in resistance to it. Both could not be the church of Jesus Christ. That was the insight that would become so fundamental in the theological discourse and call to repentance, conversion, commitment, and action of the 1985 *Kairos Document* and its valuable distinction between state theology, church theology, and prophetic theology.

Our thinking became more systemic and we discerned that the struggle was not just against the consequences of evil in general, but against an evil, highly sophisticated *system*. Consequently, the struggle should be aimed at the very pillars that upheld that system. And as we better understood apartheid as both a system of capitalist, racial domination and an evil based on a deliberate distortion of the gospel of Jesus Christ, we defined the pillars on which it was built:[32]

- Colonialism and its vile legacy, which included slavery, subjugation, dehumanization, dispossession, and generational trauma;
- Social Darwinism, expressed in customs, laws, and attitudes enshrining white superiority and black inferiority that provided the basis for South Africa's peculiar racist, pigmentocratic societal structures;
- Socio-economic exploitation inextricable from, but not exclusively based on race, but also for example on gender injustice;
- Cultural domination resting on cultural annihilation on the one hand and cultural assimilation on the other, the key being that the culture of the subjugated peoples and groups are always deemed worthless compared to the culture of the dominant groups, and therefore unworthy of consideration and contribution except when those cultural goods can be useful to the oppressor for purposes of usurpation or manipulation or both;
- Power in its different forms: psychological, physical, ideological, political, and economic; as well as the power derived from international (white) solidarity and global systems of domination;
- A belief in white innocence based on a powerful ideology of white, and in many ways a particularly Afrikaner, victimhood;
- Violence in all its forms: systemic, structural, ideological and physical violence, pervasive and total, guaranteeing and solidifying control;

---

32. See also Boesak, *Kairos, Crisis, and Global Apartheid*, 2, 3.

- And finally, and in South Africa absolutely crucial, ideologized religion (in the United States sometimes called "civil religion") and its belief systems, central to which was the belief in national exceptionalism and a predetermined "manifest destiny." In South Africa this was true in general and in particular the idea of Afrikaner chosenness with its unique and exclusive covenant with God, and its power in the justification of domination and subjugation.

Once we understood this and found the words to express it both politically and theologically, the church could reclaim its prophetic role in the struggle for justice and freedom. Pertaining to this last point, for those of us in the black churches of the Reformed tradition, and in the face of the heresy of the theology of apartheid,[33] it was of course of utmost importance to reclaim that tradition as a tradition of freedom, justice, and liberation,[34] and the Bible, as Richard Horsley et al. speak of it, as "a faithful history of resistance against empire"[35] and imperial power.

Outmaneuvered by Democracy?

Then, in 1994, for the second time in three decades, that prophetic church lost its voice. In an analysis over several pages in my *The Tenderness of Conscience: African Renaissance and the Spirituality of Politics*, I explore some of the reasons for this.[36] Respected theologian Gerald West, himself one of the key prophetic voices in South Africa, explains how successful the African National Congress leadership, from Nelson Mandela to Thabo Mbeki, had become in appropriating biblical language, stealing that language from the church so to speak, crafting it into not just the language of government but the language of the ANC itself.[37] In doing this, West argues convincingly, Mandela achieved two important things: he significantly disempowered the voice of the church in society, and he succeeded in confining the witness of

---

33 See Boesak, *Black and Reformed*.

34. See Boesak, *Kairos, Crisis, and Global Apartheid*, ch. 2.

35. See Horsley, ed., *In the Shadow of Empire*. See also Wittenberg, *Resistance Theology in the Old Testament*.

36. Boesak, *Tenderness of Conscience*, 154–59.

37. West, "People's Theology," 2–5: "Not only was Mandela the one who seems to have called for the return of religion to a national public role, he is also the one who has set the parameters of religion's public role." Mandela made clear that that role should focus on matters spiritual, working toward what the ANC called "the RDP of the soul," leaving the matters of politics, social, and economic reconstruction and development (RDP) to the state.

the church to "spiritual matters" leaving the "real life issues" of economic and social justice to the state. Our unpreparedness to deal with this strategy, coupled with those expectations that de Gruchy, correctly, calls "somewhat naïve," made the church completely lose its footing.

John de Gruchy especially identifies our "confusion" in the "anticipation of the kingdom of God" with the coming of democracy under ANC rule. Again, de Gruchy is right. The church, identified as the "prophetic church," the "church of the streets," and "the church of the struggle" did indeed tend to identify the victory of the ANC with the victory of justice. In a public discussion on this issue, theologian Tinyiko Moluleke at some point aptly suggested that we might have been "outmaneuvered by democracy."

In this regard, Dr. Martin Luther King Jr.'s dealings with Chicago mayor Richard M. Daley offer a vivid illustration of what I mean. In 1966, King came to Chicago not to march for voting rights, but to expose the segregationist politics of the North and to work for integrated housing. Chicago, is the consensus, became King's Waterloo. He failed, writes journalist Edward McClelland, because the combination of a recalcitrant but clever Daley and the "Daley-controlled black aldermen," the notorious so-called Silent Six, and the way they manipulated democracy in Chicago, completely outmaneuvered him.[38]

Unlike Southern politicians, Daley ordered his police to stop the violence—but he also went to court for an injunction limiting the size and the hours of the marches. In other words, under the cloak of "nonviolence" and making use of the democratic system, Daley proscribed the militancy of the movement and so undercut the persuasive power of one the most effective weapons at the movement's disposal. When he finally sat down to negotiate with King, they came up with an agreement in which Daley promised, among other things, to lobby for more open housing legislation and build scattered-site housing projects. King left town declaring victory. Shortly after his departure, Daley, a true embodiment of the empire whose promises can never be trusted, in his turn declared that the summit had produced nothing but a "gentlemen's agreement," an agreement he clearly never had any intention of honoring. King was furious, but there was nothing he could do about it. In Chicago, "democracy" had outmaneuvered the movement.

Looking back on this crucial moment in the civil rights struggle, some crucial lessons seem appropriate for us to ponder. One, by the time King

---

38. See Edward McClelland, "How Mayor Daley Outfoxed Martin Luther King," January 16, 2012, http://www.nbcchicago.com/blogs/ward-room/How-Mayor-Daley-Outfoxed-Martin-Luther-King-113881699.html. My thanks to my friend and colleague Dr. Curtiss Paul DeYoung, who alerted me to this article and the point it makes. See also Finley et al., *The Chicago Freedom Movement*.

came to Chicago African Americans there had been enjoying their voting rights for a hundred years. With those rights, they had put in power black representatives like the "Silent Six" who became so embroiled in the machinery of the empire, so subservient to Mayor Daley, so beholden to their own self-interests, that the larger goals of liberation became meaningless to them. In fact true liberation in Chicago would have meant the end of the profitable collaboration with the system of patronage Chicago is rightly infamous for. The people were no longer the touchstone of political authenticity. They had merely become cannon fodder for the politics of self-indulgence. In South Africa it was the Black Consciousness movement that sensitized and opened the eyes of a whole generation to these painful realities as we came to understand better the workings of apartheid through the Bantustan governments, the apartheid surrogate structures embraced by a small minority in the Indian and so-called colored communities. Now that we have won the right to a proper vote, the question looms large: what do we do with this right? In whom, and in what kind of politics, do we invest that power? Is the investment of that power an investment toward systemic change for the common good? It is a question persistently asked of the Palestinian Authority regarding their leadership disconnected from the dreams and hopes of the Palestinian people, and their submissive collaboration with the Israeli Apartheid regime's "security" demands.

Two, Mayor Richard Daley, on his own, would not have been able to outmaneuver King so easily. He could do it only with the support of his black aldermen. The black presence in the politics of Chicago was not an instrument of liberation. Rather it was a Trojan horse for the politics of deception. On every scale, and in every context, as we have learned in South Africa, the success of the empire in the oppression of the people and the thwarting of the liberation struggle is not possible without the collaboration of the oppressed themselves. In this context, we understood so much better the workings of apartheid in securing collaboration from certain persons in the black communities, bribing them with material gains and opportunities while simply using them to "prove" the success of apartheid and the "willing cooperation" of blacks as junior partners in apartheid and their own oppression.

We understood better the particular hypocrisy, deceit, and political dangers of the final gasp of apartheid reformism, the so-called Tri-cameral Parliament, proposed in South Africa's 1983 Constitution, a "solution" which purported to be a "power sharing" arrangement between whites, Indians and "coloreds" to the complete exclusion of the vast majority of South Africa's black population; an arrangement which ostensibly gave "coloreds" and Indians "voting rights" but left white political and economic power firmly intact and untouched.[39]

It is for this reason that the successful boycott of the "Indian" and "colored" elections for the National Party's Tri-Cameral Parliament in 1983, driven by a mass political, non-racial, nonviolent, militant movement, the United Democratic Front, was so important. And while it did not stop the apartheid regime from the politically desperate act of instituting that Tri-Cameral Parliament, it robbed the elections, the Parliament, and all its workings of all legitimacy. If the freedom struggle itself and Dr. King as its most visible voice had been able to secure the support from the oppressed community that was necessary for victory, "Chicago" could not have happened.

Three, this is a lesson in learning to withstand the temptations of empire and self-gratification at the cost of liberation. Although it has become almost fashionable to refer to the failure in Chicago as if it was Martin King's failure, it is not so. It is the failure of the whole movement. Chicago was not so much a personal setback for King, as it was a setback for black people as a whole, for the struggle for justice and freedom as a whole, and in the end it was a setback for the hope for America to become a freer, more democratic, more dignified society. The "Silent Six" were not the only ones. Chicago is what Chicago is, not because Martin King failed, but because too many of Chicago's black politicians and civic leaders chose profitable, palatable oppression instead of liberation, in the process rendering the right to vote virtually meaningless and abusing the power entrusted to them by the people they were supposed to serve. The question is whether we have been willing to learn from these experiences in a manner sufficient for the even greater challenges in today's so-called democratic maneuverings.

But perhaps a fourth lesson is most important of all. I think Dr. King himself learned from this experience, but it did not leave him bitter, disappointed, or paralyzed by humiliation. It radicalized him. The radical King we meet in *Where Do We Go from Here: Chaos or Community?*, Vincent Harding tells us, must be understood "in the urgent context of King's difficult experiences in Watts and Chicago."[40] Chicago was the setting for King's "fierce reminders" that the struggle was for much more than integration into American society: "Let us not think of our movement as one that seeks to integrate the Negro into all the existing values of American society." Instead, beginning to severely question those values, King urged, "Let us be those

---

39. For a discussion of the response from these communities to this political arrangement through my personal point of view Boesak, *Black and Reformed*, ch. 11; also Boesak, *Running with Horses*, Part 2.

40. See Harding, "Introduction," in *Where Do We Go from Here*, xii.

creative dissenters who will call our beloved nation to a higher destiny, to a new plateau of compassion, to a more noble expression of humanness." [41]

The King after Chicago was a very different King than the King of the Lincoln Memorial's American Dream. That King, as Cornel West has noted, had waxed exponentially in "analytical power, righteous indignation, and prophetic vision."[42] The "dissenters" King was looking for were those dissenters from the American values that held captive that greater dream, that higher destiny toward humanness. In Chicago, King saw that dream turned into a nightmare. The King of the March on Washington was the gentle, hopeful capitalist waiting for a check from the bank of the American Dream to alleviate the poverty of the masses. The King after Chicago was the prophetic, critical analyst asking the much more fundamental question: "Why are there forty million poor people in America?" recognizing that when one asks that question, "You are raising a question about the economic system, about a broader distribution of wealth. When you ask that question, you begin to question the capitalist economy." But raising those questions must of course take him further: "Who owns the oil? . . . Who owns the iron ore? . . . Why is it that people have to pay water bills in a world that's two-thirds water?"[43] These are words, King argued, that "must be said." "And I'm simply saying that more and more, we've got to begin asking questions about the whole society."[44] And by then for him "asking questions about society" inescapably meant "restructuring the whole of American society."[45]

In Chicago, King had seen the manipulation of democracy and the fatal consequences of black collaboration with a corrupt system. He had seen what it means when "freedom" is defined *for* the oppressed instead of *by* the oppressed, and he learned from it: "Freedom is not won by passive acceptance of suffering. Freedom is won by a struggle *against* suffering. By this measure, Negroes have not yet paid the full price for freedom. And whites have not yet faced the full cost of justice."[46] In chapter after chapter this King would wax in understanding, commitment, and radicality until in the final chapter he would spell out in clear, unambiguous terms what a "true revolution of values," embraced by the "creative dissenters" would mean for America and the world.[47]

41. Ibid., xviii.
42. *The Radical King*, 126.
43. Ibid., 177.
44. Ibid., 176.
45. Ibid., 176, 177.
46. King, *Where Do We Go from Here?*, 20.
47. Ibid., in the chapter titled, "The World House," 196–202.

Thus "Chicago" remains a useful illustration of the workings of power and the temptations of our need to negotiate with Pharaoh as Moses and Aaron seek to do (Exod 7:8–13) rather than to confront the pharaoh with the word from the LORD: "Let my people go!" It furthermore illustrates the need for the prophetic church to be as alert and forthright as Jesus was in his dealings with Herod, even in the face of threats, ("Go and tell that fox from me . . ." [Luke 13:32]); and with Pilate, representative of the power and might of Rome, ("You would have no power over me unless it was given you from above . . ." [John 19:11]); taking Jesus' warning seriously in our encounters with demonic powers disguised as democratic angels of light: as gentle as the dove and wise as the serpent. So Moluleke is right. However, I think there might be more to it than that:

- We forgot the lessons we have learned from our earlier understanding of the workings of power. We forgot that it is never just *who* is in power, but *how* they use their power when in power;
- More importantly perhaps, we have not reckoned with the fatal, seductive power of power and that, in its inverse imitation of God, it is not a respecter of persons;
- We forgot what John Calvin had taught us: that the true measurement of a just government is how justice is done to the poor, the wronged, and the oppressed, and how the *rights* of the poor are responded to, respected, promoted and protected.
- We confused access to political power with closeness to the throne of God.
- We exchanged our prophetic faithfulness for what we called "critical solidarity" (with a government we have elected into power and who professed to be one with us in our belief in and struggles for justice and freedom), except that our solidarity was more expedient than critical. More tragically, but unavoidably, our solidarity with those in power all too soon replaced our solidarity with the poor and the oppressed, because, in the new situation of (black) power politics in South Africa, there was so little *benefit* in it.
- We surrendered the terrain of prophetic faithfulness and allowed it to become the playground of political expediency and propaganda. So before we knew it, former president Thabo Mbeki and (former finance minister) Trevor Manuel, (and presently president Jacob Zuma and deputy-president Cyril Ramaphosa) were, and are, more at ease with using the Bible to expound their particular brand of state theology

than we were able to offer prophetic witness to the nation standing on the truth of that very same Bible.[48]

- We confused Nelson Mandela's South Africa, "a nation at peace with itself and the world" with the shalom of the kingdom of God. And we did that because as a church we no longer stood where Christ stands, and is always to be found. Instead, we found our place and took the elevated and lofty view from the hill where the Union Buildings stand, and no longer looked from the depths of the flooded valleys of misery and poverty where the neglected and the destitute still cry for freedom and justice.

- Finally and perhaps more important than we dare to admit, in ways disastrously intimate, simultaneously spiritual and political: as we became more and more mesmerized by Mr. Mandela, deeming ourselves more and more beholden to the ANC, we became more and more embarrassed by Jesus.

Unless, as I have argued earlier, we understand what Henry Highland Garnet understood about the situation of black people in the United States when he warned that "there are pharaohs on both sides of those blood-red waters,"[49] and how this reality now applies to our situations of global struggles, we might not understand that we have not only lost our edge, but that we are standing on the edge of what might be a precipice rather than at the edge of a rediscovery of our prophetic calling and of the things that make for peace in the world today. What we do need to learn and understand is we never truly "arrive." As long as God's people suffer under unjust and oppressive systems the call for prophetic wakefulness remains.

But there is a matter equally as grave. When the Truth and Reconciliation Commission started its work in South Africa, it created a terrain where the prophetic voice of the church could be, and should have been, vitally decisive. I am not speaking of the willingness or unwillingness of churches to testify before the Commission. I am, rather, speaking of bold, prophetic intervention in the processes of reconciliation itself; of taking the initiative to define reconciliation as spiritual reality and its impact on the practice of politics, not to protect the "purity" of its Christian nature, but in order to prevent it from becoming no more than a form of political pietism.[50] To ensure that a term so intrinsically biblical should not become too easily

---

48. See West, "Thabo Mbeki's Bible," 87–106; on President Jacob Zuma and Deputy President Cyril Ramaphosa and their use of the Bible, see West, "People's Theology."

49. See Garnet, "Call to Rebellion," 119.

50. For the way I use this term, see Boesak and DeYoung, *Radical Reconciliation*.

estranged from its radical character; too easily reduced to an excuse for the domestication of justice and consequently of the continuation of injustice.

We never publicly, consistently, and prophetically proclaimed reconciliation as not a handy tool for, and relatively harmless result of, politically negotiated settlements, but as a radical biblical demand even though we were aware of how reconciliation as a recognizably Christian concept became the hallmark of South Africa's reconciliation process. We did not remind the nation that if reconciliation is to be real, durable and sustainable, it has to be radical and revolutionary, and that reconciliation, in order to be real, has to be effectively and attentively translated into political and socio-economic reality with the restoration of justice at the heart of it.

We did not insist, publicly, prophetically, and consistently, what we have known from the beginning and actually preached during the struggle, that reconciliation is not possible without confrontation of evil—both the evil from the past, the evil of ongoing injustice, and the evil of acquiescing to that injustice because it is to our benefit. That reconciliation is not possible without equality, which means profound and fundamental shifts in power relations. Neither is reconciliation possible without the restoration of justice, human dignity and hope. We forgot to remind the nation that reconciliation is not possible without restitution. I do not mean the issue of reparations that has resurfaced in the debates around reconciliation in South Africa; I mean acts of systemic *restitution*, from land to opportunity to human dignity, which is hardly ever mentioned. Most importantly we did not proclaim as clearly and unambiguously as we could, that reconciliation is costly, that it is never cheap, and that a "miracle" such as we claim our transition to be becomes valueless if it is divorced from the costliness of remorse, repentance, restitution, and the restoration of justice, and the consequences of these for politics.

Forgiveness, John de Gruchy reminds us in his important work on reconciliation as "restoring justice," is a word that easily "trips off our tongue."[51] I agree. Christians use it effortlessly, ceaselessly, and thoughtlessly. We did not, consistently, publicly, and prophetically remind the nation that forgiveness is indispensable, but never sentimental; that forgiveness has personal, communal, and political dimensions; that forgiveness includes respectful room for righteous anger and that it requires a fundamental shift in power relations.

We did not insist that forgiveness is always the prerogative of the victim, never the right of the perpetrator; that it is a gift, never earned but always freely given, and that forgiveness is a soul-restoring, life-giving act,

---

51. De Gruchy, *Reconciliation*, 171.

but without the reciprocity of justice it becomes, as we have heard above, "a forgiveness that kills."[52] We did not prophesy to the nation that there are things that while they might be forgivable, are never excusable,[53] and that only through the grace of God may the inexcusable become forgivable. And we did not spell out, never even asked, what the political implications of such an understanding might be.

Elna Boesak makes the point regarding F. W. de Klerk's deplorable efforts to find excuses for apartheid as we have seen in chapter 5, to cling to his need for cheap reconciliation and his desire for the country, particularly black South Africa, to just "move on." But there is hardly a more poignant and devastating illustration of the issue of forgivability and excusability than the matter of the poisoned water in the city of Flint, Michigan, in the United States. It is now clear that the poisoned water that the city's people are forced to drink is not the result of an accident: it's the result of years of devastating free-market policies and "reforms," enduring systemic racism and cold, calculated politics of exploitation, neglect, and exclusion.[54] However, despite the fact that that the state's culpability is now beyond dispute, "the city's government continues to charge people for the poisoned water and then threatening to foreclose their homes or take their children if they refuse to pay."[55]

But here is why the matter of the poisoned water might be forgivable, assuming the officials responsible for this crime against children ever seek forgiveness, but never excusable, becomes pertinent. Michael Moore, one-time Flint resident, filmmaker, and activist for justice, in responding to those who seek to help the residents of Flint by donating bottled water explains why they cannot really "help":

52. A participant in my "Conversations on Reconciled Diversity" held during 2011 in Mangaung, Bloemfontein, under auspices of the University of the Free State's Institute for Reconciliation and Social Justice; see ch. 5.

53. Journalist Elna Boesak introduced this concept in her response to F. W. De Klerk's May 2012 public attempt to defend and justify apartheid in an interview on CNN: "Apartheid can be forgiven but not excused"; see Elna Boesak, "Time for apartheid's truth to be spoken," *Sunday Independent,* May 21, 2012, http://www.iol.co.za/sundayindependent/time-for-apartheid-s-truth-to-be-spoken-1.1301002.

54. The news items regarding this matter is a constant flow, but see, e.g., Jacob Lederman, *In These Times,* 24 January 2016. "This is a racial crime," Lederman quotes film maker/activist Michael Moore, and his own conclusion is that "Flint's poisonous water is merely the latest, and most high profile example of a bankrupt system of neoliberal governance." See http://readersupportednews.org/opinion2/277-75-34788-flint's-water-crisis-is-no-accident.

55. See John Vibes, *The Free Thought Project,* January 27, 2016, http://readersupportednews.org/news-section/2/318-66/34858-flint-residents-told-that-their-children-could-be-taken.

The reason you can't help is that you cannot reverse the irreversible brain damage that has been inflicted upon every single child in Flint. The damage is permanent. There is no medicine you can send, no doctor or scientist who has any way to undo the harm done to thousands of babies, toddlers, and children (not to mention their parents). They are ruined for life, and someone needs to tell the truth about that. They will, forever, suffer from the various neurological impediments, their IQs will be lowered by at least 20 points, they will not do as well in school and, by the time they reach adolescence, they will exhibit various behavioral problems that will land a number of them in trouble, and some in jail . . . This is a catastrophe of unimaginable proportions. There is not a terrorist organization on Earth that has yet to figure out how to poison 100,000 people every day for two years—and get away with it. That took a Governor who subscribes to an American political ideology hell-bent on widening the income inequality gap and conducting various versions of voter and electoral suppression against people of color and the poor.[56]

This is a powerful reminder of Pope Francis' observation of the "globalization of indifference," his searing critique of neoliberal capitalist policies of exclusion as well as his urgent call on us "not to be afraid to say it." Except that the secular prophet Michael Moore knows: the only way to be faithful in this situation is to "join us in revolt."

We did not publicly, consistently, and prophetically insist that whichever way one describes it, and despite its appropriation by politics or even its *necessity* for politics, forgiveness is not naturally a word from the political lexicon. One expects it rather at the end of a process of remorse, contrition, repentance, confession, and conversion, as perhaps a comma or a question mark, not simply as triumphalist exclamation mark at the end of negotiations. Forgiveness, by its very nature, belongs in the realm of the impossible, and the impossible is only possible through the grace of God and the power of the Holy Spirit.

True forgiving is not to "forgive and forget." That, Bonhoeffer reminds us, is the "cheap grace" of "live and let live" we should resist: preaching forgiveness without requiring repentance, promising absolution without personal confession. That is cheap forgiveness: without discipleship, without the cross, without Jesus Christ, living and incarnate. Elsewhere Bonhoeffer

---

56. See Michael Moore, "Do Not Send Us Bottles of Water, Instead, Join Us in Revolt," http://readersupportednews.org/opinion2/277-75/34849-focus-do-not-send-us-bottles-of-water.

expounds on the theme of forgiveness as he explores Jesus's admonition to Peter to forgive not seven times, but seventy times seven times. As long as we keep counting the old sins of the other, Bonhoeffer writes, we have not yet forgiven, and as a result, we cannot live in the freedom we desire and need. This is as important personally as it is politically. What Jesus essentially tells Peter is to "stop counting." Forgiveness is to free ourselves from counting.[57] But we must not be confused. The context of these words remains Jesus' and Peter's assumption that the perpetrator comes with repentance and contrition—every time. The context with Bonhoeffer is his steadfast rejection of "cheap grace": forgiveness without repentance, absolution without confession. "Not counting" is not the same as "forgetting" and "moving on."

So the insistence of so many South Africans that we should "move on" without embracing the costliness of repentance and forgiveness is as far from forgiveness as we can get. But it lies at the heart of our unfulfilled and incomplete reconciliation process. Simply "moving on" means never learning from the past yet remaining burdened by it, never harnessing ourselves against the onslaught of the past on that better, more humane future we are seeking. In true repentance and forgiveness we do not take the dark, sin-laden past with us, but we do take the one who offended against us with us, refusing to let go of their hand since we are now bound to fight the darkness of the past together as we are bound to seek the light of a new future together. And again, I am not sure we ever did ask what the political and socio-economic implications of *that* understanding might be. It is not the willingness to forgive that poses the danger of the dark past returning to haunt us. It is when the evil is *excused,* not repented of and therefore not forgiven; never seen as the wrong and the evil it truly was, that those crimes of the past return with a vengeance.

It is for these reasons that the South African youth, tired of being lied to, tired of empty promises, and tired of having their faith and trust betrayed are taking to the streets in such huge numbers, determined not to stop until their cry is heard.

This is the edge our theological reflection and action and our prophetic witness are called to. It makes our theology a theology at the edge because this is the edge where the people, pushed beyond endurance, burdened beyond belief, and battered beyond comprehension, are taking their stand in resistance.

---

57. Bonhoeffer, *Gesammelte Schriften*, 4:399–406.

Where Do We Go from Here?

Martin Luther King Jr.'s question not only still haunts the prophetic church today; it takes on a new sense of urgency, as do the only two alternatives that loom behind that question: it is either the creation of a beloved community of radical justice, peace, equality, inclusivity, and dignity, or it is chaos. So where do we go from here, now that South Africa's democracy is twenty-three years old but the foundational tenets of our Constitution have already come under threat and even sustained attack? Now that, as journalist Elna Boesak once remarked, we have buried the ghosts of racism, ethnocentricity, and narrow, tribal nationalisms in a grave so shallow they rise to haunt us at the slightest provocation? Is it still possible to step away from the edge of disaster, now that our foolish embrace of neoliberal capitalism has immeasurably deepened the misery of millions while immeasurably enriching the few, and the gap between rich and poor has made us one of the most unequal societies on earth?

South African economist Sampie Terreblanche, in his aptly titled book *Verdeelde Land* (*Divided Land*), after painstaking and sober economic and political analysis in six preceding chapters, speaks the prophetic language the church should speak but hardly ever does, when he exposes the facts and statistics to the light of prophetic truth:

> When the ostentatious consumerism, the waste, the greed, and the arrogance of the very rich are compared to the misery and deprivation of so many impoverished people, we have no choice but to be shocked at the vulgarity and offensiveness of the lifestyles of the rich. Are the rich and the poor really citizens of the same South Africa? Has the time not arrived for a new Codesa [Convention for a Democratic South Africa] on the question as to why so many persons are so inordinately rich and so many more persons so hopelessly poor? Why do the churches not engage in open war on behalf of those undeservedly poor and against those so undeservedly wealthy? How are we ever going to bridge the gap between rich and poor in this divided land?[58]

That is indeed the question.

Our gains in gender justice are seriously threatened and in many ways already overcome by the grim statistics that make South Africa the "rape

---

58. Terreblanche, *Verdeelde Land*, 148, my translation. Terreblance makes the point that according to Swiss bank Credit Suisse there are, amidst the shocking poverty, some 71,000 dollar-millionaires in South Africa, citing *Die Burger*, March 15, 2012. Elsewhere in the book (141, 147) Terreblanche speaks of the need for a new "Justice and Reconciliation Commission."

capital of the world." How do we regain the prophetic edge of our theology, now that our dedication to the protection and promotion of human rights, equality, and dignity for all, including those from the LGBTQI+ community are threatened, attacked, and flouted by Christian fundamentalists, ignored by judges and magistrates who pay obeisance to patriarchy but show little allegiance to equal justice; by gangs of Christian thugs who have taught us the meaning of "corrective rape" in the name of Jesus? Where do we go from here, now that carelessness, corruption, and incompetence are paralyzing services to the people and laying waste to the hopes of our elders and the dreams of our children?

As a very first priority, I should think, we must not, under the pressures of disillusionment and anger, abandon the correctness of our decision to forsake revenge, retribution, and punishment and to pursue authentic reconciliation. In fact we must publicly, consistently, and prophetically reclaim its foundational righteousness. But we must work hard to make reconciliation real, radical and revolutionary. We must step away from the temptations of political pietism and Christian quietism and the lure of cheap reconciliation, and embrace justice, dignity, and costly discipleship. We must take the restoration of justice and human dignity to its full, public, vivid, and concrete conclusions.

We must give no theological or political succor to the illusionary, deliberately created perception that the South African transition was a smooth, consensual, happy process, fair and just because we left the wealth and privileges of historically advantaged South Africans untouched, in exchange for the swift creation of a new, privileged elite of black South Africans. We must critically engage the idea and vigorously expose the lie that these arrangements are not only realistic political necessity but in fact the key to political and social harmony, and a model for other nations and societies. A theology at the edge will seriously and thoughtfully question why we are required to believe that "sunset clauses" and "the realities of the balance of power" are more expressive of reconciliation than "justice," "equity," and "restitution." We must ask much more critical questions about the secret talks and hidden negotiations that preceded the public negotiations, the so-called "end game" that dictated the rules for and content of what was to be called "reconciliation." Indeed, we must seriously challenge the very notion that the "end game" was played by a selected few in the dark, privileged exclusivity of pre-negotiations, rather than by the people, out in the open, on the streets of battle and blood, sacrifice and death.

We must resist the temptation to turn what is a history of mass struggle into a single biography. I mean this: We must combat and correct the version informed by the narrative of the dominant that claims that the miracle of our transition was the work of Mr. Mandela *all on his own*. I have already spoken to this in the previous chapter but it is worthwhile reinforcing this important point. The tendency to dishonor the people by fading their role in their own struggles for justice will only diminish the struggle itself. Only as the *people's* struggle it will become the revolution that will fundamentally challenge and overturn injustice. As an individualized reduction it will turn into individualized iconosism, leaving the revolution at the mercy of those who will use the people's sacrifices for their own self-aggrandizement and self-enrichment.

Of course, there is place for honoring our leaders and celebrating their special gifts and talents, their insights and wisdom, their leadership and courage. And we must not lack in gratitude for and pride in what we have been given in them and by them. It is upon their shoulders that we stand. But such a distortion of history, such denial of the people's ownership of their struggle and of their leader does not elevate or honor Mr. Mandela. It imprisons him all over again, leaving him at the mercy of new ideologies of domination, manipulation, and dispossession. It trivializes the struggle and diminishes the sacrifices of the people who prayed for him, fought for him, and kept our hopes and the dream of freedom alive with their blood all those twenty-seven years he was in prison. It reinforces the powers of domination, manipulation, and dispossession.

A theology on the edge of rediscovering prophetic faithfulness demands that we be honest enough to step away from the naiveté John de Gruchy has warned us against; mature enough, wise enough, and true to our prophetic calling enough to see that the result of an incomplete revolution may very well be the realization of a postponed revolution, but then with the danger of it becoming a very different kind of revolution than the nonviolent revolution we have worked, hoped, and prayed for and engaged in.

Not every revolution called by that name—as in the grand narrative of the so-called National Democratic Revolution of post-1994 South Africa or in the American version of social democracy that promises to revolutionize the American political system—is true revolution in the sense of Albert Luthuli and Martin Luther King Jr.'s understanding of it. A revolution that simply re-baptizes the existing order instead of challenging and transforming it, placing the needs of the people at its center is not revolution. And we must realize that our revolution will remain incomplete until the people's sacrifices, dreams and hopes are honored with systemic and sustainable justice. A theology from the edge will push every social revolution to this edge.

To end aggression and war; to seek a better, more just, more humane world in the undoing of injustice and the doing of justice; to save the earth from the calamities of our greed and rapaciousness; to restore human dignity as we protect and enhance human rights; to become the embodiment of hope for young and old; to believe that it is not wrong to dream and hope and work for justice; to reclaim the Bible from the distortions of those who wish to use it as justification for injustice, inhumanity, and ideologies of domination and violence: this is the edge our theology is facing.

It is also a theology with an edge of Christ-centered realism; the realism that recognizes the relentless viciousness with which the powers cling to their positions of power and privilege and the ruthlessness with which they will defend it. It is the realism with which Jesus warns his disciples of the cost of discipleship, completely honest with them about the coming persecutions: false accusations, floggings, and imprisonment; the threats of death, the betrayal they must expect from loved ones and the temptation to deny him as he sends them as "sheep among the wolves." Hence his repeated "do not be afraid of them" (Matt 10). It is the Christ-centered realism of Dietrich Bonhoeffer, who knows that when Christ calls us, he calls us to die. It is the realism of Albert Luthuli who admonishes us that the road to freedom is via the cross, and of Martin Luther King Jr. who calls on us to remember that our life is not worth living if we have not found something to die for.

As things stand, prophetic theology is not on the edge of celebrated acceptance by the political aristocracies and privileged classes of the world. Greed and power continue to feed on poverty, powerlessness, fear, and hopelessness. All over the world, people's struggles for justice are responded to with mindless, desperate brutality by deliberate, imperialistic forces from without as well as by opportunistic forces from within, both serving political and social agendas not in accordance with the deepest desires for freedom and dignity nurtured by the people.

In South Africa, the ANC of Albert Luthuli has long been bereft of life and promise by the post-Marikana heartlessness, the endless corruption and betrayals on which the ANC seems content to gorge itself. Behind its Apartheid Wall, Israel is multiplying its oppression of Palestinians with breathtaking shamelessness. In the inauguration of Donald Trump the United States and the world witnessed a spectacle many were convinced they would never see. But what we do see is the unchanging, arrogant, and frighteningly dark heart of empire, no matter who is in the White House. On the very day of his inauguration Mr. Trump, his handprint virtually still warm on the Bible, gave orders for a drone strike against defenseless Yemen, leaving at least 25 civilians dead, nine of them children, the oldest 12 years, and the youngest 3 months old.[59] And then, on April 13, the man who said

---

59. Villagers reported the victims as three-month old Asma Fahad Alu al Ameri, Aisha Mohammed Abdallah al Ameri, 4; Halima Hussein al Aifa al Emeri, Hussein Mohammed Abdallah Mabkoudt al Ameri, both 5; Mursil Abedraboh Masad al

"I love war" ordered the US military to drop the largest non-nuclear bomb in the US arsenal—"the mother of all bombs"—on Afghanistan, full of braggadocio calling the strike "very, very successful." It did not matter that the "hellish aftermath" was unimaginable destruction: splintered and uprooted trees, cars gutted, body parts strewn across the fields. "In its wake the device has left a scar on the scenic Afghan grasslands that is terrible to behold."[60]

Jack Pratt, from the Environmental Defense Fund, calls the Trump administration's relentless onslaught on environmental protection laws "the scariest legislation you've never seen," referring to the stealth with which the Republican-controlled Congress is quietly but decisively dealing with and changing environmental and safety laws in ways Americans would begin to understand fully only "when they begin to see tainted food, contaminated drugs, unhealthy pollution levels and unsafe vehicles."[61]

The politics of the new US president seems to have awakened, and emboldened, a frightening, careless hostility towards humanness, compassion, and justice. Now, all over the world, misogynists and homophobes of every stripe, creed, and color; white supremacists and unashamed racists from New Nazi's and Christian Nationalists in Europe to revived white apartheid defenders in South Africa and emboldened creators of apartheid in the State of Israel consider themselves vindicated. Predatory capitalists, worshippers of money and destroyers of the Earth have rejuvenated joy; warmongers and the makers of drones, cluster bombs, barrel bombs, land mines and all kinds of deadly chemical weapons rejoice in the temples of profiteering as they see their fortunes and stocks rise even higher this year.[62] In a perverse reversion of Isaiah's vision, they have waited upon their lord, their strength is renewed, and they are ready to mount up with wings like eagles, to run

---

Ameri, 6; Khajija Abdallah Mabkoudt al Ameri, 7; Nawar Anwar al Awlaqi, 8; Ahmed Adelilah Ahmed al Dahab, 11; Nasser Abdallah Ahmed al Dahab, 12. See Jack Moore, "The Full Details of Trump's Botched Yemen raid that Killed Nine Children", *Newsweek*, 10 February, 2017.

60. See the DailyMail.com, May 15th, 2017, citing Fox News, https://www.dailymail.co.uk/news/article-4467862. See also https://www.alternet.org/news-amp-politics-mother-all-bombs-massive-overkill

61. See http://readersupportednews.org/news-section2/318-66/43564, 5 May, 2017.

62. The US Department of Defense asked for $2 billion over five years to buy 4,000 Tomahawk cruise missiles for the US Navy in its fiscal budget in February 2017. After Trump's decision to bomb Syria, the stocks of arms manufacturing firms such as Raytheon, Lockheed Martin, General Dynamics, and Northrop Grumman rose sharply. With members of Congress insisting that it was critical to invest in more missile technology this year, "it is no surprise that defense stocks are among the top performers on Wall Street... for all of this year." See Paul R. La Monica, CNN, https://readersupportednews.org/news-section2/318-66/42918-tomahawk-maker-raytheon's-stock-rises-after-us-launches-missiles-against-syria, accessed April 11, 2017.

and not grow weary, to walk and not faint. Like Babylon, empire without peer in its day, the US Empire, in the Trump era, is saying, "I am, and there is no one besides me" (Isa 47:10).

But prophetic theology's Christ-centered realism is neither cynicism nor hopelessness. It is a theology firmly rooted in hope. But the hope in which prophetic theology is anchored is not the hope of meek acceptance of existing status quos, of resignation to the wishes of those who rule the world, who exult in the way things are, willing to do everything in their considerable power to keep things the way they are. It is rather the hope of anger and courage that is unprepared to accept the world as it is and as the powerful have made it; a hope in the reign of God that will overcome the reign of terror that rules our world, knowing that, as de Gruchy affirms, "God's reign is always on behalf of those who suffer and are oppressed." So, de Gruchy writes, "we celebrate every achievement of justice no matter how small, knowing that it is a step towards the coming of God's kingdom."[63]

As such it is a theology immersed in the struggles of the people, speaking truth from the edge of precarious existence, given its edge by the hopes of the people and the revolutionary message of Jesus. A theology on the edge of hopeful, real, durable anticipation: prepared for derision, persecution and suffering, for revilement and struggle, but unprepared, totally and resolutely, to accept the world as it is and things as they are.

---

63. De Gruchy, *Church Struggle*, xiv.

Bibliography

Alexander, Michelle. *The New Jim Crow: Mass Incarceration in the Age of Colorblindness*. New York: New, 2011.

Alexander, Neville. *An Ordinary Country: Issues in the Transition from Apartheid to Democracy in South Africa*. Scottsville: University of KwaZulu-Natal Press, 2002.

Amjad-Ali, Charles. *Islamophobia or Restorative Justice: Tearing the Veils of Ignorance*. Johannesburg: Ditshwanelo CAR'AS, 2006.

Asmal, Kader, Louise Asmal, and Ronald Suresh Roberts. *Reconciliation through Truth: A Reckoning of Apartheid's Criminal Governance*. Cape Town: Cambridge University Press, 1998.

Baldwin, Lewis V., and Rufus Burrow Jr., eds. *The Domestication of Martin Luther King Jr.: Clarence B. Jones, Right-Wing Conservatism, and the Manipulation of the King Legacy*. Eugene, OR: Cascade, 2013.

Batley, Michael. "Restorative Justice in the South African Context." In *Beyond Retribution: Prospects for Restorative Justice in South Africa*, edited by Traggy Maepa, 21–32. ISS Monograph Series; no. 111. Pretoria: Institute for Security Studies, 2005.

Battle, Michael. *Reconciliation: The Ubuntu Theology of Desmond Tutu*. Cleveland: Pilgrim, 1997.

Bell, Terry, and Dumisa Buhle Ntsebeza. *Unfinished Business: South Africa, Apartheid, and Truth*. Cape Town: RedWorks, 2001.

Bellah, Robert, et al. *Habits of the Heart: Individualism and Commitment in American Life*. Berkeley: University of California Press, 1985.

Biko, Steve. *I Write What I Like*. Edited by Aelred Stubbs. San Francisco: Harper & Row, 1986.

Boesak, Allan. "And Zacchaeus Remained in the Tree." *Verbum et Ecclesia* 29 (2008) 636–54.

———. *Black and Reformed: Apartheid, Liberation, and the Calvinist Tradition*. Edited by Leonard Sweetman. 1984. Reprint, Eugene, OR: Wipf and Stock, 2015.

———. *Comfort and Protest: The Apocalypse of John from a South African Perspective*. 1987. Reprint, Eugene OR: Wipf and Stock, 2015.

———. *Dare We Speak of Hope? Searching for a Language of Life in Faith and Politics*. Grand Rapids: Eerdmans, 2014.

———. *Die Vlug van Gods Verbeelding: Bybelverhale van die Onderkant*. Stellenbosch: SUN Press, 2005.

———. *Farewell to Innocence: A Socio-ethical Study of Black Theology and Black Power*. Maryknoll, NY: Orbis, 1977. Reprint, Eugene OR: Wipf and Stock, 2015.

———. *The Fire Within: Sermons from the Edge of Exile*. Cape Town: New World Foundation, 2004.

———. *Kairos, Crisis, and Global Apartheid: The Challenge to Prophetic Resistance*. New York: Palgrave MacMillan, 2015.

———. *Running with Horses: Reflections of an Accidental Politician*. Cape Town: Joho!, 2009.

———. *Shadows of the Light: Biblical Meditations in a Time of Trial*. Cape Town: Van Schaik, 1996.

———. *The Tenderness of Conscience: African Renaissance and the Spirituality of Politics*. Stellenbosch: SUN, 2005.

Boesak, Allan Aubrey, and Curtiss Paul DeYoung. *Radical Reconciliation: Beyond Political Pietism and Christian Quietism*. Maryknoll, NY: Orbis, 2012.

Bond, Patrick. *Elite Transition: From Apartheid to Neoliberalism in South Africa*. Pietermaritzburg: University of KwaZulu-Natal Press, 2005.

Bonhoeffer, Dietrich. *The Cost of Discipleship*. New York: Macmillan, 1960.

———. *Gesammelte Schriften*. Edited by Eberhard Bethge. 6 vols. Munich: Kaiser, 1958–74.

———. *Letters and Papers from Prison*. Edited by Eberhard Bethge. New York: Macmillan, 1971.

Bonino, José Miguez. *Toward a Christian Political Ethics*. Philadelphia: Fortress, 1983.

Branch, Taylor. *At Canaan's Edge: America in the King Years, 1965-1968*. New York: Simon and Schuster, 2006.

Brown, Kelley Delaine. "God is as Christ Does: Toward a Womanist Theology, *JRT*, 46, 1989, 12

Brueggemann, Walter. *The Prophetic Imagination*. Minneapolis: Fortress, 2001.

———. *Theology of the Old Testament: Testimony, Dispute, Advocacy*. Minneapolis: Fortress, 1997.

Calland, Richard. *Anatomy of South Africa: Who Holds the Power?* Cape Town: Zebra, 2006.

Calvin, John. *Institutes of the Christian Religion*. Translated by John Allen. Vol. 2. Philadelphia: Presbyterian Board of Christian Education, 1936.

———. *Commentaries*. Translated and edited by John King et al. 22 vols. Grand Rapids: Baker, 1981.

Carter, Warren. *Matthew and Empire: Initial Explorations*. Harrisburg, PA: Trinity Press International, 2001.

Cleage, Albert. *The Black Messiah*. Kansas City: Sheed Andrews and McMeel, 1968.

Clingan, Ralph Garlin. *Against Cheap Grace: A Study in the Hermeneutics of Adam Clayton Powell, 1865–1953, in His Intellectual Context*. New York: Peter Lang, 2002.

Cone, James H. *Black Theology and Black Power*. Minneapolis: Seabury, 1969.

———. *For My People: Black Theology and the Black Church*. Maryknoll, NY: Orbis, 1984.

———. *God of the Oppressed*. Maryknoll, NY: Orbis, 1997.

———. *Speaking the Truth*. Grand Rapids: Eerdmans, 1986.

Conradie, Ernst. "Globalisation, Consumerism, and the Call for *Status Confessionis*." In *Globalisation II: Global Crisis, Global Challenge, Global Faith; an Ongoing*

Response to the Accra Confession, edited by Allan Boesak and Len Hansen, 53–76. Stellenbosch: SUN, 2010.

Cortright, David. *Gandhi and Beyond: Nonviolence for a New Political Age*. 2nd ed. Boulder, CO: Paradigm, 2009.

Dabashi, Hamid. *The Arab Spring: The End of Postcolonialism*. London: Zed, 2012.

De Gruchy, John. *The Church Struggle in South Africa*. 25th anniversary ed. Minneapolis: Fortress, 2005.

———. *Reconciliation: Restoring Justice*. Minneapolis: Fortress, 2002.

DeGruy Leary, Joy. *Post Traumatic Slave Syndrome: America's Enduring Injury and Healing*. Baltimore: Uptone, 2005.

De La Torre, Miguel. *Liberating Jonah: Forming an Ethics of Reconciliation*. Maryknoll, NY: Orbis, 2007.

De Lange, Johnny. "The Historical Context: Legal Origins and Philosophical Foundations of the South African Truth and Reconciliation Commission." In *Looking Back, Reaching Forward*, edited by Charles Villa-Vicencio an Wilhelm Verwoerd, 14–31. Cape Town: University of Cape Town Press, 2000.

Desmond, Cosmas. *The Discarded People*. Johannesburg: Penguin African Library, 1971.

DeYoung, Curtiss Paul. *Coming Together in the 21st Century: The Bible's Message in an Age of Diversity*. Valley Forge, PA: Judson, 2009.

Dyson, Michael Eric. *I May Not Get There with You: The True Martin Luther King Jr.* New York: Simon and Schuster, 2000.

Elliott, Neill. "The Apostle Paul and Empire." In *In the Shadow of Empire: Reclaiming the Bible as a History of Faithful Resistance*, edited by Richard A. Horsley, 97–116. Louisville: Westminster John Knox, 2008.

Esterhuyse, Willie. *End Game: Secret Talks and the End of Apartheid*. Cape Town: Tafelberg, 2012.

Felder, Cain Hope. *Troubling Biblical Waters: Race, Class, and Family*. Maryknoll, NY: Orbis, 1992.

Finley, Mary Lou, et al., eds. *The Chicago Freedom Movement: Martin Luther King Jr. and Civil Rights Activism in the North*. Lexington: University Press of Kentucky, 2015.

Foner, Philip S. *Selections from the Writings of Frederick Douglass*. New York: International, 1964.

Francis, Leah Gunning. *Ferguson and Faith: Sparking Leadership and Awakening Community*. St. Louis: Chalice, 2015.

Francis, Pope. *Apostolic Exhortation Evangelii Gaudium of the Holy Father Francis to the Bishops, Clergy, Consecrated Persons and the Lay Faithful on the Proclamation of the Gospel in Today's World*. Rome: Vatican, 2015.

Freire, Paulo. *Pedagogy of the Oppressed*. New York: Penguin, 1972.

Garnet, Henry Highland. "An Address to the Slaves of the United States." In *Crossing the Danger Water: Three Hundred Years of African-American Writing*, edited by Deidre Mullane, 115–21. New York: Anchor, 1993.

———. "Call to Rebellion." In *Crossing the Danger Water: Three Hundred Years of African-American Writing*, edited by Deidre Mullane, 115–21. New York: Anchor, 1993.

Gerwel, Jakes. "National Reconciliation: Holy Grail or Secular Pact." In *Looking Back, Reaching Forward*, edited by Charles Villa-Vicencio and Wilhelm Verwoerd, 277–86. Cape Town: University of Cape Town Press, 2000.

Gilens, Martin, and Benjamin I. Page. "Testing Theories of American Politics: Elites, Interest Groups, and Average Citizens." *Perspectives on Politics* 12 (2014) 564–81.

Gobodo-Madikizela, Pumla. *A Human Being Died That Night: A South African Story of Forgiveness.* New York: Houghton Mifflin, 2003.

Gollwitzer, Helmut. "Zur 'Schwarzen Theologie.'" *Evangelische Theologie* 34 (1974) 43–69.

Graybill, Lyn S. *: Miracle or Model?* Boulder, CO: Lynne Rienner, 2002.

Griffin, Wendell L. *The Fierce Urgency of Prophetic Hope.* Valley Forge: Judson, 2017.

Halper, Jeff. *War Against the People: Israel, the Palestinians and Global Pacification.* London: Pluto, 2015.

Harding, Vincent. "Black Power and the American Christ." In *The Black Power Revolt: A Collection of Essays*, edited by Floyd B. Barbour, 85–93. Boston: P. Sargent, 1968.

Hedges, Chris. *Wages of Rebellion: The Moral Imperative of Revolt.* New York: Nation, 2015.

Hendricks, Obery M., Jr. *The Politics of Jesus: Rediscovering the Revolutionary Nature of Jesus' Teachings and How They Have Been Corrupted.* New York: Doubleday, 2006.

Herzog, William. *Jesus, Justice, and the Reign of God: A Ministry of Liberation.* Louisville: Westminster John Knox, 2000.

Hopkins, Dwight N. *Being Human: Race, Culture and Religion.* Minneapolis: Fortress, 2005.

———. *Shoes That Fit Our Feet: Sources for a Constructive Black Theology.* Maryknoll, NY: Orbis, 1993.

Horsley, Richard A., ed. *In the Shadow of Empire: Reclaiming the Bible as a History of Faithful Resistance.* Louisville: Westminster John Knox, 2008.

———. *Jesus and Empire: The Kingdom of God and the New World Disorder.* Minneapolis: Fortress, 2003.

———, ed. *Paul and Empire: Religion and Power in Roman Imperial Society.* Harrisburg, PA: Trinity Press International, 1997.

Hughes, Langston. *The Collected Poems of Langston Hughes.* Edited by Arnold Rampersad and David Roessel. New York: Vintage, 1995.

International Bank for Reconstruction and Development. *Shock Waves, Managing the Impacts of Climate Change on Poverty.* Washington, DC: The World Bank, 2016.

Jacques, Gloria, and Gwen N. Lesetedi, eds. *The New Partnership for Africa's Development: Debates, Opportunities, and Challenges.* Pretoria: Africa Institute of South Africa, 2005.

Johnson, Krista. "Liberal or Liberation Framework? The Contradictions of ANC Rule in South Africa." *Journal of Contemporary African Studies* 21 (2003) 321–28.

Jordan, June. "Poem for South African Women." In *Directed by Desire: The Collected Poems of June Jordan*, edited by Jan Heller Levy and Sarah Miles. Port Townsend, WA: Copper Canyon, 2015.

Karis, Thomas, and Gwendolen M. Carter, eds. *From Protest to Challenge: A Documentary History of African Politics in South Africa, 1882–1990.* Vol. 2, *Hope and Challenge, 1935–52.* Stanford: Stanford University Press, 1973.

Katongole, Emmanuel, and Chris Rice. *Reconciling All Things: A Christian Vision for Justice, Peace and Healing.* Downers Grove, IL: InterVarsity, 2008.

King, Martin Luther, Jr. "Beyond Vietnam: A Time to Break Silence." In *The Radical King*, edited by Cornel West, 201–17. Boston: Beacon, 2015.

———. "Let My People Go." In *The Radical King*, edited by Cornel West, 109–10. Boston: Beacon, 2015.

———. "Letter from Birmingham Jail." In *The Radical King*, edited by Cornel West, 127–46. Boston: Beacon, 2015.
———. *The Radical King*. Edited and introduced by Cornel West. Boston: Beacon, 2015.
———. *The Trumpet of Conscience*. The King Legacy. Boston: Beacon, 2010.
———. *Where Do We Go from Here: Chaos or Community?* The King Legacy. Boston: Beacon, 2010.
Klapwijk, C. *Sociaal Masochisme en Christelijk Ethos: Een Confrontatie met Th. Reik's Interpretatie van het Christendom*. Kampen: Kok, 1973.
Klein, Naomi. *The Shock Doctrine: The Rise of Disaster Capitalism*. New York: Picador, 2007.
Knox, Robert. *The Races of Men: A Fragment*. Philadelphia: Lea & Blanchard, 1850.
Kuyper, Abraham. *Calvinism: Six Stone Lectures*. New ed. Grand Rapids: Eerdmans, 1931.
Lawrence, D. H. *Studies in Classic American Literature*. Vol. 2. New York: Penguin, 1990.
Lischer, Richard. *The End of Words: The Language of Reconciliation in a Culture of Violence*. Grand Rapids: Eerdmans, 2005.
Luthuli, Albert. *Let My People Go!* Cape Town: Tafelberg, 2006.
Magona, Sindiwe. *Mother to Mother*. Cape Town: David Philip, 1998.
Magubane, Bernard. "African Renaissance in Historical Perspective." In *African Renaissance: The New Struggle*, edited by Malegapuru William Makgoba. Cape Town: Tafelberg: 1999.
Mamdani, Mahmood. "Beyond Kempton Park: Reflections on Nuremberg and the Question of Justice." Public lecture delivered at Africa Memorial Day Conference, University of the Free State, Bloemfontein, South Africa, July 14, 2010.
———. "Reconciliation without Justice." *Southern African Review of Books* 46 (1996) 3–5.
———. *When Victims Become Killers: Colonialism, Nativism and the Genocide in Rwanda*. Princeton: Princeton University Press, 2001.
Mandela, Nelson. *Long Walk to Freedom: The Autobiography of Nelson Mandela*. Boston: Little, Brown, 1994.
Mangcu, Xolela. *To the Brink: The State of Democracy in South Africa*. Scottsville: University of KwaZulu-Natal Press, 2008.
———, ed. *What Colour is Our Future?* Johannesburg: Wits University Press, 2015.
Mayer, Jane. *Dark Money: The Hidden History of the Billionaires Behind the Rise of the Radical Right*. New York: Doubleday, 2016.
Mbeki, Thabo. *Africa: The Time Has Come; Selected Speeches*. Cape Town: Tafelberg, 1998.
McMickle, Marvin A. *Where Have All the Prophets Gone? Reclaiming Prophetic Preaching in America*. Cleveland: Pilgrim, 2006.
Metz, Johann Baptist. *Faith in History and Society: Toward a Fundamental Practical Theology*. Translated by David Smith. New York: Seabury, 1980.
Moltmann, Jürgen. *God for a Secular Society: The Public Relevance of Theology*. Minneapolis: Fortress, 1999.
Moluleke, Tinyiko Sam. "May the Black God Stand Up, Please! Biko's Challenge to Religion." In *Biko Lives! Contesting the Legacies of Steve Biko*, edited by Andile Mngxitama, Amanda Alexander, and Nigel C. Gibson, 115–26. New York: Palgrave Macmillan, 2008.
Mosoetsa, Sarah. *Eating from One Pot: The Dynamics of Survival in Poor South African Households*. Johannesburg: Wits University Press, 2011.

Murove, Munyaradzi Felix, ed. *African Ethics: An Anthology of Comparative and Applied Ethics*. Scottsville: University of KwaZulu-Natal Press, 2009.

Nyirongo, L. *The Gods of Africa or the God of the Bible, The Snares of African Religions*. Potchefstroom: Institute for Reformation Studies, 1997.

Odoyoye, Mercy Amba. *Daughters of Anowa: African Women and Patriarchy*. Maryknoll, NY: Orbis, 1995.

Palmer, Parker J. *Healing the Heart of Democracy: The Courage to Create a Politics Worthy of the Human Spirit*. San Francisco: Jossey-Bass, 2011.

———. *The Politics of the Brokenhearted: On Holding the Tensions of Democracy*. Essays on Deepening the American Dream; Essay no. 8. Kalamazoo, MI: Fetzer Institute, 2005.

Paul, Nathaniel. "An Address on the Occasion of the Abolition of Slavery in New York." In *Preaching with Sacred Fire: An Anthology of African American Sermons, 1750 to the Present*, edited by Martha Simmons and Frank A. Thomas, 184–87. New York: Norton, 2010.

Pauw, Jacques. *Dances with Devils: A Journalist's Search for Truth*. Cape Town: Zebra, 2006.

Piketty, Thomas. *Capital in the Twenty-First Century*. Translated by Arthur Goldhammer. Cambridge: Belknap Press of Harvard University Press, 2014.

Pollack, Lance M. "Whose Gay Community? Social Class, Sexual Self-Expression, and Gay Community Involvement." *The Sociological Quarterly* 46 (2005) 437–56.

Praeg, Leonhard, ed. *A Report on Ubuntu*. Scottsville: University of KwaZulu-Natal Press, 2014.

Praeg, Leonhard, and Siphokazi Magadla, eds. *Ubuntu: Curating the Archive*. Scottsville: University of KwaZulu-Natal Press, 2014.

Raheb, Mitri. *Faith in the Face of Empire: The Bible through Palestinian Eyes*. Maryknoll, NY: Orbis, 2015.

Ramphele, Mamphela. *Laying Ghosts to Rest: Dilemmas of the Transformation in South Africa*. Cape Town: Tafelberg: 2008.

Samuel DeWitt Procter Conference, Inc. *Bearing Witness: A Nation in Chains, A Report of the Samuel DeWitt Proctor Conference, Findings from Nine Statewide Justice Commission hearings on Mass Incarceration*. Chicago: Samuel DeWitt Proctor Conference, 2014.

Schweitzer, Albert. *The Quest of the Historical Jesus: A Critical Study of Its Progress from Reimarus to Wrede*. New York: Macmillan, 1968.

Shakespeare, William. *Macbeth*. Edited by B. Smith. Boston: English Play, 1699.

Small, Adam. "Blackness versus Nihilism." In *Essays on Black Theology*, edited by M. Mothlabi, 14–15. Johannesburg: Ravan, 1972.

Smit, D. J. "The Doing of the Little Righteousness: On Justice in Barth's View of the Christian Life." In *Essays in Public Theology: Collected Essays 1*, edited by Ernst M. Conradie, 359–78. Stellenbosch: SUN, 2007.

Smith, Luther, Jr. *Howard Thurman: The Mystic as Prophet*. Washington, DC: University Press of America, 1981.

Sono, Themba. *Dilemmas of African Intellectuals in South Africa*. Pretoria: University of South Africa Press, 1994.

Sparks, Allister. *Tomorrow Is Another Country: The Inside Story of South Africa's Road to Change*. Johannesburg: Johnathan Ball, 1996.

St. Clair, Raquel A. "Womanist Biblical Interpretation." In *True to Our Native Land: An African American New Testament Commentary*, edited by Brian K. Blount et al., 58. Minneapolis: Fortress, 2007.
Storkey, Elaine. "Sphere Sovereignty and the Anglo-American Tradition." In *Religion, Pluralism, and Public Life*, edited by Luis E. Lugo, 189–204. Grand Rapids: Eerdmans, 2000.
Tambo, Adelaide, ed. *Preparing for Power: Oliver Tambo Speaks*. London: Hansib, 2004.
Teffo, Lesiba. "Moral Renewal and African Experiences." In *African Renaissance: The New Struggle*, edited by Malegapuru William Makgoba, 146–69. Cape Town: Tafelberg, 1998.
Terreblanche, Sampie. "Dealing with Systematic Economic Injustice." In *Looking Back, Reaching Forward*, edited by Charles Villa-Vicencio and Wilhelm Verwoerd, 265–76. Cape Town: University of Cape Town Press, 2000.
———. *A History of Inequality in South Africa, 1652–2000*. Scottsville: University of KwaZulu-Natal Press, 2000.
———. *Lost in Transformation: South Africa's Search for a New Future since 1986*. Johannesburg: KMM Review, 2012.
———. *Verdeelde Land: Hoe die Oorgang Suid Africa Faal*. Cape Town: Tafelberg, 2014.
Thomas, M. M. "Issues Concerning the Life and Work of the Church in a Revolutionary World." In *Unity of Mankind*, edited by Albert H. van den Heuvel, 89–98. Geneva: World's Student Christian Federation, 1969.
Thomas, M. M., and J. D. McCaughey. *The Christian in the World Struggle*. Geneva: World's Student Christian Federation, 1951.
Townes, Emilie M., ed. *A Troubling in My Soul: Womanist Perspectives on Evil and Suffering*. Maryknoll, NY: Orbis, 1993.
Tutu, Desmond. *No Future without Forgiveness*. New York: Doubleday, 1999.
Van Aarde, Andries. *Fatherless in Galilee: Jesus as Child of God*. Harrisburg, PA: Trinity Press International, 2001.
Van der Westhuizen, Christi. *White Power and the Rise and Fall of the National Party*. Cape Town: Zebra, 2007.
Villa-Vicencio, Charles. *Trapped in Apartheid: A Socio-theological History of the English-Speaking Churches*. Maryknoll, NY: Orbis, 1988.
———. *Walk with Us and Listen: Political Reconciliation in Africa*. Cape Town: University of Cape Town Press, 2010.
Wallis, Jim. *The Soul of Politics: A Practical and Prophetic Vision for Change*. New York: New, 1994.
Weems, Renita J. *Just a Sister Away: A Womanist Vision of Women's Relationships in the Bible*. San Diego: LuraMedia, 1988.
West, Gerald O. "Thabo Mbeki's Bible: The Role of Religion in the South African Public Realm after Liberation." In *Religion and Spirituality in South Africa: New Perspectives*, edited by Duncan Brown, 87–106. Scottsville: University of KwaZulu-Natal Press, 2009.
Williams, Reggie L. *Bonhoeffer's Black Jesus: Harlem Renaissance Theology and an Ethic of Resistance*. Waco, TX: Baylor University Press, 2014.
Wilmore, Gayraud S. *Black Religion and Black Radicalism: An Interpretation of the Religious History of African Americans*. Maryknoll, NY: Orbis, 2006.
Wink, Walter. *The Powers That Be: Theology for a New Millennium*. New York: Galilee Doubleday, 2001.

Wittenberg, Gunther. *Resistance Theology in the Old Testament: Collected Essays.* Pietermaritzburg: Cluster, 2007.

Wodak, Ruth. *The Politics of Fear: What Right-Wing Populist Discourses Mean.* London: Sage, 2015.

Wolterstorff, Nicholas. *Hearing the Call: Liturgy, Justice, Church and World.* Edited by Mark R. Gornik and Gregory Thompson. Grand Rapids: Eerdmans, 2011.

———. *Justice in Love.* Grand Rapids: Eerdmans, 2011.

———. *Justice: Rights and Wrongs.* Princeton: Princeton University Press, 2008.

Zinn, Howard. *A People's History of the United States: 1492–Present.* New York: HarperCollins, 2003.

Index

Abahlali baseMjondolo, 199
Accra Confession, the, 63n3
Acton Institute, the, 64n6
Adamson, Daniel Silas, xx
African National Congress, xiv, xxiv, 4,
    16, 22–23, 49, 60, 124, 140–41,
    145, 158, 170–71, 203, 210–11,
    216, 224
al Ameri, Asma Fahad Alu, 224n59
al Ameri, Aisha Mohammed Abdallah,
    224n59
al Ameri, Halima Hussein al Aifa,
    224n59
al Ameri, Mursil Abedrabah Masad,
    224n59
al Ameri Hussein Mohammed Abdallah
    Makboudt, 224n59
al Ameri, Khajijah Abdallah Makboudt,
    225n59
al Awlaqi, Nawar Anwar 225n59
al Dahab, Nasser Abdallah Ahmed,
    225n59
Alexander, Michelle, 59
Alexander, Neville, 155n35
Alexander the Great, 91
Amjad-Ali, Charles, 113n96
Arab Spring, 8n10, 31
Arafat, Yasser, xii
Aristotle, 91
Asmal, Kader, 160n47
Asmal, Louise, 160n47
Augustine, 83
Avnery, Uri, xix

Baal, xiv

Baldwin, Lewis V., 151n10
BaltimoreUprising, 32
BaltimoreUnited, 32
Basil of Caesarea, 75
Basson, Wouter, 177
Batley, Michael, 133, 135n63
Battle, Michael, 119n4
Belhar Confession, the, 71–72, 80, 113,
    197
Bell, Terry, 152n14
Bellah, Robert, 173n9
Berdyaev, Nicolai, 4n10
Biko, Steve, xx, 34, 111, 163–64, 206–7
Black Consciousness Movement, 34
Black Messiah, the, 86–116
BlackLivesMatter Movement, xvi, 22,
    35, 45, 50n24, 114, 147, 166
Blair, Tony, 78
Blackmon, Traci, 45
Blanqui, Louis, 4
Blood River, the battle of, xiii
Boardman, William, 38, 138
Bonino, Jose Miquez, 192
Boesak, Allan Aubrey, xxiiin19, xxvn21,
    11n25, 24n44, 26n46, 39n10,
    40n11, 43n15, 48n22, 49n23,
    56n36,37, 65n7, 69n23, 74n37,
    79n48, 83n51, 86n2, 93n23,
    104n64, 105n41, 108n77,
    112n94, 127n28, 130n40,
    132n47, 138n77, 151n12,
    153n16,17, 160n44, 170n3,
    171n5,6, 172n9, 181n30,
    186n35, 192n43,45, 198n6,
    201n10, 208n31

INDEX

Boesak, Andrea, xxv
Boesak, Elna, xxv, 74n37, 114, 186n35, 202n12, 218n53, 221
Boesak, Sarah, xxv, 60, 196–97
Bouazizi, Mohammed, 8n21, 31
Bond, Patrick, 13n27, 158n35
Bonhoeffer, Dietrich, 78, 94–97, 173, 219–20, 224
Branch, Taylor, 183
Breaky, Jessica, xxi, xxiin18, 133
Brown, Michael, 115
Brown Douglas Kelly, 93n26, 97
Brueggemann, Walter, 35, 137
Bryant, William Cullen, x
Bujanyima, Winnie, 73n31
Bujo, Benezet, 143n89
Burke, Raymond Leo, 64n6
Burrow, Rufus, 151n10
Burton, Tara Isabella, 198n5
Bush, George W., 78

Calland, Richard, 155n23, 158n35, 201n10
Calvin, John, 36–37, 82n49, 201, 215
Carruthers, Charlene, 22
Carter, Gwendolyn, 168n68
Carter, Warren, 98n38
Chatterjee, Pratap, 78n43
Cheney, Dick, 78
Chipkin Ivor, 149n6
Cleage, Albert, 92n23
Clingan, Ralph Garlin, 94n30
Coates, Ta-Nehisi, 6n15
Colvin, Claudette, 33
Cone, James H. 92n23, 104–5, 108, 113n97, 165
Congress of South African Trade Unions, xxv
Congress of the People, 18
Constantine, 91
Conradie, Ernst, 62
Crow, Jim, the new, 59
Cullen, County, 95

Dabashi, Hamid, 3, 8n21, 10, 31
Daley, Richard M., 211–14
Day, Dorothy, 78
Dawkins Richard, 198n5

Defiance Campaign, the, 17, 33, 204
De Gruy Leary, Joy, 79
De Gruchy, John W. xiii-xiv, 16, 23, 25, 58, 159n40, 199–202, 211, 217, 223, 226
De Lange, Johnny, 160
De La Torre, Miguel, 96n36, 153n18, 154
DeYoung, Curtiss Paul, xxiv, 39n10, 132n77, 170n3, 173n9, 181n30, 186n35, 201n10, 211n38
De Klerk, F.W., 48n23, 76, 151–52, 176–77, 182, 187, 218
De Kock, Eugene, 174–93
Desmond, Cosmas, 65
Douglass, Frederick, 4n21, 55, 103
Duke University Summer Institute for Reconciliation, 32, 46
Dyson, Michael Eric, 6n15, 151n10

Eisbeh, Sanier Abu, xix
Elliot, Neill, 40n12
Elijah, 41
Elisha, xii
Emmanuel, Rahm, 22
Erikson, Amanda, 64n6
Esterhuyse, Willie, 13–16

Faircloth, Zachary, xxin16
FeesMustFall Movement, 18
Felder, Cain Hope, 92n23, 108n77
Ferrell, Brittany, 45
Fernandez, Belen, 122
Finley, Mary Lou et al, 211n38
Foner, Philip, 103n61
Francis I of France, 201
Francis Leah Gunning, 36n6, 43n14, 44, 45n19, 87n1,
Frawley Bagley, Elizabeth, 121
Freire, Paulo, 148, 161–63, 168
Freedom Charter, the, 18–20, 33
Freyne, Sean, 89

Gandhi, Mahatma, 33
Garner, Eric, 115
Garnet, Henry Highland, xi, 46, 54–58, 216
Gazzera, Aurelio, 84–85

INDEX

Gilens, Martin, 10n23
Gerwel, Jakes, 173n10
Gobodo-Madikizela, Pumla, 174–75, 189
Good Samaritan, the, 26
Gollwitzer, Helmut, 103
Graybill, Lyn, 123n11, 153n16
Griffin, Wendell, 57–58
Gubash, Charlene, 77n42

Halper, Jeff, xn2
Hamer, Fannie Lou, 51n16
Hamilton, Jessica, 51n26
Harding, Vincent, 103
Hassan, Budour Youssef, xix, xx
Hawkins, Lyricia, xxin17
Hechter, Jacques, 152n16
Hedges, Chris, 4n8, 48n23, 59n43
Heltzel, Peter Goodwin, xxin17
Hendricks, Obery, xxiv, 93n23, 100–102, 107n76, 108n77
Heritage Foundation, the, 64n6
Herod, 40
Herzog, William II, 195
Holland, Lisa, 55n33
Hopkins, Dwight, 93n23, 102, 113
Horsley, Richard A., 98, 102, 210
Hughes, Langston, 95

InjusticeMustFall Movement, the, 114, 166
International Bank for Reconstruction and Development, 73n33
ISIS, 39, 77, 198

Jamieson, Alastair, 77n42
Jaycox, Edward, 67
Johnson, Krista, 4
Johnson-Jarvis, Bethany, 39
Jordan, June, 1, 21
Justice and Reconciliation Commission, 221n58

Kairos Palestine, 10n24, 27–30, 195
Kairos Document, the South African, 42, 194, 199, 209
Klapwijk, C., 44n16
Karis, Thomas, 168n68

Kasrils, Ronnie, 48n23
Katongole, Emmanuel, 158–59, 210n10
Keevy, Ilze, 123n14, 125n18, 126–28
Kessel, Michael, 6n15
Khader, Jamal, 59
King, Martin Luther Jr., xviii, 5–8, 16, 34, 47, 50–51, 53, 58, 78, 165, 183, 195, 203, 205, 211–14, 221, 223–24
Kinman, Michael, 45
Klein, Naomi, 67, 157n33
Knox, Robert, 111
Kuyper, Abraham, 198

La Monica, Paul R., 225n62
Latsoalo, Motime, 60
Lawrence, D.H., 115n100
Lawson, Dominic, 178n27
Lederman, Jacob, 218n54
LeDuc, David, 178n27
Lenin, Vladimir, 4
Leonard, Gary, S., 63n4
Lerner, Michael, 70
Lincoln, Abraham, 78
Lischer, Richard, 206
Loy, David, 63
Luthuli, Albert John Mvumbi, 17, 34, 48n22, 54–55, 145, 149, 161, 165, 167, 202, 204–6, 223–24

Magadla, Siphokazi, 123n12, n14, 124n15, 125n20, 126n25, 127n29, n30, 128n32
Magubane, Bernard, 112n92
Malan, Magnus, 176
Mandela, Nelson, xiii, xvi, 7, 16, 23, 25, 54, 58, 87, 121–22, 139, 153, 160, 165, 174–93, 195, 210, 216, 223
Malcolm X, 34, 54
Malcolm X Grassroots Movement, 52n26
Magona Sindiwe, 118n3
Mahomed, Ishmail, 133
Makogoro, Y, 125n18
Mamdani, Mahmood, 14–15, 118, 128–33, 169, 170n3, 173n11
Manuel, Trevor, 215

Mangcu, Xolela, 149
Marikana Massacre, 171
Markovitz, Eric, 59n43
Marx, Karl, 4n8
Mayer, Jane, 10n23
Mbeki, Thabo, xxiv, 48n23, 49, 150n6, 160, 210, 215
Mbetse, Mxolisi, 178
McCaughey, J.D., 1, 5
McCleland, Edward, 211
McDonald, Laquan, 50n24, 52
McMickle, Marvin, 33–34, 41, 43, 46, 58
Melvin, Don, 75n37
Merton, Thomas, 78
Metz, Johann Baptist, 44
Middleton, Waltrina, 53n31
Mofokeng, Takatso, xi, 47
Moluleke, Tinyiko Sam, 201n10, 211
Moltmann, Jurgen, 68–69
Moore, Jack, 225n59
Moore, Michael, 218
Mosoetsa, Sarah, 171n4
Motlhabi, Mokgethi, 140n82
Muedini, Fait, xxiv
Munyaka, Mluleki, 140n82
Murove, Munyaradzi Felix, 140n84, 142, 143n89
Muwakkil, Salim, 22

Nadar, Sarojini, 142n86
Nakba, the, 34
Namunane, Bernard, 75n37
Nassar, Amal, xx
Nassar, Bashira, xx
Nassar, Daher, xx
National Negro Convention, 46
National Party, 16, 155, 213
Ndlovu, Hastings, 34
Neslen, Arthur, 84
Nehru, Jawaharlal, 2
Nevins, Joseph, 152n12
Nimr al-Nimr, 77n42
Ntsebeza Dumisa Buhle, 152n14
Nussbaum, Barbara, 144n88
Nyirongo Lenard, 127

Obama, Barack, xiv, xx, xvi, 46, 52, 58, 78n43, 121–22

O'Connell, Kit, 83n52
Oduyoye, Mercy, 92n23, 126
Oppenheim, Todd, 51
Operation Ghetto Storm, 51n26
Osei-Hwedie, 127n29, 30
Oxfam, 72–73

Page, Benjamin I., 10n23
Palestine Liberation Movement, xii
Palme, Olof, 203n16
Palmer, Parker J., 190–91
Pan African Congress, 203
Parks, Rosa, 33
Paul, Nathaniel, 164–65
Pauw, Jacques, 174–78
Peterson, Hector, 34
Phiri, Isabel, 142n86
Pierce, Charles, 51
Piketty, Thomas, 72
Pillay, Suren, 149n6
Plaatjie, Sol, 160n44
Plato, 91
Pollack, Lance M., 72
Pope Francis xxiii, 61–85, 143, 218
Powell, Adam Clayton Sr., 94, 96
Praeg, Leonard, 123n12, n14, 124, 125n20, 126n25, 127n29,, n30, 128n32, 140
Pratt, Jack, 225
Pulley, Aislinn, xvi, 52, 195, 208

Qumsiyeh, Mazin, xii

Raheb, Mitri, 27
Ramaphosa, Cyril, 215
Ramodibe, Dorothy, 126
Ramose, Magobe B., 125–26, 143n89
Ramphele, Mampela 151, 189
Reconciliation, Day of, xiii
Rhodes, Cecil John, xxin18
RhodesMustFall, movement, ix, 18
Rice, Chris, 158–59, 182
Rice, Tamir, 50n24
Roberts, Ronald Suresh, 160n47
Roy, Arundhati, 75

Sachs, Albie, 125

Samuel DeWitt Proctor Conference, 44, 59
Sanders, Bernie, 38
Saul, Heather, 78n43
Sbeih, Hijazi Abu, xix
Schaberg, Jane, 111n89
Schwarzman, Steven A., 38–39
Schweitzer, Albert, 89
Sekous, Osagyefo, 45
Simon, Dean, 179
Sirico, Robert, 64n6
Shakespeare, William, 8
Sharpeville Massacre, 34, 204
Shutte, Augustine, 140
Small, Adam, 205n25
Sobukwe, Robert, 168, 202
Sono, Themba, 123
South African Communist Party, xxv
Spann, Jamell, 36, 45
Sparks, Alister, 13n27, 148
St. Clair, Raquel A., 97n37
Storkey, Elaine, 66
Strijdom, J.G., 21
Sullivan, Leon, 178

Taibbi, Matt, 70
Tambo, Oliver, 203
Teffo, Lesiba, 140n80, 81
Templeton, Alexis, 45–46, 168
Terreblanche, Sampie, 13n27, 125, 141–42, 155–59, 171n4, 201n10, 221
Thomas, M.M., xix, 1–2, 4–5, 6, 11, 19, 31
Thurman, Howard, 165
Townes, Carminah, 50n24
Townes, Emilie, 92n23
Tric-cameral Parliament, 213
Trump, Donald, 224
Truth and Reconciliation Commission, 14–16, 119, 123, 128–39, 141, 147, 151–52, 154–55, 159–61, 175–76, 182–83, 216
Tutu, Desmond, xxiii, 37, 117–22, 133–37, 139, 145, 149–52, 159n52, 171–72, 178, 178n29, 183, 184n34, 187

United Nations, 74

United Democratic Front, 166, 208, 213
United States Congress, 76–77
Utterback, Sherry, 55n3

Van Aarde, Andries, 89–116
Van der Merwe, Stiaan, ix
Van der Westhuizen, Christi, 155–56, 201n10
Van Dyke, Jason, 51
Vibes, John, 218n55
Villa-Vicencio, Charles, 121, 138–39, 140n80, 144, 154n21, 182n32, 202n32, 205
Voortrekkers, xiv
Vorster, John, 37
Vow, Day of the, xiii

Wallis, Jim, 67
Weems, Renita, 92n23
West, Cornell, 6, 216
West, Gerald, 199n7, 210
Will, George F., 63
Wilmore, Gayraud, 92n23, 105n65, 207
Williams, Reggie, l., 95
Wilson, Richard, 123
Wilson, Starsky, 45, 86
Wink, Walter, 82
Wodak, Ruth, xn2
Wooten, Jamye, 32–36, 46–47, 49–50, 52–53, 57, 60
World Alliance of Reformed Churches, 62n3
World Communion of Reformed Churches, 62n3
World Bank, the, 67, 73
World Health Organization, 74
World Meeting of Popular Movements, 79
World Student Christian Federation, 1
Wolterstorff, Nicholas, 137, 143–43, 173n12, 192n45, 206n27
Wright, Jeremiah A., 44, 57
Wright, N.T., 90

Zikode, S'bu, 198
Zinn, Howard, 76n40
Zoe-Obianga, Rose, 126
Zuma, Jacob, xxv, 60, 150n6, 161, 215

www.ingramcontent.com/pod-product-compliance
Lightning Source LLC
Chambersburg PA
CBHW030823230426
43667CB00008B/1347